FLIGHT FROM CE

Rodopi Perspectives on Modern Literature

23

Edited by
David Bevan

FLIGHT
FROM
CERTAINTY

THE DILEMMA OF
IDENTITY AND EXILE

Edited by
Anne Luyat
Francine Tolron

AMSTERDAM - NEW YORK, NY 2001

The paper on which this book is printed meets the requirements of
"ISO 9706:1994, Information and documentation - Paper for
documents - Requirements for permanence".

ISBN: 90-420-1595-0 (bound)
©Editions Rodopi B.V., Amsterdam - New York, NY 2001
Printed in The Netherlands

With special thanks to Annick Cizel

Michel Bandry, Marie-Claude Barbier, Jacques Carré, Annie Escuret, Stuart Jones, Brian Matthews, Vincent O'Sullivan, Marc Porée, Jean-Claude Redonnet, Michel Renouard, Serge Ricard, Jean Sévry.

TABLE OF CONTENTS

V. AFRICA

Introduction

The century's sense of displacement has led to a flight from certainty and timeless truths, erasing centuries-old landmarks of national and linguistic consciousness, transforming irrevocably both cultural and literary landscapes. The one certainty remaining is the degree to which the role of surprise can be counted upon to perpetuate the possibilities of further displacement and increase the number of those "living in-between." Suspended between countries, cultures, and languages, living for a present whose future is at best uncertain, authors in exile have turned to fragmented narratives in order to mirror the incoherence of the age. In their works, a distinct perception of the irony of it all co-exists with the belief in the imperative necessity of mirroring the dilemma of identity and exile in order to portray the subjective at the heart of history.

Authors, academics, and cultural historians decided to exchange their views on art, literature, history, and the meeting of cultures in order to better assess the effect of exile – whether it be imposed or voluntary, permanent or temporary – upon the individual mind as well as upon group consciousness. In spite of geographic, ethnic and linguistic differences, the essential experience was found to be similar in many respects – a sense of living apart, of an uncertain future, and of linguistic deprivation. For many participants, the experience of sharing these perceptions on a professional level was a new and a moving one, which would leave its mark on their lives.

The Puerto-Rican author, Alba Ambert, confesses that her life is spent on the edge: "The edge is a knife, a blade, the humiliation of a turned back, the sting of a slur, the rage of impotence. The edge is an end with no beginning. The characters in my novel *The Eighth Continent* inhabit an edge, a place of perpetual banishment." In describing her experience of exile, the Australian writer Gillian Bouras speaks of a "never-ending cycle, of forever re-entering atmospheres, forever adjusting and re-adjusting," all the while noting that there is a great deal to be gained from living in-between: "People who live in-between can make connections of a viable sort, and so can countries."

Dr. Miriam Frank, a neurologist who changed country and language three different times as a child, researched its troubling effect on the nervous system and confirmed the conclusions drawn by both the speakers and the audience that there exists "a thread in the centre which does not change, perhaps the pristine I."

The contributors recognize the veracity of the quotation from Horace: "You can change skies but not your soul" chosen by Russell West, an Australian writer and lecturer living in Germany. He confirms the fact that the process of identity is an on-going one. In his spatialised interpretation of Janet Turner Hospital's fiction, he implies that "a version of Australian identities emerges out of a dialogue between Australia and a transgression of geographical and national boundaries."

The authors have attempted to combine scholarship, personal experience, wit, and irony in dealing with questions which so far have gone unanswered: "How far is identity modelled by the country in which people grow up and believe they have their roots? What happens to the concept of identity when a person abandons one country to live in another?"

South African Professor, Myrtle Hooper, believes that the sentiment shared by all those who live in exile is eviction: "Africans have been forced to endure privation and oppression, yet, at a primal level they remain native. They may be denied rights in their ancestral home, yet this ancestral home is not lost to them. It remains there and theirs." The essays have a common centre. How does one recover from the trauma of exile? Is hybridity a viable form of existence? Whether they are themselves exiles writing about their own experience or observers studying its motifs, the authors seek to determine where the borders lie.

In her treatment of real and imagined homelands, Béatrice Pardini-Laurent quotes Dante Gabriel Rossetti who, when asked why he had never travelled to Italy but had chosen to write about it and to render in painting his conception of it, answered flatly: "Why bother? Got it all inside me." Korean Professor Sooyoung Chon stresses the importance of the imagination in creating new spaces, pointing out that Salman Rushdie's genius expresses itself in fortuitous and explosively imaginative trips through hybridity: "His fiction represents an expansive discourse, which seeks to create its own spaces within the context of shifting borders in the sense of cultural relocations and translations." Bombay University Professor Nilufer Bharucha explores the limits of the visible and the imaginary, quoting Martin Heideger's view that "a boundary is not at which something stops; but as the Greeks recognized, the boundary is that from which something begins its presencing."

Ruth Brown of the University of Sussex examines the virtual world of the X Generation, a world of unstable images which are distinct from a workable reality. Marty, the heroine of Maria Wickens novel *Left of Centre* can state with aplomb: "Some of my best friends are icons created by image makers." Australian academic Jennifer Rutherford concentrates on the importance of both the real and the imaginary images, needed in the process of forming a conception of identity: "Identity stems from landscape and the naturalness of belonging to it."

To the uncertain nature of fluctating images is added the difficulty brought on by the eventual multiplication of tongues. In her discussion of French speakers who inhabit the state of Maine or 'le Québec d'en bas', Priscilla Morin-Ollier of the University of Tours, quoting Romano Guardini, underlines the fact that language is as important as landscape: "The language a man speaks belongs to him in a more profound and essential way than the earth and the things he calls his country." Refusing to believe that learning a new language will suffice in dealing effectively with the problems of exile, Corinne Liotard of Nice examines the difficulties which are inevitably encountered when a person is obliged to speak more than one language: "Integration through language is always proposed, yet fluency gained in a second language does not compensate losses in the mother tongue."

Miriam Frank investigates the very real possibility that the sense of self differs in each language because of the essential role played in the perception of self by memory. For an exile who is forced to adopt a new means of expression, the sense of identity can vary to an astonishing degree from one language to another. Bernard Cros of the University of Avignon is very close to her point of view when he speaks of the surprisingly favorable image which the English language enjoys among Blacks in South Africa, that of a window open to the outside of the country, for many of them were educated at Mission Schools as well as at the College of Fort Hare, the only Black Institution of higher learning in South Africa. Living and learning in a second language enabled them to assimilate it with the positive connotation of personal achievement rather than with the negative one of oppression.

And, of course, exile ultimately entails the problem of survival. Canadian author Marianne Ackerman traces with precision and historical accuracy the changing roles of the persecuted and the persecutors as a result of forced English and French cohabitation in Canada from the end of French dominion to the present time. Neither community can claim to have been perfectly just in its treatment of the other. Both have had to survive a series of mistreatments and misconceptions. For Sarah Le Ménestrel of the Centre National de la Recherche Scientifique, the idea of survival among the descendants of displaced Acadians depends not only upon a common destiny of exile but also upon the bond of a common language. It is surprising to note that they do not share a sense of having been persecuted as their ancestors had been. Nor do they feel a sense of language deprivation in the way their ancestors would have experienced it. What does unite them is a much more abstract concept, the sense of possessing a shared memory conserved in mind and spirit over the centuries.

Florence D'Souza of the University of Lille draws a similar parallel in her analysis of the Indian novel, when she demonstrates the existence of a pole of continuity between the traditions of the past and the dislocations of the present. She believes that in spite of the sense of incertitude which is necessarily produced by their co-existence in life and literature, the two constitute the double cornerstone of post-cultural identity. In a discussion of the simultaneous exploration and subversion of various kinds of belonging in Shani Mootoo's *Cereus Blooms at Night*, Mary Conde of Queen Mary and Westfield College, London, insists upon the necessity of evading certainty in order to avoid the tyranny of categories. She indicates, as well, that it is necessary to question the traditional role of inherited categories, and to invert the customary notions of the real and the imaginary. Geetha Ganapathy-Doré from the University of Paris quotes Julia Kristeva's assertion that to be a citizen is to be an alien at the beginning of the twenty first century and reinforces this claim in her discussion of Sri Lankan writer Jean Arasanayagam, who feels that "she has no country now but self."

In his essay "The Exile of the Mind," New Zealand dramatist, author and critic Vincent O'Sullivan speaks of the "groundswell from the past which rises continuously in the fiction of Katherine Mansfield and enables her to refashion it. He feels that at the heart of her creation is the desire to escape, at least momentarily, from the exile which she felt was detrimental to her work: "I'm sure that it does a writer no good to be transplanted." The conception of mental exile is further explored by University of Toulouse Professor Xavier Pons, who examines Australian writer Patrick White's assertion that the mind's exile can be beneficial: "...death by torture in the country of the mind is part of the process which turns an alien place into a home."

The transformation which must take place for the alien place to become a home is discussed by Francine Tolron from the University of Avignon. The imagined and the imaginary homelands of colonists in New Zealand blend the impenetrable forests of totara and rimu with the gracious oaks of England. What had only been imagined in England becomes real in New Zealand: what formerly constituted reality recedes into the imaginary world of a half forgotten past. Avignon lecturer Madelena Gonzalez insists upon the necessity of squarely facing the uncertainties inherent in the condition of exile. In her treatment of Salman Rushdie's philosophy of constant becoming, she demonstrates that exile is identity, the most productive form of identity – an intellectual exile from fixed truths. With Salman Rushdie, she believes that the organizing principle of intellectual exile seems to be uncertainty.

It would seem, as the French-Rumanian philosopher Cioran has suggested, that the uncertainties of exile, once experienced, can never be forgotten by a writer. For the implications reach deep into the recesses of mind and spirit, to the furthest corners of the conscious and the unconscious, transforming expression as the native tongue slowly becomes a strange one and the exile discovers a new sense of selfhood. In spite of the initial suffering engendered, there are gains as well as losses. For, as Cioran understood so well, lucidity is at least in part the consequence of being acutely aware of loss. We should not be surprised, therefore, to discover that the exile is both a far-seeing and eloquent being, whose very solitude allows him to mirror the subjective nature of his experience by creating a language and space of his own.

Part I
THE EIGHTH CONTINENT

1
The Eighth Continent or Living on the Edge

Reflecting on the fictional characters in my work, I discuss the novel *A Perfect Silence* and narratives from *The Eighth Continent and Other Stories* which explore the ambivalent identity and sense of exile among Puerto Ricans in the United States. The characters in these works inhabit an "eighth continent:" an emotional and psychic limbo teeming with people who do not belong where they are and who can no longer return to the place where they came from. My characters reflect my own condition of perpetual exile.

The edge of the tongue, the edge of the mind, the edge of consciousness. Flapping like a rag over the border and back, never knowing quite where that border ends or begins. Not knowing what the border consists of. What is a border, anyway?

What does it mean to live on the edge, to subsist on knives and blades and shards of glass? What does it mean to step ever so carefully, all the time afraid of stumbling over one's own tongue? The edge is not a shore or a frontier. The edge is a knife, a blade. The edge is the humiliation of a turned back, the sting of a slur, the rage of impotence. The edge is an end with no beginning. The edge is living the jabber of a foreign language.

The characters in my book *The Eighth Continent and Other Stories* inhabit that edge. They live the cutting experiences of a place they never anticipated inhabiting. A place of perpetual banishment. They are caught drifting aimlessly in a continent of marginal people coming together in a babble of languages, a cacophony of traditions, but never quite merging with any sense of belonging. Always looking back, far back, to the impossible return. One of the most unforgiving attributes of the eighth continent is that impossibility of going back. There is no possible return from the eighth continent. Finally, the eighth continent is living in the silence of one's language.

I was in Lille some years ago on a frosty February day when the North Sea wind cut into my face like a switchblade. Shivering, I took refuge in a café and plopped down at a table with a comfortingly hot and foamy double espresso. Rain came down heavily and made me glad to be indoors. I remember sitting quietly, looking out at a paved street that glistened under the pewter sky. I was lost in thought, but I became aware of a dramatic shift in the lifeless Musak that had been streaming from the speakers. It was like surfacing from the deep black sea into a windless day. There in Lille, a French city near the Belgium border, I heard the unmistakable voice of La Lupe, belting out *Teatro* a lusty Caribbean *bolero*.

The lyrics were drenched with meaning for me. The blend of the words, the voice, the rhythm – a fortuitous blend – transported me thousands of miles away, a lifetime away. But it was the words of the *bolero* that had the most impact. The passionate words, in Spanish, had the magic of flinging me back, far back into the curve of time and space.

Instantly, I was a little girl in the South Bronx. I was running up the stairs of the tenement building where we lived on 138th Street, hearing the *boleros*, the *rancheras*, the *salsa* that poured from other apartments. These melodies filled the stairwell with words of love, passion and death. The stuff from which fiction and poetry are wrought.

While I sat at the café in Lille, the *bolero* triggered memories of rice and beans, of oregano, garlic, cilantro and peppercorns, of a fragrant *sofrito* sizzling in the *caldero*. These culinary memories triggered others. I was flooded with memories. So at that café, I began writing the following description of the South Bronx that would eventually become part of my novel *A Perfect Silence*.

On 138th Street, men of the barrio, bandannas tied around their foreheads, roll dice. Empty-faced spectators hover on stoop steps, pulling hard on cigarettes and warm cans of beer. Someone flips a joke. Lethargic laughter rattles up to the sweaty women bent over window sills, arms crossed on folded towels. The women sniff the camphor air and watch the action on the stoops. They keep an eye on the ash-soaked boys pitching pennies at brick walls.

The heat is thick. Bongos and conga drums pulsate in the buckled air. The heat awakens atavistic yearnings for faraway suns. Heat drenches the South Bronx skies with sweat. Desolation. Alienation. Hunger. Apathy. A wick drenched in wrath ready to blaze violence.

Everyone waits – the dropouts, the laid-off, the janitors, bellhops, dishwashers – men and women who live with the insults that are constantly thrown at their feet, so they must look down. Weary of scrubbing toilets and scavenging trash cans, they wait out the long hours it takes to live through a day.

They flock to the streets seeking relief from the windowless, cheerless scorch of cold-water tenements. They bunch up in street corners shrinking from the cockroaches, the crying infants, the shrieking radios in their rooms. They skirt the garbage in the yards, the stench of urine clinging to stairwells, the harsh smell of smog. The street pushes its wares. Heroine and rum. Men snuffle and spit and squint under the hazy sun. They stare through the women who walk by, skirts hot as broth. A scuffle breaks out in the heat. A switchblade glints. A man gambles his life. It is worth so little.

At a distance, the mournful voice of Felipe Rodríguez, La Voz, makes an unusual appeal for wine: "Bartender, pour my wine in a broken glass. I want to bleed drop by drop the poison of her treacherous kiss." For even kisses kindle pain in the barrio. The jukebox bellow songs of agony and wrath. There is little hope embroidered in the notes that weave indolently through the days and the nights (46–47).

So, at that café in Lille, so far away from it all, I was able to go back to the ghetto on a blistering summer afternoon and relive it. Words from a *bolero*, words that I did not remember I remembered, brought it all back. Such is the power of language.

Our native language, or as I prefer to call it, our mother tongue, is the language that nurtures us when we are infants, when we are at our most vulnerable. The mother tongue is the coffer that holds the treasure of our mother's voice, her intonation, the gentle cadence of her words in the innermost sanctuary of the self. The mother tongue endures in that first precious word we hear, in the first concept we transform into a word, thus capturing the nature of meaning. Our mother tongue allows us, as infants, to grasp the meaning of the world which surrounds us. A world that can seem so enormous, uncontainable and hostile, but also welcoming and caring. Our mother tongue offers us the gift to name that world and everything in it. It allows us to make sense of the universe. Our mother tongue endows us with the magic of speaking the first word we ever speak. Yes, our mother tongue gives us the power to name.

Deceptively simple words in that primordial language, have the force to elicit potent memories, to stir the most meaningful of evocations. A word can bring back the aroma of freshly-baked bread, the scent of our mother's breast, the sounds of crickets chanting in the night. A word can elicit feelings of pain, loss, desolation and elation. A word can bring us back to a time we may have thought forgotten, but that exists in our brain, unerasable, enduring. Words have the power to contain within them all that we are. This is why the loss of a language is such a terrible tragedy.

The eighth continent is a state of infinite longing deeply embedded, I think, in the native language. The eighth continent is a state that results from having been expelled from the familiar, the loved, from having lost the primordial language. The pain of this loss is quite evident in the writer, who like me, lives the ultimate exile of writing in a language that is not her own.

Puerto Rico has been a colony of the United States for a century. As a result of the political, social, economic and cultural colonization of Puerto Ricans, we are exiles at our place of birth. Whether born on the island or the ghettos of New York City, where millions of us have flocked since the 1940s, we are born in exile. The English language, with its culture of domination, has invaded our lives. As Puerto Ricans rise to express ourselves, shunting between Spanish, our mother tongue, and English, the language of the colonizers, we are split in half and remain forever poised in the emotional limbo that exists between the two worlds. We're not quite Latin Americans, not quite North Americans. We inhabit the no man's land of the eighth continent, a land of alienation, of exile. In the eighth continent, we have forever lost our capacity to return home. There is no home to return to. Whatever we left, is no longer there.

The stories in my most recent book, *The Eighth Continent and Other Stories*, explore issues of race, language and the sense of exile of Puerto Ricans living in the United States. But it is the title of one of the stories that describes perfectly how Puerto Ricans in the US are perceived. The story *You Ain't Black, You Ain't White, You Ain't Shit* is a story about not fitting into a society that, when it does decide to peel the layers of invisibility from Puerto Ricans, sees us as the vicious gang members of *West Side Story*, the drug-addled prostitutes of *Fort Apache, the Bronx* or the cold-blooded murderer of Paul Simon's *Capeman*. We're never black enough, never white enough to fit into the mainstream. But we are invisible enough to forever inhabit the nether world of poverty, ignorance and criminality that racism and colonization have spawned.

The following are passages from the story *You Ain't Black, You Ain't White, You Ain't Shit* where the protagonist ponders on her feelings of anxiety when she moved from Puerto Rico to Boston and had to learn English, while fearing the loss of her mother tongue.

I came to New York to run away. Into my own mind. Before that I lived in Boston for many years. Boston's a cold city. Even in August when the weather is so hot you can fry an egg on the pavement, a chill, deep in my bones, was always there, reminding me of my absolute loneliness. The interminable winters were hard, snow crusting the streets like a biker's helmet, a snow so drab it made my eyes hurt and tear just to look at it. The gales of Boston tunnel between buildings all winter long, sharp as knives, cutting into your face and vulnerabilities. I used to gaze at the gray Charles River, take long walks down Fresh Pond, bicycle through the Cambridge Common, but I was blind to the beauty other people saw in the city. I always felt outside of myself there, having strange doubts about my identity. It was in Boston that I was forced to define who I was and couldn't find the vocabulary. It was there that I began to doubt myself, to see myself in the angry eyes of strangers who refused to see, to know, to acknowledge the person that I was. My mind wasn't free to really reach into itself and roam its interior landscape. I was always distracted fighting something or other out there where I didn't want to be in the first place. In Boston I felt like a graft that doesn't take.

...Amita was the first friend I made when my mother and I moved from Puerto Rico to Boston. I was only ten then. Amita and I met at Cambridge Alternative Elementary School. My mother was always putting me into alternative things. It's a hangup she has from the 60's.

...I truly hated school, especially when I was forced to learn English. I struggled so hard not to get lost in the harshness of the language. I also feared deprivations I was sure I would suffer when I learned it. I became even more terrified of English when my grandmother, who came to visit us from Puerto Rico, hear me practicing some words I had learned in the new language. She hugged me and said sadly, "When you learn English, Teresa, I'll never be able to speak to you again.

When I started speaking English well, I realized that often I'd forget the names of common things in Spanish. No matter how hard I tried to remember, the Spanish words just wouldn't be there perfectly arranged in my mind the way they used to be. I was so distressed about this that one day I went to school and refused to speak at all. I didn't speak for weeks, months. My mother was practically pulling her hair out, but it wasn't so bad. Since I wasn't distracted by words, everything seemed sharp and vivid. All my senses seemed to have awakened from a deep sleep. That's when I began roaming in my own mind, searching for hidden rooms, furniture covered with white sheets, and the dusty attics of memory (161–162, 173–174).

I came to my bilingualism at an early age, in a rather oppressive and severe environment. I was born in a shantytown in San Juan, Puerto Rico, and at the age of two arrived in the South Bronx, a Puerto Rican ghetto where everyone in the neighborhood spoke Spanish. By the time it was my turn to go to school, I had had very little exposure to English. So there I was at P.S. 9 on 138th Street: A Spanish-speaking Puerto Rican girl in the South Bronx. As typically happened in those days, my education began in a class for the mentally retarded. Mysteriously, I was no longer retarded when I learned English. So I was plucked from my dim-eyed friends and placed in a class where I finally learned to read – in English, the language I knew least. The first grade class at P.S. 9 read out of sheer fright, most of us spoke little or no English. So our teacher used unorthodox teaching methods. I remember her well. She was a dark-haired tyrant with scarlet nails and when we struggled to read a word we had never heard before, she pulled at our collars and braids and dug her red nails into our arms. To consolidate her power, she boasted possession of two eyes behind her head, hidden under her hair, so even when facing the blackboard, she could see our every move. Of course, she would never allow the use of Spanish in the classroom. So between those eyes we believed she had in the back of her head and the ruler blows she administered liberally when we spoke Spanish, we were a bunch of silent kids, let me tell you.

Because of this sink or swim method of instruction, instead of learning to read in Spanish, the only language I knew, and then transferring my reading skills to English once I learned it, I wasted several years just trying to make sense out of the language of books. Learning to read was a terrifying experience for me and it is a tribute to my subsequent teachers who instilled in me the love of books, that I was able to overcome my fear of school, of reading and writing and eventually I taught myself to read in Spanish. After some years, we moved back to Puerto Rico, in a phenomenon common with Puerto Ricans in which we flit back and forth between the U.S. and the island depending on economic circumstances. I eventually moved back to the United States to do graduate studies and then settled in Europe where I have lived for over fifteen years.

The first story I ever wrote in English is entitled *Dusks*. I wrote this story while living in Athens where my longing for the impossible return intensified. This story marks the moment when I realized that because of the emotional impact of certain themes, it was best if I wrote about them in English, my language of exile. Up to that point, my creative work had been written in Spanish. I never could have written *Dusks* in Spanish, though. Spanish is the language of the flesh, the language that flutters under my skin like a heart. To write in Spanish is to write with no clothes on, stark naked. The story *Dusks* is about the devastating impact of the loss of my mother when I was a child. It was much too painful to write about this in the language of the flesh.

English offered me the distance I needed to write this story. When I write in English, I do so with my clothes on, properly dressed to face friends and strangers. English is a language of geometries, of lines, of bones and scaffolds, of angles, of frontiers, of barriers. A hard language of sharp consonants and edges, it is also a supple, rich language, with lots of muscle. In English I can write about anything at all, regardless of the pain, longing, agony, and still feel at a distance. Because of the alienation in which I exist when writing in English, the themes of loss and longing which I frequently write about are not so painful to tackle.

English is also my language of disguise. When I write in English, I'm not really writing about me, but that other self that inhabits me and can take off into tangents I don't care to look at. English is absence, English is my metaphor for exile. It's the language of rage and frustration. Of weeping into the darkest recess of the night.

In the act of writing in English, I am lost in the different layers that underlie the language and I see myself as constantly translating my self. I translate the self that I truly am into the one that I become when functioning in English. But if I am constantly translating myself, how effective is this translation, I wonder? At times I don't know which is the translation and which the original.

A separation from my essential self is evident when I write in English and I often confront the language with suspicion. Am I really expressing what's in me when writing in English? Or is the English language so separate from my innermost self, that it fails to express who I am, what I feel? In my circumstances, English is the language of repression. The language which constrains my naked emotions and holds them in check. The language which censors. The language which punishes my flights into metaphorically rich landscapes and constricts my incursions into the lush rain forests of expression. I often wonder what degrees of separation exist between me and the writer who writes in English. So living in a language that is not my own, which is what I am doing now, creates a deep sense of exile. I really don't know where I stand. I feel a deep sense of *anomie*, of not belonging anywhere.

I'd like to end with an excerpt from the story *Rage Is A Fallen Angel* which I think best describes what it's like to live and write in the eighth continent.

In this place I'm finally grasping the true meaning of silence. A concept that echoes in my mind like a nightmare. There's a place at my core where words don't exist. Where I discovered the multiple dimensions of pain. The core of desolation, loss and rage. It's what was left after my little girl died and my pain had no words. There's nothing worse than the inability to name your hurt. Will I ever be able to attach words to my loss?

That's when I rage. And I hate and I rave and I pound on the table and scream, no more, I won't take any more. And I cut myself with knives, and when they take away the knives, I cut myself with plastic forks, whatever there is to hurt myself more. And then they hide everything from me, but I find a plastic cup and I crush it in my hand like a freshly laid egg and there I find that in the mess, there is always an edge. That's all I need to open my flesh, to make blood flow from myself. To feel relief from the terrible rage (142).

Alba Ambert
Richmond, The American International
University in London

Works Cited

Ambert, Alba. *A Perfect Silence*. Houston: Arte Público Press, 1995.

————. *The Eighth Continent and Other Stories*. Houston: Arte Público Press, 1997.

2

Memories of Living In-between

Rudyard Kipling is reputed to have said that there are two kinds of people: those who stay at home and those who do not. For all Australians except the Aborigines, emigration and immigration are facts of life and history, as is the concept of exile. The formative centre is located elsewhere, making memory and inherited memory extremely important. The way in which exile affects identity and the way in which the past becomes *myth* and the present *reality* is examined. Attention is paid to *cross-cultural living: living in-between* becomes a matter of balancing the tensions between cultures, languages and world views. The advantage that cross-cultural bilingual people have is that they are automatically able to view each relevant culture as a *subject* rather than as an *object*. Some countries, as well as some people, can be said to be *living in-between*.

My memories of Australia, my not infrequent returns to that place of my birth, my life in Greece, measuring nearly eighteen years now, and an attempt to start and maintain a parallel life in London, all mean that I am forever living in-between, forever re-entering atmospheres, forever adjusting and readjusting.It will be obvious that there is a certain pressure involved in this process: nomads of whatever sort inevitably find their hearts and minds becoming rather crowded, and a certain amount of splitting, tearing and bleeding seems to be unavoidable. But there is a certain convenience, too. Australia, for example, is always with me, the country of my mind; it doesn't matter, particularly, that there is a gap between the Australia of the present and my memories. Feeling homesick for Australia when in Greece, as I often do, I once wrote:

> Going back is easy. One blink and I am there, seeing, not rocks, tufted mountains, olive trees and cypresses, but a maze of suburban streets edged by clipped nature strips, each of which had a prunus planted at its centre.

I am a product of township and suburbia, but one Christmas I booked an air ticket after receiving a specifically Australian card, from which koala and kangaroos in fur-trimmed hats were mercifully absent. I spent some time writing about this card:

> A water-colour horse and cart pause on a narrow dirt track beside a post-and-rail fence, a verandah'd homestead beckons in the middle distance, a mountain makes a purple shadow against white-grey smudges of cloud. Gum trees, dead giants, skinny saplings, mature stalwarts, cast shadows on the stubbled paddocks, and the whole is dappled and stippled with muted, tinted light. Gold? Peach? Sand? Dust-coloured? I cannot decide. The name of the painting is Coming Home. This is one card I am likely to find in a scrapbook twenty years hence. Like so many suburban Australians I have been seduced by a rural scene.

We are suspended between the myth and the reality, not quite sure who we are or where we fit.

But then it seems to me, even though I am no theorist and certainly no academic, that there is a modern or post-modern preoccupation with the concepts of *identity* and *place*. Were people in previous generations as concerned? I am not sure, and was recently relieved to note that writer Theodore Zeldin considers that 'the idea of a sense of identity was invented for people who wanted the world to be less complicated.' (*An Intimate History of Humanity*, Minerva 1996, 380) Consider the case of the great historian Lewis Namier, who was a European Jew in the age of Hitler. John Vincent, another historian, tells us that Namier came from a part of rural Poland that was then Austrian. His first wife was of uncertain East European origin, his second Russian, and he spoke English with a foreign accent. And he was the world's greatest authority on the reign of George III of England. It should come as no surprise that Namier, in accepting multiple identity as a normal human condition, was very much aware of the pathology which calls itself nationalism.

Mario Vargas Llosa has memorably remarked that one's native land is an accident in life. In a sense, my three sons, whose father is Greek, have had two accidents and therefore have two native lands, Australia and Greece. They slip in and out of each country and each society with the greatest of ease: at least that's the way it seems to me. (If they were here now they would affect to moan about my exploitation of them, for I am always talking about them, always writing about them: they give me to understand that they need the equivalent of a modern Greek Lord

Shaftesbury to protect them, and I live in dread of a bill arriving.) Their dual heritage is, of course, reflected in the fact that they are bi-lingual. When my middle son visited England for the first time in 1988, an English girl said to him, 'I didn't know you spoke English.' 'Of course I do,' he replied, 'I'm Australian.' In 1992 that same boy was in Australia, and a Greek man remarked,' I didn't know you spoke Greek.' 'Of course I do,' came the answer, 'I'm Greek.'

It has been said that Australians are the hardest people in the world to categorise. It could also be said that my generation, the last of its kind, is the easiest to categorise. I am an Anglo-Celt Australian, born at the end of the war. If you grew up in country Victoria as I did, life was apparently mono-cultural and apparently simple: you knew who you were. You also knew <u>where</u> you were and where you were going. You were set for a received life, following the pattern your parents had set for you. There was home, there was school and there was church. Your ancestors had been part of what Australian historian Manning Clark called the transplantation of a mighty culture from one end of the earth to the other.

I think it is fair to say that for a certain type of personality this upheaval was, if not too much, at least enough. We are what we are. My own grandparents led quiet, contented lives of almost immutable routine. In his youth my grandfather had spent four years in the trenches of France and Belgium; those same years my grandmother spent in Port Hedland, Western Australia, a foreign land indeed in comparison with the Victorian Murray River township she had left. On their return from these places they had no real desire to leave home again; their lives seemed to be divided into sections with their early adventures taking on the status of myth. I always remember them as being a little tired, even though they were quite young grandparents. This memory interests me, almost as if the contrast, my being continually on the move, reminds me that I am alive, even though I, too, am a little tired. (Kipling remarked that there are only two kinds of people: those who stay at home and those who do not.) I know which sort I am, for I do not find the idea of settling, of being in one place or even in one culture necessarily natural. There is, after all, not much room to move in the grave and plenty of time to rest.

The idea of mono-cultural Australia, as it was thought to be way back then, needs to be and has been modified. We can only be, any of us, what we are, but what we are is complicated. (Even in the township where I grew up in the 50s there was a strong German element, and we also had an Austrian baker and a Chinese vegetable man). My great-great-grand-parents, in their various alliances, produced mongrels, as a Scot married a Cornishman, as a Gaelic speaker married someone who spoke only English, and as more Scots mixed with the products of Ireland and East Anglia. Many of these people experienced an isolation they had never experienced before as they moved from close-knit villages to lonely farmhouses. Their isolation was physical; mine, as I migrated from middle-class suburbia to a Peloponnesian village, was psychical: an interesting pattern. My ancestors also established contact with cultures they knew little about One great-great-grandmother lived in the Buckland Valley, then a remote part of NE Victoria, where she acted as midwife to the few Chinese women who were on the goldfields; her husband saved the lives of several Chinese miners during the Buckland Valley riots, and in turn, some time later, had his life saved by a Chinese man.

I have mentioned my grandmother's years in Port Hedland, Western Australia; she was there because her brother was a Presbyterian minister working for the Australian Inland Mission at that time. They both developed close contact with the Aboriginal communities there, a fact which it may not be politically correct to mention: people's lives are being continually reconstructed. My grandmother died too soon for me to ask the questions needed to penetrate the myth and to establish some sort of reality out of what seemed to me (I was very young) to be a romantic adventure.

Illegal immigration was also part of this long story, as a sailor forebear believed himself a murderer after he felled his petty officer with a deck-scrubber in a fit of pique. It was rather convenient that the ship on which this drama took place was moored off Adelaide: he swam ashore, and family legend as it that his hair turned white overnight. Twenty years later he saw the man he thought he had killed: he actually walked right past him in Collins Street, Melbourne.

I have already suggested that the concept of settling is not necessarily a natural one. Much can be said for patterned migration as being natural: can trillions of birds be wrong? I ask myself as I pack my suitcase yet again. It has also been contended that migratory species are less aggressive than sedentary ones, and now that I have lived, or at least stayed, in small communities in three countries, I can well subscribe to this theory. It is, however, a very common human desire to want to belong somewhere, somehow, yet writers return again and again to the impossibility of achieving this goal. Dickens, wanting it all, as usual, wrote that the journey is ever onward, or we have no place here: he combines the idea of belonging – and not. The same man saw one of his sons off on a voyage to Australia, and said, "This life is half made up of partings and we must learn to bear them." What his son said is not recorded; as far as I can ascertain they never met again.

Returns are also difficult: the great Greek poet George Seferis wrote of miserable homecomings to Greece in terms of parallel monologues and also wrote, very touchingly, of an attachment about which he felt profoundly ambivalent: "Opou kai na taxithepso, I Ellatha me pligoni. Wherever I go, Greece wounds me." (I know exactly how he felt.) But change itself makes foreigners of us all, of course, ensures that we do not belong, and David Malouf has written that we are all exiles, even those of us who have never left home. Age makes foreigners of us all: I occasionally think of St Peter and Charos as being passport control officers sitting waiting behind their respective windows rather than at the Pearly Gates or by the Styx. The Greek novelist Kazantzakis knew a great deal about not belonging, and maintained that loneliness is the natural climate or atmosphere of man. The Orthodox Church forbade him burial in a churchyard; his grave is atop the walls of Heraklion, and his epitaph reads: "Then elpizo tipota. Then fovamai tipota. Eimai eleftheros. I hope for nothing. I fear nothing. I am free". Solomos, who wrote the Greek national anthem, did not visit the Greek mainland.

But Australian writers such as Henry Handel Richardson, Martin Boyd and Patrick White had intimate knowledge of living in-between, and had, generally speaking, the whole business thrust upon them: Patrick White, for example, was born an Australian London gentleman, a very rare breed. Later writers such as George Johnston and Charmian Clift actively sought the condition of living in-between. More than thirty years ago Johnston and Clift escaped what they construed as the narrowness of Australian society and eventually went to live on the Greek island of Hydra. In the long-run, however, where they sought escape and balance, they found the particular chaos that goes with displacement, for problems of whatever type are almost always exacerbated by distance and isolation. It is a bitter lesson, and one I have had to learn, that many an attempt at reinvention or expansion of self, can eventually involve a contraction of that same self and the abandonment of a dream. While achieving very considerably, Johnston and Clift paid a high price for living in-between, but perhaps they would have paid it anyway, even if they had never set out on their great adventure. Returning to Australia was no help, for they had been away too long, had, in effect, lost two homes and found no substitutes. They tried valiantly to balance the tensions, but for whatever reason or reasons, the imbalance was, in the end, too striking and too prolonged.

As I have tried to suggest, much depends on personality, on family dynamics, on a whole host of factors. The Australian writer Glenda Adams lived in New York for some time and loved the whole experience of pottering around in that enormous city where there is no prescribed way of living one's life. In a sense she was living in-between in a particular way. Of course we all live poised between the past and the future, but the migrant is poised between expectation and reality, and, quite literally, I think, trembles in the present, in the endless moment usually in a state of utter and continuing exhaustion, as she constantly improvises in order to cope with each new set of circumstances. All this sounds quite negative: the positives are a chance to reinvent oneself at least to some extent, and the bracing effect of the new/culture shock which, after an interval, subsides into the sort of strain which is quite good for one. Of course I have to believe in this theory, don't I? Living in-between means living more intensely. Well, I have to believe in that idea, too.

I have to tell myself these things because, in the eighteen years I have spent in a Peloponnesian village, I have found myself living in-between in very particular ways, in that I did not merely swap countries. I swapped suburbia for an agricultural community, I moved from the tradition of Nonconformity in which I had been raised to the baffling mystery of Orthodoxy, and shifted from an educated middle-class family to live, at least for a time, with my mother-in-law, who was the widow of an Orthodox priest. She was illiterate and lived the completely traditional life: children, chooks, goats, donkey, the full catastrophe. From being reasonably articulate and competent, I was reduced to the fairly helpless level of the three year old as a result of being plunged into the specific and strange language world of a Greek village.

I was also caught, I now realise, between two life views, that of the pioneer as opposed to that of the peasant, the view of life as being <u>invented</u> and the view of life as being received, prescribed. Auden's poem "The Shield of Achilles" developed a particular significance for me, as I learned, slowly and painfully, that appearances in a strange country are always of a very provisional nature. The poem is directly applicable to the whole business of living in-between, to the gap between expectation and reality: poor

Thetis cries out in dismay as she sees what the thin-lipped armourer, Hephaestos, has finally wrought for Achilles.

> She looked over his shoulder
> For vines and olive trees,
> Marble well-governed cities
> And ships upon untamed seas,
> But there on the shining metal
> His hands had put instead
> An artificial wilderness
> And a sky like lead.[1]

Living in-between, like life itself, is so much more and so much less than we expect.

My sons, I am almost certain, do not have the same consciousness of this in-between-ness, being further along the continuum, as it were. Their lives involve a kind of pendulum swing rather than a linear progression. They seem to take being bi-lingual and cross-cultural for granted, at least at this stage of their lives. Their hearts are not divided the way mine is. They seem, rather, to be twice-blessed, and so far rather fortunate in not being as muddled as their mother is.

Comparisons must not be strained, but there are many that can be made between Greece and Australia. The geographical position of both countries is quite literally one of being in-between, with effects for both on the concept of identity. Both countries developed with the idea of the formative centre being located <u>outside</u>. The French historian Braudel considered that men can be crushed by the huge weight of distant origins. Constantinople is still at the heart of Greek consciousness, is a spiritual home in the way that Britain was once the spiritual home of white Australia.

Looking in the other direction requires great efforts for Greeks: I think this may also be the case for many Australians, as political and economic necessities force them to look in the direction of Asia. Greek parents still tell their small children to eat up their vegetables: "*If you don't grow up to be big, strong boys, how are we going to re-take the City?*" My sons have all been told by a female high-school principal that they must be prepared to shed their last drop of blood for Ellatha and the instruction has always reminded me of Andrew Fisher, Australia's Prime Minister at the outbreak of war in 1914, who pledged that Australia would defend Britain to the last man and the last shilling.

Arnold Toynbee considered that "human beings awake to consciousness to find themselves in chaos. They then try to impose order on this chaos in order to make life endurable. We cannot verify whether the chart we make of the mysterious universe corresponds to the elusive reality, but in order to live we have to make this chart, realising it is an act of faith which is also an act of preservation." Charts are, of course, instruments of navigation, and are particularly necessary for people, and even countries, who are neither one thing nor the other. It is interesting to remember that it was Toynbee who wrote of the centrality of first the Mediterranean and then Europe. Now historians seem to be considering the marginalisation of Europe. For individuals the pull of the past, childhood, religion and culture gets stronger as they age. I think the same is probably true of countries. If it is, then white Australia should not neglect the inner child of Europe/Britain, whether or not these places are now marginal.

Theodore Zeldin suggests that the traditional emphasis on the metaphor of roots is an indication of an old-fashioned interpretation of botany. We must remember, he urges, the importance of leaves. The foliage of a tree is, after all, extremely important. For Zeldin, roots represent the past, while leaves represent the future, an open-ness to light and life.

Writer Oliver Sacks sees each of us as 'a singular narrative. To be ourselves, we must have ourselves – possess, if need be repossess – our life stories, 'recollect' ourselves, recollect the inner drama, the narrative of ourselves.' The Australian critic Helen Daniel extended this metaphor when she maintained that 'this holds for countries and communities as well as individuals. Australia, too, is a narrative which is being continually constructed.' To be ourselves we must possess or repossess our life stories. We must recollect our British and European past even as we look, of necessity, and also from desire, towards Asia. We should no longer feel crushed by the weight of distant origins, but regard them instead as a source of great richness and power. Living in-between, balancing the tensions, can help us, I think, transform Seferis's parallel monologues into some sort of dialogue. We must not neglect the myth while looking forward – along the narrative continuum, if you like – to what we are pleased to call reality.

To end on a maternal and also an exploitative note, as my sons would have it, let us say that people who live in-between can make enviable connections of an unexpected sort. My youngest son was eleven when he visited London for the first time. He saw his very first squirrel in St James's

Park, and was caught half-way between fear and excitement as this cheeky little creature ran up his leg. But he rallied quickly. 'Smaller than your average possum, Mum?' he asked, and in that moment I knew that he was checking his particular myth against the reality of the moment and that the graft, Australia on to Greece, had taken, and that there is a great deal to be gained from living in-between. People who live in-between can make connections of a viable sort.

Gillian Bourras
Australian writer

Notes

1. Auden, W.H., "The Shield of Achilles", in *New Golden Treasury of English Verse*, Leeson Edward (ed), London: Pan-Macmillan, 1981.

3

A Rediscovery of The Dislocated Self
Through Literary Translation

In *High Wind in Jamaica*, by Richard Hughes, variable aspects of a ten year old girl's behaviour in widely different circumstances point to a changing perception of the self. The same phenomenon was experienced by myself following repeated uprooting in my childhood. My translation from Spanish into English of a work by the Argentinean author, Héctor Tizón, bridged the break between my Mexican and New Zealand selves, and brought into focus the intimate connection between language and identity. In short, identity is seen to be a variable, shifting state dependent on surroundings, social pressures and language, among other factors, around a central fulcrum of the constant, basic self.

Somewhere in the middle of Richard Hughes' novel *High Wind in Jamaica*, in which a group of children are stranded in a schooner with the pirates who have abducted them on their way from Jamaica to England, the young heroine – who liked to climb up the ship's mast and sit on a perch at the top to pass the time surveying the ocean around her – was suddenly struck one day by the amazing thought that, out of all the people in the world, she was *she*. With her legs entwined around the mast, she looked down under her dress to examine what she could see of her body, and then rubbed the side of her face against the hollow of her shoulder trying to work out whether she felt the sensation of that caress through her cheek or her shoulder, and all the while she was thinking with astonishment, "this is *me*".

The second part of *High Wind in Jamaica* I vividly recall is the ending of the book. The ten year old girl this time is sitting in court, being interrogated before a jury, with the pirates in the dock, back in the civilized world of England. In response to the heavy pressure from this, to her, new society – different from her colonial life in lush Jamaica, or her experience at sea with the gentle pirates – she complies with what is expected of her from all those around her and ends up describing in the most convincing, graphic details a bloody murder that didn't take place, sending her friends to the gallows. The reader is left feeling an uncomfortable witness to the various, complicated aspects of the child's identity, from the girl we first meet growing up as part of a genteel, English colonial family in wild, tropical Jamaica in the throes of a hurricane, and then watch as the happy, carefree tomboy, exploring, fantasizing, and enjoying the natural elements around her on the ship with the pirates, along with the human interactions which develop between them, and now *this* person who, in response to the demands of her new social environs, coldly, without thought or care, as though acting in yet another private make-believe game of her own, betrays her innocent friends condemning them to their deaths. This perplexing, changing picture of a human being, a child, as she moves from one milieu and circumstance to another, seemed to me to be thrown up in sharp relief against the *moment* – so beautifully described by Hughes – of the girl's sudden, incisive awareness of her Self as she sits high on the ship's mast surrounded by nothing but air and water, unencumbered by all the paraphernalia of nations, culture and society: the clear, unadulterated 'I'.

Looking back now, I can better understand the impact on me by those particular passages of that novel, as I read it at a time when I too was fully engrossed in my efforts to come to terms with my new life and surroundings in a new country, New Zealand – where my reduced family had recently emigrated – while trying at the same time to deal with the loss of my old world in Mexico. In my confusion, I was trying to understand where I stood in the midst of all those changes, what was happening to the *me* I had felt I was up till very recently, and what I had to do, what transformations I had to undergo, to be taken up into my new surroundings. It was a time too, when the reasons for our earlier move, from France to Mexico when I was five, were beginning to dawn on me: the full force of the Shoa with all its implications, the sense that we had escaped, but so many others had not, and the role of friendship and treachery in times of war, the nature of loyalty and its breakdown under social pressure, or more extremely, under torture, were all questions I was trying to grapple with – for all these things are fundamental to what one is, to our identity.

In *High Wind in Jamaica*, Richard Hughes seemed to be exposing the raw, unretouched mind of a child at the mercy of changing natural surroundings and, more conflictingly, changing adults' expectations. Among other things, Hughes appeared to be throwing into some kind of perspective the enigmatic, in some sense even ephemeral, nature of this thing we call 'identity'. Is it, in essence, anything we can catch, ensnare, examine, define?

A few years ago, following a lecturing visit at a congress of my medical specialty in Buenos Aires, unlike many of my colleagues who disappeared to spend some days in Barriloche, the "Switzerland of Argentina", according to the brochures we were handed out, I preferred instead to visit the remote, little known area in the northwest of the country, in the Andes, close to the Chilean and Bolivian borders, where the local population still includes descendants of the indigenous people from the days before the Spanish Conquest. Here, in San Salvador de Jujuy, and in the mountains and plains I visited further north, I was bewitched by the otherworldly aura I came across – the slow, timeless rhythm of life and landscape; the calm, olive lake of Yala in the hollow of a summit; the twisted *seibo* trees with their crimson flowers; the violet, pink and sepia of the stratified hills of Purmamarca; the direct, open friendliness of everyone I came into contact – and, on my return to London, in my quest to learn more about that area, an Anglo-Argentine journalist friend lent me the books of a writer he knew from San Salvador de Jujuy. I turned to the first page and read,

> *Aquí la tierra es dura y estéril; el cielo está más cerca que en ninguna otra parte y es azul y vacío. No llueve, pero cuando el cielo ruge su voz es aterradora, implacable, colérica. Sobre esta tierra, en donde es penoso respirar, la gente depende en muchos dioses. Ya no hay aquí hombres extraordinarios y seguramente no los habrá jamás. Ahora uno se parece a otro como dos ojas de un mismo árbol y el paisaje es igual al hombre. Todo se confunde y va muriendo.*

> Here the earth is hard and barren. The sky is closer than it is anywhere else, and is blue and empty. It does not rain. Yet when the sky roars, its voice is terrifying, wrathful, implacable. In this land, where air is scarce, the people rely on many gods. Men of distinction are no longer found here, and surely will never be again. Now, one man is like another as two leaves from a single tree and the landscape is similar to man. Everything is mixed up and slowly dying.

In some peculiar way I could not explain, these words hooked me. The starkness and strength of Héctor Tizón's writing in combination with mysterious, often ambiguous nuances and the remarkable sense of discovery provoked by its every phrase, stirred me deeply. The Spanish of Tizón's novel, *Fuego en Casabindo*, turned out to be a difficult mix of archaic idioms, reflecting the remoteness of that region until the advent of the railway at the turn of the twentieth century; local prehispanic terms which had found their way into the language; and finally and not least, Tizón's own inimitable construction of expression. During my determined efforts to capture the breadth and depth of Tizón's meaning, I found myself laboriously examining each phrase and translating it into English – the language I had become more familiar with over the years – that I might grasp it better. My task became a passion, and as the extraordinary story of life on that high, barren plateau in the Andes, with its myths, wild contrasts and closeness to the elements: the dust, the wind, the thunder and lightning, the colour, music and dance, the strange hybrid rituals which fused the Christian with the pre-Columbian, and the harshness of everyday life, as all this was unfolding and being transformed into English words and constructions in my mind, my own two worlds of a primitive Mexican village where I grew up, and the genteel Anglo-Saxon world of New Zealand into which I was abruptly transplanted in my early adolescence, suddenly met.

That meeting of those two, up till then, very separate worlds within me, was like an earthquake: a shaking, cathartic experience. The rift between my early life, which I had experienced in Spain, France and Mexico, and of which all my memories and associations were intimately bound with the Spanish and French languages, and my subsequent life in New Zealand and later in London, which I experienced and expressed in English, was being bridged, resolved, healed by the actual process of translating Tizón's work. Though by then I had spoken English for by far the greater part of my life – I had done my secondary schooling and my medical and postgraduate studies all in English, as well as all my reading and writing, which included scientific papers, yet my earliest experiences of this language were intimately associated with my distress and disorientation at my abrupt dislocation from my lush, intense, colourful Mexican world, to the unfamiliar, grey, flat world of Christchurch, New Zealand. English, for me, had turned into a language of repression, the language in which I formed all my new associations during my struggles to adjust to that foreign land as I had to learn and use it to communicate in my new surroundings, while at the same time I was trying to deal with the loss of all the vitality and sensuality of my Mexican world – in other words, a crushing of what to that point had been my Self. Although I had mastered English, I resented it, I kept it at arm's length, I felt uneasy with it. And now, I was discovering that in going through the task of refashioning that remote, harsh, magical world of Tizón in the Andean plains into the English language, in the painstaking searching of words and phrases and rhythms and sounds in English, that I might convey that ambience with its vague but strong echoes of the Mexico I had loved and lost.

I was stretching a soothing link across the two. I was making friends with English, learning to love it, to get pleasure in my use of it. I began to understand too the powerfully emotive relationship we have with language. I remembered, for instance, how the sound of German – my mother's native tongue which I had frequently heard in the background as she conversed with her friends during my early childhood in Barcelona and in France during times of war – would evoke feelings of warmth and tenderness as it elicited my mother's voice, yet as I grew older and heard the Gestapo's shrill commands in films and documentaries, that same language began to give me a sense of dread.

And more: I was also experiencing the essential part language plays in our sense of self, for with my change of language, I saw now that I had undergone a whole new system of thinking, a new view of the world experienced through different sounds and associations, another grammar and vocabulary, so that the image of who I am in one language differs from my self image in another. It seemed as though each language has its own, particular, separate, nervous network, or circuitry of associations, in the brain, each making up a whole inner world in our mind, which was the 'I' in that language, and that these different networks, in parallel, were being bridged every time we switch from one language to another, as when translating. And – maybe – the more established and numerous these neuronal bridges between them, the more integrated be our identity. As all these ideas came into focus while I continued with my translation, the relationship between my own flimsy 'roots' and the memories I carry within me also began to emerge, and I started understanding that all my nostalgia for countries in my past was nothing more than a mirage. For I had not, after all, lost a part of myself in my beloved Mexican village, Acapancingo, but it all existed still within me, and my 'roots' do not reside outside myself, in some geographic location or even as part of a defined group of people, but are actually made up of the sum total of all my memories and experiences which I carry within me, and all the richer for spreading across so many cultures and continents. Indeed, I was beginning to feel privileged to have experienced such an extravagant wealth of first-hand material which I could sift around and think about, in my contemplation of the nature and wonder of identity.

Tizón, on the other hand, was born and grew up in San Salvador de Jujuy and the nearby village of Yala, and has a very strong sense of his definitive, geographical and cultural roots. In *Fuego en Casabindo*, which I was translating, he brings to life the people of his land along with their rigours and celebrations, legends and history – and this is *his* world, that which he loves and to which he always returns, whether he has been abroad working in his country's diplomatic service, or in exile from his country's brutal regimes. For this is the place where, as he says, he feels *himself*, surrounded by his familiar landscape and the people he understands. In another of his novels, *La Casa y el Viento*, (the house and the wind), he writes about his pain of separation from these deeply felt roots.

Desde que me negué a dormir entre violentos y asesinos, los años pasan. Todo parece simple y claro a lo lejos, pero al recordarlo mis palabras se convierten en piedras y soy como un borracho que hubiera asesinado a su memoria. Como es posible que lo que quiero narrar -el derrotero de mi propia vida: una huella minúscula y difusa en la trama de otras vidas- sea tan difícil? La soledad también enseña a gobernar la lengua. Pero ya no quiero estar solo, ni olvidar ni callar. No quiero que la noche me sorprenda con mi propio rencor. Cuando decidí partir, dejar lo que amaba y era mío, sabía que era para siempre, que no iba ser una simple ausencia sino un acto irreparable, penoso y vergonzante, como una fuga. Creo que es la única manera de irse. Pero antes de huir quería ver lo que dejaba, cargar mi corazón de imágenes para no contar ya mi vida en años sino en montañas, en gestos, en infinitos rostros; nunca en cifras sino en ternuras, en furores, en penas y alegrías. La áspera historia de mi pueblo.

Since I refused to sleep among brutes and murderers, the years pass on. All seems clear and simple from afar, but on recalling it my words are turned into stones and I feel like a drunk who would shoot down his own memory. How is it possible that what I wish to relate – the course of my own life, a minute, diffuse imprint in the chain link of other lives – should be so difficult? Solitude teaches us also to guard our tongue. But I no longer want to be alone, to forget, to keep silent. I don't want the night to surprise me with my own rancour. When I decided to go, to leave behind what I loved and was mine, I knew that it would be forever; that it was not going to be a simple absence, but an irreparable act, painful and shameful, like taking flight. In reality, all my departures have been flights. I think that is the only way to go. But before escaping, I wanted to see what I was leaving, to fill my heart with images, that I may no longer measure my life in years but in mountains, gestures, infinite faces; never in numbers but in tender moments, in furies, in pains and joys. The harsh story of my people.

So here too, speaking thr-ough the character in his novel, Tizón has the urge to "fill his heart", to engrave in his memory all the images of his land, that he might take a blueprint of his 'roots' to a new home in unfamiliar ground.

In the commonly hostile world of exile – especially when it arises from circumstances which themselves have called in question, or worse, outrightly condemned aspects intimately related to our identity, be they racial, ideological or political – questions of *who* or *what* we are, are thrown into sharp relief. In the experience of this inner conflict born from misplacement, while trying to deal with the break with the past and the adjustment to the new, these questions begin to haunt and trouble us. Are we what we were? Or are we this new emerging self? Is there maybe a running thread in our centre which does not change? Perhaps the pristine 'I' which the girl in the pirate ship suddenly recognised ...

I once watched with fascination speeded up images of developing nerves caught in film through a powerful microscope, in which the nerve axons, or filaments, could be seen budding, growing and stretching towards other nerve cells and making new synapses, in relation to new stimuli experienced by the organism. Here was a beautiful picture demonstrating the actual changes taking place in the developing, central nervous system in response to new sensations received by the individual, suggesting that each experience is in fact incorporated, however subtly, in the structure and circuitry of the brain. So we are, indeed, what we have experienced, yet always subject to further change, bearing in mind too that our potential, over and above our initial genetic typecasting, must be vast, if not infinite, which suggests to me that what we become – that is our identity – is to a large measure a result of chance and circumstance, making things like wars based on patriotism, or religious disagreement, or presumed racial superiority, in essence, absurd – looked at from this angle.

Our behaviour also forms an integral part of this thing we define as the Self. Add to that, our morality and our philosophy. Remember the girl who betrayed her friends, the pirates, in her new surroundings, when the Atlantic ocean was replaced by an English court. And it is in exile, again, that our response to new demands and circumstances, and our interaction with a new group of people, are placed under greater strain, when the pain of the sense of 'not belonging' might tempt us to compromise our integrity that we be accepted, lose sight of that central 'I', and in turn and paradoxically double our struggles in our attempt to recover it.

I have tried to give a sense of the profound revelations my translation of Tizón's work opened up for me in terms of my identity and its inseparable relation with language. It gave me a greater understanding of the part played in my perception of my self by my memories and all I have experienced in my motley life so far, of the flux and flow of what one perceives as Self in response to changing surroundings, every day and moment even, and the possibility of transcending that shifting image to maybe reach a central core, rather like the eye of a storm, the serene, constant, essential 'I' where common humanity and the universal meet.

Miriam Frank
Senior Lecturer and Consultant in Anaesthesia
Royal London Hospital

Works Cited

Hughes, Richard. *High Wind in Jamaica*. London: Chatto and Windus, 1929.

Tizón, Héctor. *Fuego en Casabindo*. Buenos Aires: Galerna, 1969.

———. *Fire in Casabindo*. Trans. Miriam Frank. London: Quartet Books, 1993.

———. *La casa y el Viento*. Buenos Aires: Legasa, 1984.

4

The Dream of a Victorian Quattrocento: D.G. Rossetti's Answer to the Dilemma of His Anglo-Italian Identity

As an "Italian from England", the painter-poet D.G. Rossetti (1828–1882) was equally influenced by his Italian ancestry and by his English contemporaries. His allegiance, in turn to the spirit of Quattrocento artists and to that of British poets, can be traced in most of his painted work up to about 1870. After that period however, Rossetti's two main sources of inspiration seem to blend into the careful balance that became characteristic of his later works: the artist had created an iconography suited to his needs, one that fully acknowledged his cross-cultural identity.

As it is suggested in the title of this paper, Dante Gabriel Rossetti's exile took place in time as well as in space; however it was not a physical one but one of the mind. The sense of rootlessness due to his double origins led the poet-artist to strive to achieve the symbiosis of the time periods and cultural influences he felt close to. In examining a corpus of 62 works produced between 1849 and 1880[1], it appears that these are divided in almost equal proportion between Italian and English inspiration. The predominance of one source over the other alternated, and thus four distinct phases can be observed. The early part of the painter's career shows an endeavour to identify himself: first as an Italian Quattrocentist until 1856, then as a predominantly British Victorian artist during the 'Jovial Campaign' of 1857. After 1859 he went back to Italian sources but slowly adapted them until they reflected his dual identity. During the last ten years of his life as an artist, Rossetti alternated Italian and English titles for his paintings, but it seems that his inspiration had come to rely less and less on either nation's literary background. He had managed to create for himself the dream-world that incorporated the essence of both.

Italian aspects

Dante Gabriel Rossetti (1828–1882) was an English painter, poet and translator of Italian descent. His father had migrated to England in 1824, as a political exile. His maternal grandfather, Gaetano Polidori, was also Italian.

Rossetti's Christian names were in fact Gabriel Charles Dante. It would thus seem that his parents had wanted to anglicize the name of the father: Gabriele. Gabriel was the name which his friends and family always called him, and the name which he used to sign his letters. When he had to sign *The Girlhood of Mary Virgin* (1849), his first major oil painting however, he reversed and italianized his Christian names into Dante Gabriele. The dropping of Charles, which may have sounded too English to him (and reminded him of his godfather Charles Lyell, with whom he did not get on well), together with the addition of a final "e" to Gabriel and the emphasis on Dante would seem to indicate that the young artist wanted to assert his Italian origins. Later he reverted to Gabriel as a middle name, thus forming the Anglo-Italian name by which he became famous.

The influence of Italy on the young man can be traced in his physical appearance – in his biography, Stanley Weintraub insists on Rossetti's "Latin grace" (Weintraub 82) – and in the fact that many Italian exiles visited the Rossetti home, thus re-creating a continental microcosm. But the most important Italian aspects of Rossetti were his mastery of the Italian language, and his fascination for Dante Alighieri, both inherited from his father who was a Professor of Italian at King's College as well as a life-long Dante scholar. Therefore Rossetti was at an early age connected, via his father's studies, with Italy's late medieval and early Renaissance poets. Of these, Dante had the most powerful and longer lasting influence. Rossetti stated in the preface to his translations "the first associations I have are connected with my father's devoted studies ... Thus, in those early days, all around me partook of the influence of the great Florentine" (Hunt 75). Rossetti's fascination for his 14th century namesake was such that it grew in his imaginative mind that he must be some sort of reincarnation of the great Italian, and that somewhere his own Beatrice was awaiting him. This is what he implied when, in a poem he addressed his father thus:

> And didst thou know indeed, when at the font
> Together with thy name thou gav'st me his,

That also on thy son must Beatrice
Decline her eyes according to her wont ...? *Dantis Tenebrae* (1861)

The influence of Dante pervaded most of Rossetti's iconographical production from 1849 until 1856 (8 out of 14 works listed in the Appendix). Many water-colours, small in format but highly finished in detail prove his obsession for rendering the mood of the 14th century poet. *Beatrice Meeting Dante at a Marriage Feast Denies him her Salutation* (1851) or *The First Anniversary of the Death of Beatrice* (1853) are good examples of his production of that period. The gem-like colours Rossetti obtained by using very little water, and occasionally mixing his pigments with glue, were quite new to the Victorian public used to the tarrish browns which appeared regularly on the walls of the Royal Academy. The colours in *Beatrice Meeting Dante at a Marriage Feast Denies him her Salutation* appealed to the influential art critic John Ruskin who declared it "a most glorious piece of colour"; "The breadth of blue – green – fragmentary gold" was to him "a perfect feast" (Whiteley 48). Upon seeing *The First Anniversary of the Death of Beatrice*, the author of *Modern Painters* sent Rossetti a letter which marked the beginning of their friendship. "I think it a thoroughly glorious work" he wrote "– the most perfect piece of Italy, in the accessory parts, I have ever seen in my life"[2].

At the time he wrote to Rossetti for the first time, John Ruskin was a specialist in early Italian art, and he was able to recognize in the small water colours the glorious pigments and the unmistakably Italian touch of the artist who, unlike himself, had no first hand experience of Italy. Indeed, despite his environment, influences, and the recognition of John Ruskin who described him as "a great Italian tormented in the Inferno of London", Rossetti could only feel Latin in his imagination. Mary Bradford Whiting remarked that "Italian as he was by birth and by nature, he had never watched the yellow Arno washing the palace walls of Florence, he had never seen the glow of the sunshine on the white colonnades and pillared loggias that he loved to paint; for him the grey-green olive and the dark pointing finger of the cypress existed only in imagination." (Whiting 278). Rossetti had never physically travelled to Italy[3].

English Aspects

Because he was born and educated in London, Rossetti felt at home in England. The culture he had acquired from his childhood readings – full of chivalric adventures by Sir Walter Scott, tragedies by Shakespeare, gothic tales by Byron and Maturin, as well as old English and Scottish ballads[4] – made it possible for him to develop an Anglo-Saxon imagination. Mrs Helen Angeli, Rossetti's niece, wrote of him that he was "noticeably English in attitude and tastes" (*Rossetti and the Pre-Raphaelite Brotherhood* 93) and in fact Rossetti as a social man was well integrated in Victorian London: he had many English friends, eventually married Elizabeth Siddall, an English-born girl, he was recognized and championed by the most famous English art critic of his time. His Englishness was due to his perfect mastery of the language, to his "Anglo-Saxon wit" (Weintraub 82) , to his down-to-earth Victorian businessman's concern about the price of his paintings;

Moreover, Dante Gabriel Rossetti had found in the poet and painter William Blake another possible prior possessor of his soul. Blake's poetry had become accessible to a larger public from 1839 when *Songs of Innocence* were first printed in ordinary type. Therefore it is not surprising that when Rossetti, at the age of 18, was offered the chance of buying Blake's own note-book for ten shillings, he enthusiastically accepted. He kept the precious volume with him for the rest of his life. Obviously, "the 58 leaves crammed full of Blake's sketches and scribblings" (Preston 43) had a deep and lasting influence on the young painter-poet, whose imagination had come to dwell on an intriguing coincidence: Blake had passed away on 12th August 1827, whereas he, Rossetti, was born on 12th May 1828, exactly nine months later. Could it be possible that the soul of Blake had been intercepted at the moment of his conception? K. Preston suggests that Rossetti fondled the idea that he could be a reincarnation of Blake (38–41).

Indeed, it seems that just like William Blake before him, Rossetti was unable to find inspiration in the contemporary scene: the one "social subject" he ever tackled was that of prostitution, and he never finished painting *Found*, with which he struggled from about 1854 until the end of his life. No matter how English he felt, "the ordinary world of vision scarcely supplied any inspiration to him" (Doughty 157). One notable instance of Rossetti borrowing from Blake in his iconography can be seen in the winged spirit of Love escaping from the hand of the female figure in *La Donna della Fiamma* (1870).

Finally, the most obvious element that contributed to the Englishness of Dante Gabriel Rossetti was his attraction for, and frequent treatment of the Arthurian legends. Subjects drawn either from Malory or from the new Tennyson version of the Arthurian cycle inspired 8 out of the 14 works produced between 1856 and 1859 listed in the appendix. This interest, possibly initiated by William Morris, reached a climax at Oxford in 1857 where Rossetti had planned to decorate the walls of the Union building with illustrations of the tales of King Arthur and the Knights of the Round Table. Rossetti was to paint three out of the ten panels himself, but eventually only painted one, *Sir Lancelot's Vision of the Sanc Grael* (1857). The pen and ink drawing of *Sir Lancelot in the Queen's Chamber* (1857) could have been intended for another compartment. After the Oxford episode, Rossetti's interest in the Arthurian legends did not abate: seven years after the "Jovial Campaign" he was still influenced by the medieval Arthurian theme and painted *How Sir Galahad, Sir Bors, and Sir Percival were fed with the Sanc Grael; but Sir Percival's Sister died by the Way* (1864) – a watercolour based on one of the murals. His enthusiasm for putting his art at the service of contemporary craftmanship did not fade either: in 1857 he was involved in the illustration of the Moxon edition of Tennyson's poems on the Arthurian legends, for which he contributed five designs, and in 1859 he painted a watercolour, *Sir Galahad at the Ruined Chapel* which is an expanded version of one of them. He also took part in his friend's firm, Morris, Marshall, Faulkner and Company, for which he produced designs for *The Story of St George and the Dragon* (circa 1861–1862), a series of six stained-glass panels. In most of his contributions to what was then called utilitarian craftmanship, Rossetti drew upon the English theme of Saint George, as well as British literature, both traditional and contemporary, ranging from Malory and Shakespeare to Tennyson and Coleridge.

Alternation

Rossetti belonged to two different cultures, which at different moments of his life became predominant: the first seven years (1849–56) of his artistic career were devoted mainly to the illustration of Dante's *Vita Nuova* – which he also translated –, while the following three years (1857–59) were marked by inspiration from English lore. From 1860 until 1870, he reverted mostly to Italian inspiration, whereas during the last decade of his life Italian and English sources alternated and eventually blended. Yet, while belonging to two cultures, Rossetti actually belonged to neither: the titles of some of his poems, such as *Birth-Bond, The Landmark, Lost on Both Sides* betray the quest for identity which occupied him throughout his life.

The first two periods, based respectively on Italian and then Anglo-Saxon heritage, show an effort of the artist to define his art by establishing an artistic tradition.This tradition took the form of the two successive phases of the Pre-Raphaelite Brotherhood.

In 1848, Rossetti took part in the founding of the Pre-Raphaelite Brotherhood, together with two fellow-students from the Royal Academy School: W. Holman Hunt and J. Everett Millais. The name Rossetti coined for their association, which included seven young men, shows his conciliatory effort to bring together English and Italian traditions, as well as two different time periods: the Pre-Raphaelite Brotherhood had the "romantic, conspirational connotations" of a 19th century secret society, "as well as the ring of the early Christian monastic tradition" (Weintraub 29) which the young artists saw in 14th and 15th century art. It also brought together the Italian tradition of the painters who had preceded Raphael, and the British taste for clubs.

Dante Gabriel Rossetti's attempt to solve the dilemma of his dual background consisted in re-creating a past in which he could bring together the two parts of his identity. . His solution was an effort to merge English and Italian cultures into an ideal synthetic past which he constructed to fit his own needs, and which gave him a justification as an Anglo-Italian in his own right. This ideal Anglo-Italian medieval past was painted in powerful Italian colours, but used English models. Within the frame of his constructed ancestry, Rossetti invented an imaginary artistic tradition which he could draw upon for inspiration, and which he could perpetuate. Characteristically, the Brethren, under the impulse of Rossetti, needed to stipulate, at the founding of the Brotherhood, the tradition in which they situated themselves and the heroes who became the object of their creed. A document, "the list of the Immortals" was therefore produced (Hueffer 105–106). It formed an almost completely Anglo-Italian pantheon (40 out of 57 "Immortals" were either English or Italian), allowing for the insertion of three biblical characters, certainly to please William Holman Hunt, and a few outsiders such as Homer, Joan of Arc, and Cervantes. It is interesting to note that in the bulk of English and Italian entries, no doubt largely the work of Rossetti – for Hunt and Millais were little versed in literature or art history – the English are twice as numerous as the Italians. The former are mainly writers – including Romantic and Victorian poets such as Byron, Wordsworth, Keats, Shelley, Elizabeth and Robert Browning, Coventry Patmore, Thackeray and Tennyson – whereas the latter are predominantly Quattrocento artists: Raphael,

Michael Angelo, Giovanni Bellini, Giorgioni, Titian, Ghiberti, Fra Angelico and Leonardo da Vinci. Therefore, the tradition which Dante Gabriel Rossetti was trying to establish drew heavily upon Anglo-Saxon literature but considered itself the successor of the early Italian masters.

After the first Brotherhood was dissolved in 1853, Rossetti still felt the urge to belong to a community, and he found an emotional and artistic compensation in his art teaching at the Working Men's College. In 1857, however, an unofficial second Brotherhood was formed with William Morris and Edward Burne-Jones as the main disciples and Rossetti abandoned for a while his Dantesque obsession and developped an interest in the Arthurian Legends. In Oxford, where the two new disciples were students, was the newly-built Oxford Union which had an octogonal reading gallery with large wall surfaces, pierced by attractive six-leaved windows. Rossetti asked Woodward, the architect, for permission to gather a few painters to decorate the walls in an endeavour that would certainly be "an experiment", since mural painting of this kind had never been done in England. "Woodward was greatly delighted with the idea," Rossetti related in a letter of June 1861, "as his principle was that of the medieval builders to avail himself in any building of as much decoration as circumstances permitted at the time" (That Ne'er shall Meet again 101).

Thus, once again, a group of seven dedicated young men was brought together – Rossetti's "brothers" from the first Pre-Raphaelite Brotherhood had declined the invitation – and they spent an unforgettable summer (which is still referred to as the 'Jovial Campaign') decorating the walls of the Union with subjects from Malory's *Morte d'Arthur*. Rossetti had never worked in wall-painting, and does not seem to have enquired about fresco techniques. Perhaps he felt reassured that his Italian ancestry would lead him unconsciously to rediscover instinctive gestures. The choice of mural painting seems emblematic of Rossetti's quest both for Italy and for the Quattrocento. He had discovered in 1848 engravings of famous frescoes of the Campo Santo in Pisa by Giotto, Orcagna and Gozzoli, in a book by Lasinio, which had filled him with enthusiasm. Typically, in enlumining a contemporary English building, which itself was Gothic in architecture, with paintings of Italian inspiration but illustrating ancient English legends, in the communal spirit of the old Italian masters or of the Round Table, Rossetti was doing more than just decorating the Oxford Union Debating Hall. He was enacting the effort that he had been making spriritually for a long time, which consisted in adapting his inherited Italian culture to the Victorian context of his life. But at this stage, the merging of both cultures had not yet been achieved and his efforts resulted in a superposition of Italian colours and mood over English literary subjects. This contributed certainly to the success of his illustrations of the Arthurian legends, which seemed traditional, and at the same time new and exotic.

Thus, the solution provided by the second Brotherhood was only a transitory one, and after his marriage to Elizabeth Siddall in 1860, Rossetti went back to his early influences, and titles such as *Dantis Amor* (1860) or *Bonifazio's Mistress* (1860) evoke the Italian atmosphere of his youth.

The Rossettian Dream World

Rossetti's sense of displacement increased after the suicidal death of his wife in 1862 and led him to seek escape within himself. As an obvious consequence of the creation of his imaginary past, Rossetti came to build an imaginary world, different both in time and space from the one he lived in.

The 1860s can be considered as a period of transition during which Rossetti still drew heavily upon the Italian tradition (11 out of 16 works in our corpus), even though the exact source of his inspiration became increasingly difficult to identify. His art from then on was less the illustration of other poets' verses than an expression of his own soul. This is certainly the case of *Beata Beatrix*, begun in 1863.

It would seem that the artist had achieved in his mind the dream of a perfect Victorian Quattrocento, the vision of which soothed his sufferings after the death of his wife and solved the dilemma of his identity. This was the dream he called forth for inspiration: Rossetti wrote "I shut myself within my soul / And the shapes come eddying forth" (Versicles and Fragments, VI, 379). The artist's soul therefore became his ultimate place of retreat where he felt so much at home that no more effort was needed to produce art. His task as an artist was then simply to copy the visions he had inside. Whether the shapes belonged to England or Italy had little meaning to him, they came from his inscape[5], where both cultures had been blended. Rossetti in his later works represented a far country in ancient times which came from his visions. Sometimes the paintings were without a subject, such as *Veronica Veronese*(1872) or *The Bower Meadow* (1872). Only the title makes it possible to classify them as Italian or English. The first one, "a study of varied greens", is a portrait of Alexa

Wilding, one of his favourite models, in a setting so absolutely out of time and space that the Italian title provides the only landmark. The landscape for *The Bower Meadow* was painted at Knole, near Sevenoaks, and yet, despite the Englishness of the title and the setting, the composition bears a resemblance to the 15th century Italian tradition of the "dancing in the garden scenes", the most famous of which is Botticelli's *Spring*.

His later paintings portray an idealistic and sensuous dream-world, which had become the real world for the artist: "I do not wrap myself up in my own imaginings, it is they that envelop me from the outer world whether I will or no" he said, thus emphasizing the opposition between his 'inscape' – a mixture of medieval England and Italy – and the outer world of Victorian London.

After a first mental crisis in 1872, he became more and more "a solitary prisoner of his own dream of a world", as Pater wrote (Hunt 98). His paintings from then on portrayed gigantic, sensuous and cruel women, with pouting lips, masses of wavy hair and columnar necks. These are now the paintings for which Dante Gabriel Rossetti's name is still remembered by the general public. As Rossetti gained autonomy from the Italian and English sources which had inspired him in his youth, his later paintings were accompanied by poems of his own composition. Whether their titles have an Italian or English ring, is as irrelevant as the language in which the accompanying poem was written. *Proserpine* (1872–82), of which there are eight versions, was sometimes painted with the appended sonnet in Italian (the 1874 version, which now hangs in the Tate Gallery, shows the poem and an inscription "Dante Gabriele Rossetti ritrasse nel capodanno del 1874", both in Italian. In the inscription, the artist reverted to the Italian name which he had used for the signature of *The Girlhood of Mary Virgin* in 1849), while sometimes the sonnet appears in English, such as in the 1882 version on which the artist was still working a few days before his death.

As the artist's sense of national identity became increasingly blurred, his paintings frequently incorporated simultaneously pieces of England and Italy. One version of *The Blessed Damozel* (1875–8), which is now at the Fogg Museum of Art, shows a maiden inspired by Dante's Beatrice who is looking down from heaven, not on her poet-lover as could be expected, but on an Arthurian hero with a dagger at his side, lying in a suspiciously English-looking countryside. The poem is in English. In 1875, Rossetti painted *La Bella Mano*, a very large portrait of Alexa Wilding as 'the Virgin of beauty and modesty'. This oil, despite its Italian title and elevated imagery, looks rather odd because, far from the austere settings of the early Italians, it features a crowded, "unmistakably bourgeois Victorian interior" (Rodgers 118). The majority of the works produced in the last period show a reconciliation of two influences which seemed almost incompatible with one another : the paintings of the 1870s appear to have transcended the dilemma of their creator's identity. *Astarte Syriaca* (1877) portrays Jane Morris as a love goddess, in a sphere "betwixt the sun and moon", where the notion of national identity has clearly become meaningless.

It seems that D.G. Rossetti managed to create in his imagination, and occasionnally bring to life in his art, a world that suited his needs, which borrowed aspects of England and Italy, of the 15th century artists and 19th century poets, and reconciled his two artistic models: Dante and Blake. This is possibly the reason why he never lived in Italy. Rossetti's exile was not a geographical one as his father's had been. It was a place and time of retreat and solace for his mind. While living his earthly life in Victorian London, he felt he had incorporated the spirit of medieval Italy. When asked why he had never travelled to Italy but had only painted it and written about it, Rossetti allegedly answered "Why bother? Got it all inside me" (Beerbohm 11).

Béatrice Pardini-Laurent
Université d'Avignon et des Pays de Vaucluse

Works Cited

Beerbohm, Max. *Rossetti and His Circle*. New Haven and London: Yale U. P., 1987.

Doughty, Oswald. "Rossetti's Conception of the 'Poetic'" (1953). *In Pre-Raphaelitism, a Collection of Critical Essays*, ed. J. Sambrook. Chicago and London: University of Chicago Press, 1974.

Fleming, G.H. *Rossetti and the Pre-Raphaelite Brotherhood*. London: Rupert Hart-Davis, 1967.

———. *That Ne'er Shall Meet Again*. London: Michael Joseph, 1971.

Hueffer, Ford Madox. *The Pre-Raphaelite Brotherhood*. London: Duckworth & Co, New York: E.P. Dutton & Co, n.d.

Hunt, John Dixon. *The Pre-Raphaelite Imagination 1848-1900*. London: Routledge and Kegan Paul Ltd, 1968.

Preston, Kerrison. *Blake and Rossetti*. London: A. Moring Ltd., The de la More Press, 1944.

Rodgers, David. *Rossetti*. London: Phaidon Press, 1996.

Rossetti, D.G. "Hand and Soul". In *The Germ*, no. 1 (January 1850). London: Aylott & Jones.

Savarit, Jacques. *Tendances mystiques et ésotériques chez Dante-Gabriel Rossetti*. Paris: Librairie Didier, 1961.

Sonstroem, David. *Rossetti and the Fair Lady*. Middletown, Connecticut: Wesleyan U. P. , 1970.

Surtees, Virginia. *The Paintings and Drawings of Dante Gabriel Rossetti. A Catalogue Raisonne*, 2 vols. Oxford: Clarendon, 1971.

Weintraub, Stanley. Four Rossettis, *A Victorian Biography*. London: W.H. Allen, 1978.

Whiteley, Jon. *Oxford and the Pre-Raphaelites*. Oxford: Ashmolean Museum, 1993.

Whiting, Mary Bradford. "Beata Beatrix". In *Temple Bar*, no. CXXVI (September 1902), London.

Wood, Christopher. *The Pre-Raphaelites*. London: Weidenfeld and Nicolson, 1981.

Notes

1. See appendix. The corpus is based on Virginia Surtee's Catalogue raisonné.

2. Ruskin to Rossetti (12 April 1853), in *That Ne'er shall Meet again*, 63.

3. It has been written in some books that Rossetti visited Italy in 1847, at the age of 19 (Langlade, Jacques (de). *Dante Gabriel Rossetti*. Paris: Editions Mazarine, 1985, 38–39) Apparently this information is solely supported by quoting the first sentence in the final section of Rossetti's tale "Hand and Soul", which ran "In the Spring of 1847 I was at Florence" (*The Germ*, Aylott & Jones, London, No. 1, January 1850, 32). There is no biographical evidence that Rossetti ever went to Italy, whereas his journeys to France and Belgium are recorded in poems and letters. Therefore, the quotation should be put back in its fictional context, and not taken at face value. Preston stresses the fact that the realistic details, footnotes and references to a catalogue included in the tale led some readers to assume that it was based on a real journey and an existing picture, whereas in fact every element was imaginary (Preston 85).

4. William Michael Rossetti, indicates the following list as representative of his brother's youthful readings: "Hamlet and other Shakespearian tragedies and

histories, Sir Walter Scott (*The Arabian Night, Ivanhoe* ...), series entitled *Brig-and Tales, The Iliad*, Scottish and English ballads, Allan Cunningham's *Legends of Terror*, Bürger's *Lenore*, Byron, Maturin, Monk *Lewis's Tales of Wonder*, Mein-hold's *Sidonia the Sorceress*" (Sonstroem 9).

5. "Gerard Manley Hopkins used the word to denote the self-hood of a particular thing, its conformation, its design, its shape" (Elizabeth Rothenstein quoted in Savarit, 118).

APPENDIX

Title	Date	Inspiration Ital.	Engl.	Source
The First Anniversary of the Death...	1849	x		Dante
Benedick and Beatrice	1850		x	Shakespeare
The Return of Tibullus to Delia	1851	x		Tibullus
Beatrice Meeting Dante at a Marriage ...	1851	x		Dante
"Hist!", said Kate the Queen	1851		x	Browning
Giotto Painting the Portrait of Dante	1852	x		Dante
Dante at Verona	1852	x		Dante
Hesterna Rosa	1853	x	x	Sir Henry Taylor
Found	1854–		x	W. Bell Scott
Ballad of Fair Annie	1855		x	English ballad
Dante's Vision of Matilda Gathering ...	1855	x		Dante
Dante's Vision of Rachel and Leah	1855	x		Dante
Paolo and Francesca da Rimini	1855	x		Dante
Dante's Dream at the time...	1856	x		Dante
The Lady of Shalott	1856–7		x	Tennyson
Mariana in the South	1856–7		x	Tennyson
The Damsel of the Sanct Grael	1857		x	Malory
Sir Lancelot's Vision of the Sanct Grael	1857		x	Malory
Sir Galahad, Sir Bors and Sir Percival ...	1857		x	Malory
Sir Lancelot in the Queen's chamber	1857		x	Malory
The wedding of St George ...	1857		x	Malory
The gate of Memory	1857		x	W. Bell Scott
The Skeleton in Armour	1857–8		x	Longfellow
Hamlet and Ophelia	1858		x	Shakespeare
My Lady Greensleeves	1859		x	English ballad
Sir Galahad at the Ruined Chapel	1859		x	Tennyson
The Salutation of Beatrice	1859	x		Dante
Bocca Baciata	1859	x		Boccaccio

Title	Date			Source
Dantis Amor	1860	x		Dante
Bonifazio's Mistress	1860	x		
Fair Rosamund	1861		x	English history
Fazio's Mistress	1863	x		
How Sir Galhad, Sir Bors, and Sir …	1864		x	Malory
Beata Beatrix	1864	x		Dante
The First Madness of Ophelia	1864		x	Shakespeare
Monna Pomona	1864	x		
Venus Verticordia	1864–8	x		
King René's Honeymoon	1864		x	Sir Walter Scott
Monna Vanna	1866	x		Dante
Fiammetta	1866	x		Boccaccio
Sibylla Palmifera	1866–70	x		
Monna Rosa	1867	x		Poliziano
Sir Tristam and la Belle Iseult…	1867		x	Malory
La Pia de' Tolomei	1868–80	x		Dante
Mariana	1870		x	Shakespeare
La Donna della Fiamma	1870	x		Dante
Perlascura	1871	x		
Water Willow	1871		x	
Veronica Veronese	1872	x		
Proserpine	1872–82	x	x	
Ghirlandata	1873	x		
Marigolds	1874		x	
La Bella Mano	1875	x		
The Death of Lady Macbeth	1875		x	Shakespeare
The Blessed Damozel	1875–8	x	x	Dante
Orpheus and Eurydice	1875	x		Virgil
A Sea-Spell	1877		x	Coleridge
Forced Music	1877		x	Watts-Dunton
Astarte Syriaca	1877	x		
Desdemona's Death Song	1878–81		x	Shakespeare
La Donna della Finestra	1879	x		Dante
The Day Dream/Monna Primavera	1880	x	x	

Classification of works according to Italian or English inspiration has been made considering the nationality of the literary author of the source. When no source is indicated, it must be assumed that Rossetti drew upon either ancient mythology – in which case the Italian influence is the strongest, as the myths transited via Italy before being integrated by other civilisations – or Rossetti's own inspiration. The language in which the title was chosen has then been used as a further reference for classification. Occasionally a single painting is known under two different titles, one English and one Italian. In that case, both inspirations have been mentioned. Similarly, when the nationality of the author and the language of the title do not match, both inspirations have been mentioned.

Part II
THE INDIAN SUBCONTINENT

5

Real and Imagined Worlds: Salman Rushdie as a Writer of the Indian Diaspora

Living in diaspora entails existing on at least two different planes. The diasporic person lives simultaneously in the past and the present. S/he is a member of the new/host community and at the same time hasn't severed ties with the old/originating community. Salman Rushdie's writing is an excellent example of this dual existence, this double vision. Rushdie's Indian sub-continental past continues to haunt his British present. This imparts his texts with what he himself has called a periscopic vision, that comes from an insider-outsider location. This is not in itself a handicap and Rushdie has turned this into a strength that permeates his discourse at all levels. This chapter contextualises Rushdie's novels within the general Indian diaspora and then examines how their location provides these texts with a unique voice.

Salman Rushdie is a writer of the Indian diaspora which is a result of the colonisation of India by Britain and the resultant displacement of her peoples through means forced and voluntary. After the official end of slavery, Indian peasants were transported to the Caribbean and the Fiji islands to fill the gaping holes in the work force on sugar plantations there. Indian labour was also used to construct railways and roads in Africa and to work in the rubber and tea plantations in Mauritius, Sri Lanka and Malaysia. Robin Cohen (1997) calls this the 'labour diaspora' (57). This diaspora was meant to replace slavery with cheap labour from the colonies. However, there was a difference between the indentured labour from the colonies and the black slaves. The indentured labourers could not be bought or sold like the slaves and at the end of their contract period had to be given a free/sponsored passage back home or given an opportunity to be re-indentured with a promise to be set free at the end of their renewed indentures. However, as V.S. Naipaul (1964) has noted, very few Indians taken to the Caribbean as indentured labourers, took the passage back home – for most of them the journey to Trinidad 'had been final' (31). It is possible that after having lost caste by crossing the ocean – *Kaala Pani*, the black waters – the mainly Hindu labourers would have been reluctant to return home and live as outcastes in their villages.

This forced diaspora was followed by voluntary migrations to these countries by small-time entrepreneurs who followed the imperial flag in search of trade. This marks the transformation of the constitution of the Indian diaspora from labour to petty bourgeoise. After the end of Empire and the Africanisation programmes of several countries on the African continent and the covert and overt racism practised in the Caribbean islands, led large sections of Indians there to once again migrate, this time to either the 'Mother' country Britain or Canada. In this context it would be worthwhile to note that the story of race in the original sense is the Manichean opposition of Black and White, noted by Frantz Fanon (1952, 1986) and Edward Said (1978). In India the brown races occupied the position of the Blacks, although they were often called the Natives as well. In the African/Caribbean spaces the opposition was between the White colonisers and the Black Africans/Afro-Caribbeans. The diasporic brown races complicated the situation and were in time treated as a colonial elite by the Europeans and hence earned the ire of the Blacks, who thought of them as colonial stooges. This situation was compounded by the economic power the Indian diasporic people began to acquire. This after decolonisation in the 1950s and 60s, led first to discrimination and then as in Uganda, to expulsion of the descendents of the indentured Indian labourers and traders. The expelled Indians and those who voluntarily left the African/ Caribbean countries, once again did not exercise the option to return to India. The reasons this time being materialistic rather than related to caste.

From Postcolonial India too in the 1950s and 60s there has been a move to the West in search of jobs as well as for higher education. Postcolonial India has also seen a petro-dollar diaspora in which a huge number of Indians, originally from the Indian state of Kerala and now from other states too, went to the Gulf countries to man their oil rigs and 'woman' their health services. In the Caribbean, African countries, Fiji, Singapore, Malaysia, Kuwait, Bahrain, Dubai, Saudi Arabia, Britain and Canada today there are well established 'Little Indias', with second and third generation of persons of Indian ethnic origins. These diverse diasporas which began in the Ninteenth Century with the first group of indentured labourers being transported to Mauritius in the 1830s are now over a hundred and fifty years old.

Living in diaspora means living in forced or voluntary exile and living in exile usually leads to severe identity confusion and problems of identification with and alienation from the old and new cultures and homelands. As Salman Rushdie has put it in *Imaginary Homelands* (1991), the position of 'the exile or immigrant' is one of 'profound uncertainities' (10). The diasporic person is at home neither in the West nor in India and is thus 'unhomed' in the most essential sense of the term. However as the Postcolonial theorist Homi Bhabha has pointed out in *The Location of Culture* (1994), 'To be unhomed is not to be homeless' (9). When the realisation of being unhomed strikes one 'the world first shrinks...and then expands enormously' (9). 'The unhomely moment relates the traumatic ambivalence of a personal, psychic history to the wider disjunctions of political existence' (11). This relation of personal and psychic trauma to the disjunctions of political existence is clearly evident in the writing of Salman Rushdie.

This chapter is focussed on his work and considers how it grapples with these problems. The preferred term used here to describe the Indian writer who lives outside India is 'diaspora' – the term related to the ancient Jewish diaspora as it gives a proper sense of dispersement, loss, nostalgia and is thus more evocative than the terms exile or expatriate. However as Vijay Mishra (1996: 424–25) has pointed the Indian diaspora lacks several important parameters of the Jewish diaspora. The most important one being the searing desire to return to the Homeland. As noted earlier there is little of that evident in the Indian diaspora. To quote V.S. Naipaul (1961, 1969: 19) again, Indians in the West Indies would talk nostalgically about India but when offered the opportunity to return there, would refuse to take it up. However a 'Return to the Homeland' need not take place in actual terms. As Stuart Hall (1990: 401) has noted, for those in diaspora, such a return is usually metaphorical. Even though the Indian diaspora has not subscribed to the Homeland myth of the Jewish diaspora, it is not deficient in feelings of nostalgia and attachment for India. As Parekh (1994: 603–20) has pointed out, Hindus in diaspora kept alive their religion and heritage by inviting holy men and learned speakers from India to speak to them. They also adopted the *Ramayana* as their key religious text.

Diasporic Indians like other diasporic peoples thus have strong links to their homeland, but they also display a keen desire to assimilate and belong to their current place of abode. This creates counter-pulls in the psyches of the diasporans and is reflected in the literature they produce.

Salman Rushdie, however, is not just a writer of the Indian Diaspora, his texts can also be placed within the broader parameters of the Modernist tradition of Metropolitan Literature. The Modernists had made the city the focus of their writing and often used it as a metaphor for moral, social and cultural decadence – the city as the archetypal wasteland. Rushdie's cities at first reading appear to mimic these Modernist tropes but at the subtextual level they transcend realistic boundaries and move into Post-modernist and Postcolonial terrains of fable, magic, allegory, loss, fragmentation of self and exile. The cities Rushdie has depicted – Bombay in *Midnight's Children* (1981) and *The Moor's Last Sigh* (1995), Karachi and Quetta in *Shame* (1983), Bombay and London in *The Satanic Verses* (1988) and *East West Stories* (1994) and Bombay, London and New York in *The Ground Beneath Her Feet* (1999) – are as much real as they are imagined, as much visible as they are invisible. Rushdie has an explanation for this phenomenon in The *Imaginary Homelands* – the profound uncertainties of being in diaspora leads such writers to 'create fictions, not of actual cities or villages, but invisible ones...' (10). The cities of Bombay, Karachi and Quetta are cities of Rushdie's past and belong to his 'imagined homelands' – India and Pakistan. London, however, is the city of his present. Yet he is as much an 'insider-outsider' in London as he is in the cities of Bombay or Karachi. If the cities of the Indian subcontinent are not 'home', neither is London. Rushdie, the diasporic writer is 'unhomed' both in the East and the West. Furthermore it is interesting to note that while Rushdie has dealt to some extent with London in *The Satanic Verses* and *East West Stories*, the usual setting of his books is the lands of the past. This is not unusual as most persons in diaspora are haunted by the past and have an overwhelming desire to look back rather than forward. Also many diasporic writers hesitate to write about their new homelands because if they did, they would write as outsiders – as persons who do not belong. There has however been a shift in *The Ground Beneath Her Feet*, in which though the city of Bombay is foregrounded in the first quarter of the text, the rest of the novel is set in London and then in New York. This novel seems to be the turning point in Rushdie's career in which, post-*Fatwa* and India's lead in banning *The Satanic Verses*, he appears to have made a conscious decision to move away from India – 'India, fount of my imagination, source of my savagery, breaker of my heart. Goodbye' (*Ground Beneath Her Feet*, 1999: 249). Also in an interview with Maya Jaggi Rushdie has said that his physical distancing from India in the post-fatwa period has intensified the gradual wearing down of that link and 'in the artistic context, I don't think I have much more to say about that India I cared about and that I felt belonged to me as a writer.... Bombay has been transformed into Mumbai. I'm not interested in Mumbai; I was interested in another city in that space, which isn't really there now.... The ideas that come up and seem rich and capture me do seem, for the moment, to have turned away from the East. I'm not going to stop being a person who was born an Indian and brought up an Indian and was completely shaped by it.... But my interests have changed'. (*The Age on Sunday*, 25 April 1999). Rushdie has been known to have made similar emotional statements earlier and only the contents of his next book will reveal whether he has really turned away from the East. However, even if Rushdie's subsequent novels will be located in the West, upon his own above admission, he will not cease being an Indian writer in diaspora, whose Western cities going by the evidence so far, will more likely than not, continue to be an amalgamation of real and imagined worlds.

When diasporic writing tries to reflect real and imagined worlds it 'is obliged to deal in broken mirrors, some of whose fragments have been lost' (*Imaginary Homelands*, 10–11). However, this could also be seen as the strength of diasporic texts – that they are incomplete, the fact that they do claim to offer the ulitmate truth – the fact that they deal with alternatives rather than essentials. It is these alternatives histories and narratives that Rushdie had offered us in *Midnight's Children*. Further as Stuart Hall has observed colonisation leads to a 'break' with the past and in a post-colonial context this past is 'always constructed through fantasy, narrative and myth' (395).

Midnight's Children is one of the most important literary texts of recent times. With its publication the entire corpus of Indian Literature in English became redefined and underlined in a most emphatic manner. This novel appeared at a most propitious time when the first Postcolonial and Post-imperial generations came of age in the former colonies and in Britain. Hence the desire on the part of both to recapture and repossess their histories coincided most auspiciously. Rushdie, however, is not just a Postcolonial writer, he is also heir to the Postmodernist tradition and the narrative mode of Magical Realism. *Midnight's Children* legitimised and privileged the till then marginalised 'other' and stood the conventional notions of the centre and margins on their respective heads. This text proclaimed the arrival of a new type of postcolonial – not the Mimic

Man – not one who has accepted the 'givens' of history and politics, but one who subverted and rewrote histories, smashed the whole sorry scheme of things and moulded new realities. These realities included not just alternative world views but a new language in which to express them. So Rushdie's texts revelled in not just alternative realities and subaltern histories but also in linguistic hybridity – a hybridity that enabled the postcolonial writer to be his/her own person, even if in the language of the erstwhile colonisers. Here was the appropriation of a language that had in the colonial period been used to subordinate the Calibans and lure the Ariels into submission.

In *Midnight's Children* Rushdie has offered us alternatives to the master narrative of recent Indian history as mediated by the Western coloniser. The text leads us into the very processes of history-making as the author who is 'handcuffed to history', tells us the stories of India from 1915 to 1977, using almost all the weapons in the Postmodernist and Postcolonial armoury – parody, pastiche, intertextuality, alternative narratives, self-reflexivity, hybridity in language, problematising of history and magical realism. This wonderful 'Bombay Mix', challenges the Grand Narratives of High Modernism, Colonialism and Postcolonialism, Nationalism and even Religions. The text is thus almost a paen of freedom and against totalisation of any kind.

History in *Midnight's Children* is not a macro-narrative it is instead presented in the form of several minor narratives – a multitude of stories, stories which clamour to be told. Stories told in diverse voices and diverse traditions that assert the heterogeneity and intertwining of peoples, cultures, traditions, heritages and languages. Stories which are larger than linear narratives, stories which demand the reader 'swallow a lot' and suspend all disbelief. So Saleem Sinai, the narrator, combines in himself several ethnicities, religions and cultural traditions. He is a Kashmiri, who is not really a Kashmiri. He is the son of a father who is not really his father. He is both Indian and English, black and white at the same time. His stories are in the Scherazadic tradition of the thousand and one tales but are only more fantastic than any *djins* which troubled the peoples of the worlds created by the desperate Scherezade.

The Islamic elements in Saleem's stories are mixed up with Hindu beliefs and he of the huge nose is also linked with the elephant-headed Hindu god Ganesha, who was the scribe of the Indian epic *Mahabharata*. Further, none of Saleem's stories are 'whole' or 'complete'. They are fragments out of which he tries to create his own myth of India. This is an India of magic, where reality is not of much use, where the Nineteenth Century European tradition of Rationality is but a thin veneer over thousands and thousands of years of time which stretches back into the darkness of an unfathomable past.

So Saleem spins his stories, his dreams, his fables which are juxtaposed and come into collision with much older myths, very old dreams which pre-date colonialism. Realistic narratives cannot cope with fabular time and mythic traditions. Only the special attributes of magical realism which can push back the frontiers of traditional realism, can possibly do justice to Saleem and his horde of one thousand and one Midnight's Children. Through this device Rushdie has narrated his own version of India's history and repossessed his past.

At the midnight hour of 15 August 1947, India made her 'tryst with destiny' and the Midnight's Children came into existence. They were born at 'the best of times and the worst of times'. They should have been the children of freedom, of light, of new beginnings; but spawned out of darkness, they were the children of the dreaded *Kali Yug* – the age of darkness (196–97). They were doomed even before they were born, creatures who were 'brilliant' but not always 'good'.

Leading this band of the midnight born are Saleem and Shiva – symbolic of the binary oppositions: 'Hindu/Muslim, Old/New, Preservation/Destruction' (196–97). Born out of confusion, conspiracies, bitterness, bloodshed and broken promises the midnight's children grow up creating their own new darknesses. Saleem the scribe is their spokesperson, the convenor of the Midnight Conference, which through magical means takes place inside his own head. His narration, however, is unreliable, it is based on selective memory (207). In fact it could almost be dismissed as complete fabrication, *Maya*. However, if all is illusion then there is no given truth, no definitive version of history, or language, or culture which can be privileged above all others. This is distinctly subversive and cuts at the very roots of colonial theories of racial, cultural and even moral superiority.

In addition to being unreliable, Saleem's very identity is fluid and mysterious. He is the illegitimately sired son of the Englishman Methwold – a parting gift to the new nation and symbolic of the continuing hold of the coloniser over the decolonised world. Saleem's genesis is also symbolic of the new nations of India and Pakistan, born of an illegitimate coupling of Imperial Britain and pre-colonial India.

Saleem's childhood is spent in Bombay and the city has been power-fully evoked right from its earliest beginnings as a fishing village that was gifted to King Charles I by his Portuguese bride, Princess Catherine d'Bra-ganza. The island city of Bombay/Mumbai clings to the Indian subconti-nent, forever different, changeable, the very quintessence of multitudinous realities, full of *Maya* and very fittingly the home of Indian cinema – that magnificently magical and non-realist construct, whose language of juxta-position, long shots, close ups and freezes is often invoked by Saleem in his own stories.

The Bombay years of Saleem's early childhood are interwoven with momentous events in the history of Postcolonial India. There is the 1962 war with China, the increasing erosion of Nehruvian secularism and the rise of the Jan Sangh (the present day BJP). Saleem's Muslim family in spite of being resident in the then tolerant Bombay, feels insecure enough to migrate to Pakistan – the Land of the Pure.

For Saleem, being pitchforked from the relative cosmopolitanism of Bombay into the conservatism of Pakistan, is traumatic. He feels he is in exile (274) and finds the single-minded devotion to Islam that is expected from him difficult to profess (301). So through many twists and turns of fate, which includes fighting in the Indo-Pak war of 1971 that leads to the creation of Bangla Desh, Saleem is with the help of the other children of midnight, returned to India. However, this is an India over which the Widow (Mrs. Indira Gandhi) presides in a rather malevolent fashion. This Widow, her Son (Sanjay Gandhi) and the Widow's hand (Mrs. Gandhi's election symbol), are the unholy trinity which causes a cloak of darkness to fall upon the land of freedom. Another midnight's hour is evoked and just as Saleem's (actually Shiva's son) is born, on June 25, 1975, the Widow declares an Emergency, suspends the constitution and all the fundamental rights assured by it. Saleem is once again asked to give a pledge of uni-lateral allegiance – the worship of goddess Indira. He feels unequal to this task of single-minded, blind faith (422).

So he retreats to the pickle factory of his old nurse, Mary, the one who had exchanged him with Shiva at birth and meets his Padma – the lotus flower that blooms in the muck. The lotus is of symbolic value in Hindu and Buddhist lore. It is contemplated by Vishnu and Brahma and is en-twined between the fingers of the Buddha. With the assistance of Padma, Saleem pickles history, pickles the past and bottles truth or *Maya* in bot-tles – one each for each year of India's independent existence (444). The past can be repossessed in diverse ways, different versions of the past are available but the future however is unknown (444). With the thirty jars lined upon the shelves, Saleem encompassing within himself the fractures and faults of histories, ends his stories of the brood of 1001 children of midnight.

Shame (1983) does for Pakistan what *Midnight's Children* did for India. Using fact, fiction, irony, parody, allegory and fairy tales Rushdie has traced the history of Pakistan in the 60s and 70s. Even way back in 1983, Rushdie knew that the very act of writing *Shame* was dangerous and problematic – "if I'd been writing a book of a realistic nature it would have done me no good to protest that I was writing universally, not only about Pakistan. This book would have been banned, dumped in the rubbish bin.... Realism can break a writer's heart.... I am only writing a modern fairy tale...Nobody need get upset.... No drastic action need be taken either...' (70). However, since then Rushdie has found out to his cost that fairy tales do not really provide protection against irate governments and clerics and that peoples do get upset and most tragically he has also learnt that they do 'take drastic action'. From 14 February 1989, Rushdie has been under a death threat which is the result of a *fatwa* (religious edict) issued against him by the now deceased Ayotallah Ruhollah Khomeni of Iran, for having written allegedly blasphemous things in *The Satanic Verses* about the Prophet Mohommed. The Ayotallah considered Rushdie's book shameful and the writer deserving of the most severe punishment. Its ironic that this should be considered so, because in *Shame*, Rushdie has elaborated at length upon the several facets of 'shame' or the lack of it and evoked all the complex meanings it has within the Indian subcontinent. To these complex meanings of shame, could be added both Rushdie's own 'shame' as well as that of those who have sentenced him to death. For shame is a two-edged sword and cuts both ways. As Rushdie himself has said in his novel *Shame*, shame is a beast which ultimately self-destructs and takes with it all who are around it.

Rushdie has pointed out that in Urdu, the word shame has denser connotations than it does in English. The nearest English equivalent would be the medieval chivalric notion of 'dishonour'. In Rushdie's text his several protagonists have reason to feel ashamed on several counts. First of all there is the dishonour of the three Shakeel sisters who 'jointly' give birth to one and then another son, without the benefit of wedlock. Then there is the dishonour of financial ruin, aristocratic penury, which stared the three sisters in the face when their father died penniless and in debt.

There is the dishonour brought upon the Indian subcontinent by the shameful acts wrought by both Hindus and Muslims during the Partitioning of the country. This is the shame of Bilquis Hyder who was stripped naked by the communal mobs. There is the shame of profligacy which is the dishonour of Sikander Harappa, which has to be unjustly shared by his wife Rani Harappa. Rani avenges this undeserved shame by revealing to the world on eighteen embroidered shawls, the shame of her husband's regime. There is also the shame of not having rendered to God what is his due. This is the shame that drives Raza Hyder to pray so often that his forehead is marked with all the pressings to the ground it receives. Above all there is the shame of gender itself. This is the shame of being born a woman, the shame of missing male genitalia. This is the shame of Sufia Zenobia, the daughter of Raza and Bilquis Hyder, who should have been born a male. This is the shame which stunts her mental growth – the reductiveness of being born woman – and turns her into a beast who consumes all in its frightful rage.

Interwoven into these dark and sordid stories of shame are the dishonours brought upon the God-fearing who live in the land of the infidel – England. This is the shame of the Migrant. The narrator in the text is a migrant, who uses the trick of traditional Nineteenth Century omniscient author not just to narrate the tales of Pakistan, or rather 'Peccavistan', but also uses his power to interpolate these tales of Asian fathers and brothers in England who kill their daughters and sisters for having brought shame upon their families by consorting with white boys. At another level this is also the shame of the former colonisers who 'condemn' the 'barbaric' acts of their Asian co-citizens. Thus the shame of one becomes the shame of all.

In *The Moor's Last Sigh*, Rushdie has once again most powerfully asserted his right to his Indian heritage. This text is a complex saga of a Jewish-Christian family. The narrator cherishes his rich and varied inheritance and sees himself as 'a Cathjewnut, a stewpot, a mongrel cur'. The trouble is that India does not seem to value such 'both or nothings' anymore. So this is also a text that critiques those who seek to destroy India's multiple identities and above all a scathing indictment of those who appear to seek the destruction of Rushdie's birthplace – Bombay.

The Moor's Last Sigh is a quintessential Bombay book. From his own incarcerating exile, engendered by Islamic Fundamentalism, Rushdie has written most poignantly of the city of his birth, grappling with Hindu Fundamentalism. By writing about Bombay he has reasserted his right to the city. Even more importantly he has focussed upon the fact that the smaller minorities of India have as much right to being Indians and to 'Indianness' as do what he calls 'Majority, that mighty elephant, and her sidekick Major-minority...' (87).

This is Rushdie's most self-conscious novel to date and in the opening line itself, he has written himself into the narrative – 'On St. Valentine's Day, 1989, the last day of her life, the legendary pop singer Vina Apsara woke up from a dream of human sacrifice in which she had been the intended victim' (3). The last day of Vina's life was the first day of Rushdie's own uneviable experience of living under the death sentence pronounced on him by the Iranian cleric-President Ayotallah Khomeni on 14 February 1989. The Ayotallah himself puts in a guest appearance in the text as the Christopher Plummer look-alike who grips the dreaming Vina's wrists and ankles and prepares her for torture and ritualistic death.

The Ground Beneath Her Feet thus opens with a flashback in which the personal is interwoven with the fictional and the factional. Vina's premonition of her own death, ties in with Rushdie's *fatwa* and her character is a composite construct in which a little known pop-star of Indian origins, Asha Puthli, who had some success in the New York of the 1970s, is a major ingredient. As for Ormus Cama, her only true love, he is a thinly veiled Freddy Mercury, the lead singer of the pop group Queen. Rushdie has admitted that 'Freddy Mercury was quite helpful to me' (Jaggi, 1999), but has denied a one-to-one resemblance between his Ormus and the late Mercury. After all even though both Cama and Mercury were Bombay Parsis, Cama was a heterosexual and Mercury was a homosexual. But the important commonality between them was that both, although they did not deny their origins, did nothing to make them known. As a result very few of the Queen fans knew that Freddy Mercury was born Farrokh Balsara and had spent his youth in Bombay. As Rushdie has said in his interview with Jaggi, 'I've no idea why Mercury made those decisions, but I suspect it's because he didn't want to be put in an ethnic ghetto. He wanted to be a mainstream star .... That led me to the idea of transcending your skin, going past the frontier of the skin...'.

In spite of the physical and psychic struggles involved in being dislocated and having to relocate across boundaries the ultimate feeling one gets about the work of Rushdie is its positive nature. His texts are not merely about being unhomed, they, in the manner of Martin Heidegger,

HeiHalso acknowledge that 'A boundary is not that at which something stops, but as the Greeks recognised, the boundary is that from which something begins its presencing' (152–3). In the final analysis Rushdie's fiction is expansive discourse, which seeks to create its own spaces within the context of shifting borders, in the sense of cultural relocations and translations.

Nilufer E. Bharucha
University of Mumbay

Works Cited

Bhabha, Homi. *The Location of Culture*, London: Routledge, 1994.

Cohen, Robin. *Global Diasporas: An Introduction*, London: UCL Press, 1997, 57.

Fanon, Frantz. *Black Skin, White Masks*, 1952, London: Pluto Press, 1986.

Hall, Stuart. 'Cultural Identity and Diaspora', *Identity: Community, Culture, Difference*, ed. J. Rutherford, London: Lawrence & Wishart, 1990, 227–37.

Heiddeger, Martin. 'Building, Dwelling, Thinking', *Poetry, Language, Thought*, New York: Harper & Row, 1971, 152–3.

Jaggi, Maya. 'Rushdie, The Ground Beneath His Feet', *The Age on Sunday*, 25 April 1999, extracted online from amazon.com.uk.

Mishra, Vijay. 'The Diasporic Imaginary: Theorizing the Indian Diaspora', *Textual Practice*, 10 (3), (1996), 421–447.

Naipaul, V.S. *A House for Mr. Biswas*. 1961, London: Penguin, 1969, 19.

———. *An Area of Darkness*, London: Andre Deutsch, 1964, 31.

Parekh, B. 'Some Reflections on the Hindu Diaspora, *Textual Practice* 10 (3), 1966, 421–447.

Rushdie, Salman. *Midnight's Children*, 1981. London: Picador, 1982

———. *Shame*, 1983. Calcutta: Rupa & Co., 1983.

———. *Satanic Verses*. London: Viking, 1988.

———. *Imaginary Homelands*, 1991. London: Granta Books, 1992.

———. *East West Stories*. London: Jonathan Cape, 1994.

———. *The Moor's Last Sigh*. New York: Pantheon Books, 1995.

———. *The Ground Beneath Her Feet*. London: Jonathan Cape, 1999.

Said, Edward. *Orientalism*, 1978, London: Penguin, 1987.

Sharma, L.K. 'Interview with Salman Rushdie', Times of India, Bombay, 10 Sept. 1995.

6

The Flight from Certainty in Shani Mootoo's
Cereus Blooms at Night

Shani Mootoo's novel *Cereus Blooms at Night* constitutes a flight from
certainty in its subversion of the conventional categories of time and
space, age and gender.

The flight from certainty begins with the contemplation of Shani Mootoo's identity as a writer. She was born in Dublin of Indian parents in
1957, but left at the age of three months, spending the next eighteen years
in Trinidad, where her parents and a sibling still live. Yet she is not legally
a Trinidadian, because of her birthplace, and is now a Canadian citizen.
She thinks of herself as Canadian rather than Trinidadian, and feels that
she could not have written her novel *Cereus Blooms at Night*, published in
1996, if she had stayed in Trinidad, needing the distance, "climate of permission" and openness of Canada; she was helped with a grant from the
Canada Council while she was writing the novel, and was nominated for
the B.C. Book Prize, and the Giller Prize, and shortlisted for the *Books in
Canada* First Novel Award.

Further complications of Mootoo's identity are that her three other
siblings live in England, that she feels she gained much from a very "British" literary education, that she lives not only in Vancouver but also in
Brooklyn, and that she could (but chooses not to) gain extra publicity as a
woman of colour and as a lesbian. In addition, her father is a Hindu, the
son of a Catholic, and her mother is from a Christian family: at times of
crisis, she would perform a Hindu puja one day and invite the local nuns
to tea the next. Mootoo herself is a convert to Buddhism.

Mootoo's novel, besides narrowly missing the shortlist for the British
Booker Prize has also, fittingly for such a multicultural product, achieved

publication in twelve countries. What it brilliantly achieves is the evasion
of certainties in its simultaneous exploration and subversion of various
categories of belonging. Trinidad, for example, is not the setting of the
book, but Lantanacamara, which is a mythical version of Trinidad, like
Brenda Flanagan's Santabella in *You Alone Are Dancing* (1990). Just as
Paule Marshall's Triunion in *Daughters* (1992) is and is not Barbados and
Merle Collins' Paz in *The Colour of Forgetting* (1995) is and is not Gre-
nada, so Lantanacamara subverts the categories of "real" and "imaginary".
The setting of *Cereus Blooms at Night* is more specifically a small town
called Paradise, a name which in itself suggests a defiance of human cate-
gories.

The opening narrator of the novel, Nurse Tyler, despite a desperate
desire "to be – and be treated as – nothing more than ordinary" (22) is
miserably conscious of evading categories as "neither properly man nor
woman but some in-between, unnamed thing" (71). When guarding the
supposed madwoman Miss Ramchandin, he takes a perverse pleasure in
being offered a broom by Sister:

> I took the broom, proud that it was not assumed that I, the only man among
> the nurses, ought to be strong and fearless and without need of protection
> (10).

When he trains abroad, in the Shivering Northern Wetlands, he is aston-
ished to encounter other male nurses (6).

The Shivering Northern Wetlands, across the ocean from Canada,
"that cold country" (249), is probably to be associated with Britain, although rather an archaic Britain, whose inhabitants use phrases like

> "I'd be very much obliged, Chandin, my good fellow ..."
> "... upon your honour!"... "how infinitely superior ..." (38).

There is a deliberate haziness about the novel's setting in time as well as
place: Mootoo has said that she thought of the story as beginning a little
before 1900, but with Canada at a different historical stage. The discovery
that the Shivering Northern Wetlands boasts a Prince Rupert II (207) suggests, rather startlingly, that time and place coalesce to produce an attack
on colonialism which is heavily laced with a nostalgic makebelieve.

Tyler is the opening and closing narrator of the novel, and in enabling
its publication is placing his trust, as he tells us in its first sentence, "in the
power of the printed word to reach many people" (3). He rather archly

deprecates his own intrusion into the story, since he claims that his intention "is not to bring notice to myself or my own plight" (3); however, not only does his nursing of Miss Ramchandin eventually lead to his happy romance with the transsexual Otoh, and, even initially, to what he calls "my own ballooning sense of self" (17), but it is his involvement in her story and his narrative control of it which he sees as a triumphant assertion of his own identity. As he says, mock-dispassionately,

> It is an interesting quirk of fate, I think, that for all the prattling by almost everyone at that time, sowing and tilling and reaping idle rumours about the Ramchandin family, and for all the scant attention paid my presence, I am the one who ended up knowing the truth, the whole truth, every significant *and* insignificant bit of it. And I am the one who is putting it all to good use by recording it here ... (6–7).

Tyler's interest in the Ramchandin family begins when he is about ten. As one might expect in a Caribbean novel, it begins with a conversation with a grandmother, his Cigarette Smoking Nana as opposed to his Bible Quoting Nana, and it arises through Tyler's interest in categories. He asks Cigarette Smoking Nana if it is possible for your father to be your father and grandfather at the same time, and this leads into the story of Mala Ramchandin, who is forced to sleep with her own father after his wife runs off with another woman, or, as the townspeople put it,

> whose father had obviously mistaken her for his wife, and whose mother had obviously mistaken another woman for her husband (109).

Once the narrative moves from Tyler it becomes omniscient, and is composed of unchronological fragments which only form a coherent whole when they are reassembled in retrospect. It cannot, of course, be said that Mootoo is subverting a category in writing like this, since stories told in strict chronological order are extremely rare, but her method does help to conceal the way in which her characters are abruptly deprived of sympathy or significance. Mala's mother Sarah and her lover Lavinia, for example, never reappear once they have eloped together, even though they never originally intended to abandon Sarah's children, and this failure to reappear is given little attention. (In interview, Mootoo merely remarked that returning would have been too dangerous.) By contrast, Mala's sister Asha, who also abandons her, has written a shoeboxful of letters to Mala which have never been delivered to her (243), much like Nettie's Letters to Celie in *The Color Purple*; Tyler hopes that the narrative of *Cereus Blooms at Night* itself will help to locate Asha (7, 249).

Chandin Ramchandin, once his wife Sarah has left him, becomes a spiteful, violent monster, and yet before this happens, he himself was caught up in the tyranny of categories. He is removed from his father, an indentured field labourer from India, and adopted by the Wetlandish Reverend Thoroughly so that he can become a Christian teacher, theologian and missionary. As a condition, Chandin's parents are supposed to convert to Christianity, a proposition which is treated in a way reminiscent of Olive Senior's short story "Arrival of the Snake Woman". Villagers debate it in a Chorus-like exchange:

> "... I can't do that. No. I just don't want to do that."
> "What you talking? What you mean you don't want to do that! If it is the only way for your child to get education and not have to work like a horse sweating and breaking back in the hot sun for hardly nothing, you wouldn't convert? ..." (28)

As soon as Chandin leaves to live with the Thoroughlys, his mother takes down the brass crucifix the Reverend has given her, and the number of statues of Hindu gods and goddesses on her walls increases (30), perhaps reflecting the pragmatism Mootoo had observed in her own childhood.

The Reverend does not move beyond caricature; his name, Ernest Thoroughly, is presumably intended to indicate that he is thoroughly earnest, but he is also a materialist, openly rejoicing when his daughter Lavinia gets engaged to a man who will "inherit a rather large estate" (45), and a hypocrite as well, who uses family rather than racial categories as an excuse in telling Chandin that he cannot be in love with Lavinia because she is his sister, although as Chandin mumbles to himself, "... She is not my sister. It's not really wrong, is it? It can't be." (37)

Lavinia, a rather fleeting presence in the novel, defies categories, not only in her elopement with Sarah, but in her insistence that snails have souls, who will return to protect the people who have protected them. This propels the little girl Pohpoh, and then the old woman Mala she becomes, into an obsessive interest in snails. The little girl and her childhood companion Boyie collect snails to save them from the school bully Walter Bissey, a character who appears in the first pages of the novel as the judge who refuses to try Mala Ramchandin for the murder of her father. Mala in her old age plants snailshells as a kind of fortification round her ruined house, a house which contains the Gothic secret of her father's corpse, and meets the appropriately Gothic fate of being burnt to the ground by Otoh. The burning house creates a suffocating cloud which hangs over Paradise for several days, a visible metaphor for Paradise's wilful ignorance.

Otoh's decisive action is in a sense out of character, since undecisiveness is an integral part of his character to which he owes his name:

> Ever since the days of early high school, where he excelled in thinking but not in doing, this trait of weighing "on the one hand" with "but on the other" earned him a name change. He began, though through no choice of his own, to be called Otoh-boto, shortened in time to Otoh, a nickname to which he still answered (110).

This ability to see both sides of the question presumably originated in the reason for his first name-change, from Ambrosia to Ambrose: his changing from a girl to a "boy". His final name-change, to Otty, as Tyler's beloved, signals a final, if rather convoluted, choice of sexuality for himself. Up to this point, one of Otoh's functions in the novel is to subvert categories of age and sex, being:

> the object of desire of almost every Lantanacamaran woman, regardless of her age. (It is also noteworthy that a number of men were shocked and annoyed by their own naggingly lascivious thoughts of him.) (135)

Sometimes men do openly flirt with Otoh, like the "amorous out-of-towner" with his "brick-red face" (149) who stops to pick Otoh up in his car, and only gives up when Otoh tells him he is on his way to court a woman. He exclaims that his intentions were of the purest sort:

> "Oh, you courting her. You? You courting a woman! I see. Is a lady you courting, eh. Uhuh. Well, I better not keep you back, because I have to go and meet my wife to take she to matinee. And my children coming with us too. What I was asking you was to come to the pictures with my family. You understand, na." (149)

The reader, like Otoh, is amused at his admirer's hasty re-insertion of himself into a respectable category, but the statement which prompts it is rather a curious and complex one. Otoh is indeed going to court Mala Ramchandin. Although he is a young man and she is an old woman, in the sense that, dressed in his father's clothes and having effectively become a walking memory of his father, he is taken by Mala to be the suitor of her girlhood, Boyie.

There is a suggestion of the Sleeping Beauty in Mala Ramchandin's discovery by Otoh, who seems to be unlike any woman he had ever seen:

> She sat in a rocking chair beside the tree, her eyes closed. Her figure was all
> but lost in the blueness of the mudra's trunk. She wore a petticoat, greens
> and browns and light blues, that blended into the background of leaves and
> gnarled, twisted limbs ....
> She was unlike any woman he had ever seen. It was as though he had stum-
> bled unexpectedly on a lost jungle, and except for the odours he would have
> sworn he was in a paradise. (155)

Although Otoh is in the town of Paradise, he is not in an actual paradise,
and the traditional happy ending of the fairytale is subverted by Mala's
abandonment by Otoh, just as she has previously been abandoned by her
mother, and her sister, and her suitor Boyie, despite the idyllic courtship
of that "black lord and his poor brown princess" (209). In a perverse variation of the Sleeping Beauty story, it is Boyie who awakens from his long
sleep, but he is abandoned in his turn by his longsuffering wife Elsie, who
leaves him a terse note: "You was simpler when you was sleeping" (239).

Boyie is to some extent another version of Wetlandish corruption, like
Chandin. Both marry wives they do not love in reaction to being deprived
of the woman they love obsessively, and both take it upon themselves to
correct their wives' language in the light of Wetlandish standards. When
Boyie finds Elsie's farewell note, he is saddened but does nor forget to
correct the grammar mistakes it contains with a red pen:

> he shed a few tears, after which he took a red pen, made corrections to her
> grammar and saved the paper, just in case she were to return some day and
> he could explain the errors to her (239).

When Chandin angrily asks his wife Sarah what the Wetlandish Lavinia
will think of her uneducated speech, she spiritedly replies,

> "If you still so concerned with she, why didn't you wait until she returned
> from abroad to marry? You and I married now, boy. Ask her if she still inter-
> ested in you. Ask her. Besides she never correcting how I speak. Is only you
> who always correcting me" (53).

Sarah and Lavinia, who love each other, are comfortably at home together
in their language, as are Mala and Boyie during their courtship, even though
Boyie delights in displaying his Wetlandish eloquence (197), and is seen
admiringly by Mala in Wetlandish terms:

> more dapper than even the Wetlandish Reverends and white plantation own-
> ers who had not visited their home countries in many years. Except for his
> skin colour he looked like a man in a foreign magazine, and with a little twist
> of her imagination she could picture him fair skinned (196).

It is precisely Boyie's Wetlandish glamour, indeed, that makes Mala dream of herself in fairytale terms,

> as the lady who would one day be rescued by him and revealed to all the world as a princess stolen by commoners at birth (208).

Yet Boyie is not only fully alert to Wetlandish racism (198), but has turned away from the Christian ministry, consistently viewed by Mootoo as authoritarian and oppressive, to plans for tourism, through which he aims to display the exotic wonders of Lantanacamara to foreign visitors. He, unlike Chandin, is aware of the magical beauty of his own island, of the birds that "appear to have escaped the pages of a fairy tale" (200), and he attributes the awakening of this awareness to Mala herself.

Mala is the character who comes the closest to being a personification of Lantanacamara: she blends into the background of its vegetation, and can imitate perfectly the cries of its birds, crickets and frogs (24). She, like the island, is left again and again by those who leave home for the Shivering Northern Wetlands (192–194). She, "the twinkling star of Lantanacamara" (209), is particularly associated with the cereus, which annually blooms at night, sending out a heady perfume which is in turn associated with the courting rituals of the island (134–136). The fact that Mootoo writes that these traditions operate "even now" (134) suggests a nostalgia which is encapsulated by the dual existence in the novel, and in Mala's mind, of the little girl Pohpoh and the old woman she has become. Mala has, over the years, grown fond of the little girl, even though "she had rather disliked her many years before when they were one and the same" (173).

Just as the cereus blooms only one night in every year, so Mala, the embodiment of Lantanacamara, experiences only very brief intervals of happiness with the mother, sister, and lover who all desert her. Only very limited attempts are ever made to protect or care for her. She has made a fetish of her own past by embodying it in a small child she fantasizes she can save from harm, and she lives, before her removal to the Paradise Alms House, in an atmosphere of stench and corruption. She has internalized alien standards of beauty, and seems to have found impossible what was a demonstrably possible escape from the most hateful patriarchal tyranny.

In telling Mala's story Shani Mootoo takes a flight from certainty to subvert the categories of "real" and "imaginary". Mala's story is also the story of a Caribbean island, narrated both with stinging criticism and passionate affection, and one which clearly identifies itself as a plea for a rescue from history, and from the tyranny of categories, and certainty.

Mary Condé
School of English & Drama
Queen Mary, University of London

Works Cited

Collins, Merle. *The Colour of Forgetting*. London: Virago, 1995.

Flanagan, Brenda. *You Alone Are Dancing*. Leeds: Peepal Tree, 1990.

Marshall, Paule. *Daughters*. London: Serpent's Tail, 1992.

Mootoo, Shani. *Cereus Blooms at Night*. Vancouver: Press Gang, 1996.

Senior, Olive. *Arrival of the Snake Woman and Other Stories*. London: Longman, 1989.

Walker, Alice. *The Color Purple*. London: Women's Press, 1982.

7

Hybridity as a Mode of Postcolonial Existence in Rushdie's *The Satanic Verses*

In the postcolonial era, when redeeming the authentic cultural identity is impossible for the formerly colonized, the concept of hybridity, which can be summed up as a negotiable space existing between boundaries of identity, promises to be a useful tool in analyzing various problems of post-colonial cultures. In fact according to Homi Bhabha, one of the first proponents of this concept, there is no such thing as pure or authentic identity for any race, nation, gender or even individual. Every identity is hybridized. And every beginning is a fusion and adoption of existing identities. This study applies ramifications of the concept of hybridity to Salman Rushdie's controversial work *The Satanic Verses*. Bhabha rightly calls Rushdie, who exists in the crepuscular cultural space between the subcontinent and Europe, a hybridizing writer, and provides a few brilliant insights into hybridizing moments in *The Satanic Verses* in both *Nation and Narration* and *The Location of Culture*.

"Hybridity" is a concept defining an identity of the postcolonial self in Homi Bhabha's theory. To put it in a reductively simple form, it is an idea that there is no such thing as a pure, originary, and essential colonial or postcolonial self. Like any other sign in poststructuralist discussions, it is simply a space created by differentiation. Its boundaries fluctuate continually, and it is an adulterated space ceaselessly negotiating and exchanging its attributes across its boundaries. Since postcolonialism's focus of interest is national identity rather than individual identity, Bhabha uses this term mostly in reference to national identity.

The concept negates the strict dichotomy between the colonizer and the colonized or between the ex-colonizer and the ex-colonized in its struggle against ex-colonizers, since it posits subject positions that are ambivalent, that is, hybridized, for both the colonizer and the colonized. Because of this emphasis on ambivalence, it tends to dull the belligerent edge of the ex-colonized self, and thus dissatisfies critics like Benita Parry who prefers Fanon's method of maintaining the dichotomized "polarities devised by a dominant centre" in its course to "repossessing the signifying function appropriated by colonialist representation." In Fanon, because the chronic psychological conditions of a colonized native was created exactly by internalizing "the colonizer's address to its other as darkness and negation," the way to recover normal psychological condition is to overcome the hybridization and to constitute "a self-identity where native difference is validated and which empowers the native to rebel" (Parry 28–30). However, in the present, most postcolonial situations throughout the world, are with a few exceptions past stages that call for direct political rebellion and one wouldn't know where to direct the belligerent energy generated by the validation of native difference. The generator of the neo-colonialist economic oppression is so vague and invisible that it becomes a difficult target to aim one's activism at. And for most postcolonial nations, enough problems of their own have accumulated apart from those rooted in the colonial past, that the struggle against the ex-colonizer alone is an anachronistic and partial way of facing their present dilemma. Besides, in the same way that Western nations cannot go back to the pre-industrialized stage however strong their nostalgia for pollution free and idyllic environment may be, postcolonial nations cannot recover their authentic pre-colonial past. They have to live with the cultural and material legacies left by the colonizing powers, in the same way that the metropolis London has to live with its numerous citizens from its ex-colonies, and that Indian restaurants are now almost an authentic part of London culture. Hybridization of national identity is a condition one has to embrace whether one likes it or not.

The concept of hybridity, which seems to reject the Self/Other dichotomy prevalent in the works of early postcolonial theorists like Edward Said, is actually found in a seminal form in Said's *Orientalism*. Said's idea was that it is impossible to talk about the fixed identity of the Orient, and despite Said's own dependence on the dichotomy of the Western self and the Oriental other in his arguments, his ultimate position is that the practice of dividing human beings into such generalities as the Westerners and the Orientals "has been...usually towards not especially admirable ends." (*Orientalism* 45) In his "Afterword" to *Orientalism* written in 1994, he declares that his aim in writing *Orientalism* has been far from encouraging

Arab nationalism and Islamic fundamentalism. (*Orientalism*, 339) For him cultures are "hybrid and heterogeneous" and his aim is "the re-thinking of what had for centuries been believed to be an unbridgeable chasm separating East from West" and "to challenge the notion that difference implies hostility, a frozen reified set of opposed essences, and a whole adversarial knowledge built out of those things." (*Orientalism*, 352)

In this chapter, I would like to apply this concept of "hybridity" to Salman Rushidie's controversial novel *The Satanic Verses*. Homi Bhabha himself labels Rushdie a "hybridizing writer" (*Nation and Narration*, 6) and provides some very keen insights into the interpretation of *The Satanic Verses* in both *Nation and Narration* and *The Location of Culture*. Hybridity provides a useful handle for grasping and controlling the seemingly chaotic, prodigal, and elusive world of *The Satanic Verses*. Rushdie himself seems to have been conscious of this concept as one of the germinating ideas of this novel. The two protagonists of the novel Gibreel and Saladin each artificially endowed with the angelic and satanic identities in their new life in England find it impossible to keep their newly-given identities exclusively intact from the first. They experience their fluid identities interpenetrating each other. In the first scene where Gibreel Farishita and Saladin Chamcha fall from the Bostan, Chamcha feels himself becoming "hybrid, ...growing into" Gibreel. The "Hybrid cloud-creatures" in the form of "gigantic flowers with human breasts dangling from fleshy stalks, winged cats" (*The Satanic Verses*, 6) etc. mirror the hybrid nature of the protagonists' identities and of all identities for that matter.

The first scene thus begins with the problematizing of the traditional dichotomy between the angelic and the satanic, in other words, good and evil. And throughout the novel, Rushdie extends this questioning of identities to roughly three areas: that is, the English identity, the Islamic identity, and the Indian identity. Thus the concept of hybridity is used to question the epistemological legitimacy not only of the dominant culture, but also of the so-far oppressed alternative cultures. Its critical edge cuts both ways. And for the postcolonial self it becomes an important tool for self-reflection and self-interrogation in addition to being a tool for correcting the epistemic violence of the dominant culture.

Concerning the hybridizing of the English national identity, Homi Bhabha makes some very pertinent observations. S. S. Sisodia's remark "The trouble with the English is that their...history happened overseas, so they...don't know what it means." (*The Satanic Verses*, 343) is taken by

Bhabha as a comment on the need for rethinking the traditional boundary of a nation. Rosa Diamond whose phantom visions of the battle of
Hastings seems to give solidity and unity to this creature of "cracks and
absences she knew herself to be." (*The Satanic Verses*, 130) represents for
Bhabha the English identity. (*Nation and Narration*, 317) She dreams of
the phantasmic arrival of the conqueror William's fleet. William's conquest
of England was the last historical event that consolidated the identity of
modern England as a nation. It was the last invasion, and the invading
force has been since incorporated into the mainstream of English life.
However, this historical event that gives unity and solidity to the English
identity itself shows that the unity was achieved by the influx of an external element.

Near Rosa Diamond's house, the shoreline has changed since the
Norman Conquest, and the first Norman Castle that had once stood on
the seashore now stands inland as if to symbolize the incorporation of the
Norman culture in English life. Even the change in nature suggests that
what had had abandoned his Indian identity in order to become a first class
citizen of England with an English wife and a mansion of his own, Saladin
witnesses the underside of the English society while he goes through the
humiliating roughhandling in the hands of the shoreguards. The England
he experiences as an arrested illegal alien is not the England of democracy,
liberty, and human rights protection he knew it o be. This "new" England
is responsible for the much maligned monsters Saladin meets in the special hospital where Africans, Asians, and other non-Europeans who have
been partly transformed into animal forms under the gaze of the prejudiced English are interned.

However, the moment Saladin is freed from the hospital, he notices
that he himself is not free from the same racial prejudice as the English.
Hyacinth, the black nurse, who assisted the escape of the hospital inmates
transforms into a nightmarish vision of ugliness and threat in Saladin's
eyes the moment her role as a rescuer is over. Hyacinth herself begins to
look at Saladin not as a fellow sufferer but as an ugly monster. Saladin
himself with his denigrating perception of his own Indianness and other
non-Europeans seems to be partly responsible for his continued existence
in a devilish form.

Saladin had always been more English in his ideological identification
with its rulers than his English wife Pamela. He views the Falklands War
as England's just punishment for the invaders of home, whereas Pamela

thinks of it as the two parties claiming their rights to the island but the English first raising its violent hand. After all, Saladin had chosen Pamela for her aristocratic English countryside background, and Pamela had chosen Saladin for everything that was not her background. And it is Pamela and her lover Jumpy Joshy who die as martyrs to expose the suspicious transformation of aliens at the hospital for the aliens. This is another example of the national identity not quite coinciding with its border.

This shifting and sharing of the responsibility for prejudices continues in Rushdie's probing of the Islamic identity. It is not only the English who claims its authentic and unified identity in the face of contradictory evidences. Rushdie uses Gibreel's dream vision generated by his psychotic condition to problematize the Islamic grand narrative, an alternative to the Western European narrative of its own superior rationality. In his dream vision, he is the archangel Gibreel who had inspired Mahound (the name of the Mahomet character in the novel) to become a prophet. But he himself is not certain of his role as an archangel. Various prophets including Mahound and his successors such as Imam and Ayesha claim that revelations were made to them by Gibreel, but Gibreel feels he himself was never the source of the words or graces the prophets claim to have received from him. Rather it seems that the prophets have wrestled and forced the necessary inspirations from him.

Gibreel as the archangel in Jahilia is not only uncertain of himself as the unified and originary source of inspiration for the Islamic religion. He functions sometimes as a camera eye spanning the whole of Jahilia, or sometimes zooming on a focused individual's life. At other times, he feels as if he were a film audience watching the goings on in Jahilia (108) His subject is not only split; it occupies different positions and performs different functions depending on the circumstances. Gibreel at times even feels that he is Mahound himself in the novel. (108) These are all fictional inventions on the part of Rushdie to drive home his point about the cracks in identity. However, Rushdie also reminds us that the historical Mahomet himself doubted his own sanity when he first received God's messages from the archangel and tried to commit suicide out of despair. It was his wife Kadija who gave him conviction about his own righteousness. (92) Mahound and his followers forgot the cracks and doubts in the origin of their religion and became doctrinaire.

The historical background for the birth of the Islamic religion provides enough evidence of its non-originary and hybridized birth. By the time historical Mahomet came, the nomadic Arabs had begun to settle down for a city life and their livelihood had come to depend heavily on commerce. In the commercialized cities individualism and mammonism began to dominate, while the nomadic life had evolved around the ethics of solidarity, compassion, and mutual support. Mahomet himself was an orphan whose survival had depended on the care of his nomadic community, and he was acutely aware of the need of compassion for the weak and the unprotected. Mahomet combined the nomadic Arab tradition of mutual support and compassion, with the Judeo-Christian tradition of monotheism, last judgment, and belief in the next world to provide correctives for the moral depravity of the new commercial culture. In the novel the individualism of the commercial culture and its scattering nature are represented by the sand worship in decadent Jahilia and the new unitary culture of Islam by the importance attributed to the consolidating substance water in the new austere religion.

The often repeated questions in the novel "How does newness come into the world? How is it born?/Of what fusions, translations, and conjoinings is it made?" (8) remind one that all beginnings are non-originary, and this applies to the beginning of the Islam as well. And the charge of non-originariness does not denigrate the Islamic religion since all beginnings and all identities are hybrid for Rushdie. He is only urging for the need to be modest and self-reflective in one's beliefs and claims, by drawing attention to the cracks in the origin and identity of everything under the sun.

The very title of the novel *The Satanic Verses* points right to the crack in the origin of Islam. Before the historical Mahomet introduced the monotheistic idea borrowed from the Judeo-Christian tradition to the Arabs, they worshipped numerous gods and goddesses, and Mahomet had difficulty persuading people to accept monotheism. At one time, for the sake of expanding his religious influence, he acknowledged the divinity of three aboriginal goddesses in addition to Allah. Later he contradicted himself and returned to absolute monotheist by saying that it was revealed to him that his previous message concerning the three goddesses was the message from Satan which he mistook for that from Gibreel.

In the novel, the dissonance at the origin is further complicated by Mahound's scribe Salman's intervention. In order to test Mahound's authenticity, Salman intentionally forges some parts of the message and Mahound does not recognize the forged part, which he should have done if he were conveying God's sacred words. At least in the fictional version of the story, this makes Quran a rather doubtful source for the absolute truth. Thus the ideas sprung from the cracked origin are transmitted through the unreliable medium of human communication to the posterity, and the implication is that it is naturally absurd to claim the literal application of Quranic dictates to the contemporary life. It is from this perspective that Rushdie satirizes the Islamic fundamentalist Imam with his declaration of war against the change brought by time, and the visionary prophet Ayesha who agrees to the execution of an innocent baby because it is evident that she is a product of an immoral union. Rushdie's sense of irony reaches its climax when he describes Imam, a staunch anti-Americanist and Islamic fundamentalist drinking water constantly "one glass every five minutes, to keep himself clean;" and simultaneously reveals that "the water itself is cleansed of impurities, before he sips, in an American filtration machine." (209) Obviously Imam is dictating impossibilities to his followers. Even he himself cannot help using modern gadgets despite his insistence on fixing the clock at Mahomet's time in the seventh century.

The question of Indian identity provides a guideline for how an individual in his daily life can define and function with the identity that is supposed to be cracked in its origin and fluctuating constantly. And the character who struggles with the question of his Indian identity most intensely in the novel is Saladin Chamcha. He begins by rejecting the Indian identity and adopting the British identity. His father's comments on this behavior, "A man untrue to himself becomes a two legged lie, and such beasts are Shaitan's best work," (48) and "A man who sets out to make himself up is taking on the Creator's role, according to one way of seeing things: he's unnatural, a blasphemer, an abomination of abomination," are faintly echoed in Mimi's complaint that Saladin feels like a hollow man. Abandoning one's native identity and forging a completely new identity for himself is not the solution Rushdie suggests for solving the perplexing problem of living with one's identity in the hybridizing world.

However, returning to the pure orthodox Indian identity is not possible either since, as Zeeny Vakil claims in her book *The Only Good Indian* (meaning that it is a dead Indian) the entire national culture was "based on the principle of borrowing whatsoever clothes seemed to fit, Aryan, Mughal, British ..." (52) and there is no such thing as an orthodox and pure Indian identity. On the other hand, uncritical eclecticism is not an answer either. Hind Suyfan, in her admiration for her husband Muhammad's pluralistic openness of mind, imitates the pluralism by experimenting with cooking and eating all the diversity of multicultural dishes of the sub-continent and as a result "began to resemble the wide rolling land mass [of the subcontinent] itself." (246) Her husband, who didn't gain a single ounce while subsisting on the same food, quietly comments "Restraint is also part of our traditions." (246) He embraces pluralistic openness of mind, but not forgetting the noble aspects of the traditional culture. He is uprooted from his life in India and becomes an unwilling exile in London because of his government's intolerance of his communist sympathy, but he continues to live a life of restraint, charity, and openness, even as an unhappy exile in London. Therefore, in spite of the cracked and hybrid-ized nature of identity, Rushdie seems to acknowledge the existence of a benign and productive core of one's identity from which compassion and charity for other human beings emanate. As in Gibreel's song, his shoes may be Japanese, and his trousers English, and on his head a red Russian hat, but his "heart's Indian for all that" (5), Rushdie's ideas of openness and hybridity don't quite do away with the center, however fluctuating it may be.

Later Muhammad Suifan's principles of life are inherited by his daugh-ter Mishal and his son-in-law Hanif. As products of multi-cultural educa-tion, they have the instruments and lever to move the English life to fit their needs. And Mishal may look like a punk with her spiky hair dyed in rainbow colors and her tank top fashion, but equipped with better tools she continues to serve the Indian society in London in the same way his father did with the limited means as an owner of the Shandaar Cafe.

It is also significant that the novel ends with the prodigal Indian Saladin Chamcha's return to India and the conclusion of his enmity for his father. His first act upon his return to India is to join the demonstration in sup-port of national integration, in which the participants form a human chain across Bombay. This effort at integration has a different meaning than creating dogmatic nationalistic identity. It arises from the critical intro-spection on Indian people's own racial and religious prejudices against Indians: "How to accuse others of being prejudiced when our own hands are so dirty?" (518) The terrorists, members of a minority group in India, who hijacked the jetliner Bostan, after all, were asking for an "independent homeland, religious freedom, release of political detainees, justice ..." among other things. And the novel makes frank references to color preju-dices in India, and the massacres committed in the name of religion within India.

Despite the prodigious impression of the novel, its messages for openness, tolerance, self-reflection, charity, and human solidarity are not very difficult to pick up. Although, I must admit that Rushdie's genius lies in all the fortuitous and explosively imaginative trips through hybridity he takes us on towards these simple and basic principles of life.

Sooyoung Chon
Ewha Womans University

Works Cited

Ashcroft, Bill. Griffiths, Gareth. Tiffin, Helen. *The Empire Writes Back*. London/ New York: Routledge, 1989.

Bhabha, Homi. *The Location of Culture*. London/New York: Routledge, 1994.

———. ed. *Nation and Narration*. London/New York: Routledge, 1990.

Fanon, Frantz. *Black Skin White Masks*. London: Pluto, 1986.

JanMohamed, Abdul R. "The Economy of Manichean Allegory" Henry Louis Gates, Jr. ed., *"Race," Writing and Difference*. Chicago: University of Chicago Press, 1986.

MacDough, Steve ed. *The Rushdie Letters: Freedom to Speak, Freedom to Write*. Kerry, Ireland: Brandon, 1993.

Parry, Benita. "Problems in Current Theories of Colonial Discourse" *Kunapipi* Vol. xi, No. 1, 1989, 27–58.

Said, Edward. *Orientalism: Western Conceptions of the Orient*. Harmondsworth: Penguin, 1995.

Spivak, Gayatri Chakravorty. *The Post-Colonial Critic: Interview, Strategies, Dialogues*. Sarah Harasym ed. New York/London: Routledge, 1990.

Olson, James S. ed. *Historical Dictionary of European Imperialism*. New York/London: Greenwood, 1991.

Rushdie, Salman. *The Satanic Verses*. Dover, Delaware: The Consortium, Inc., 1992.

Watt, W. Montgomery. *Muhammad: Prophet and Statesman*. London/Oxford/New York: Oxford UP, 1961.

8

Becoming Oneself in Amit Chaudhuri's Novels

Amit Chaudhuri uses postcolonial appropriations of the English language, certain poetic images drawn from universal folklore and everyday sights as well as evocations of music to anchor his fictional texts astride the double axis of postcolonial identity, expressing a yearning for continuity with the past, together with the uncertainties and open interrogations of the future.

We all write and speak from a particular place and time, from a history and a culture which is specific. What we say is always 'in context', positioned (…) all discourse is 'placed', and the heart has its reasons. (…) We cannot speak for very long, with any exactness, about 'one experience', 'one identity', without acknowledging its other side – the ruptures and discontinuities …. Cultural identity in this second sense is a matter of 'becoming' as well as of 'being'. It belongs to the future as much as to the past. (…) Far from being grounded in mere 'recovery' of the past, which is waiting to be found, and which when found, will secure our sense of ourselves into eternity, identities are the names we give to the different ways we are positioned by, and position ourselves within, the narratives of the past.

Stuart Hall, *Cultural Identity and Diaspora*[1]

For post-colonial individuals, a common experience is a feeling of exile from oneself, which makes the question of positioning and identity crucial. This is underlined by Stuart Hall as essential in understanding cultural identity. It constitutes a fundamental aspect of the becoming of the fictional characters in Amit Chaudhuri's three novels: *A Strange & Sublime Address, Afternoon Raag* and *Freedom Song*.[2] Whether his narrative deals with childhood holiday memories with cousins in Calcutta or student experiences in Oxford with a home base in Bombay and Calcutta, or the trajectories of the members of three families from Sylhet in East Bengal/ Bangla Desh over more than fifty years, the ongoing exploration of identity is central. In order to follow the author's representation of this complex, never complete process, we will first look at the stable, continuous frames of reference that structure it, before moving on to the contradictions, cross-overs and instabilities that accompany the constant re-positioning entailed in the becoming of and reconciliation with oneself.

The stable frames of reference in Amit Chaudhuri's novels, the importance of the family is striking. In *A Strange & Sublime Address*, the third person omniscient narrator recounts the idyllic school holidays of the ten-year old protagonist Sandeep in a secure and all-encompassing family network. His first trip to Calcutta was separated from his second by an interval of eighteen months (S&SA, 97). Even though the second trip was heightened by the presence of Sandeep's company executive father which meant that he lodged with his parents at the Grand Hotel on Chowringhee instead of in his mother's family homestead with his cousins and availed of the service of the company car, while his Calcutta uncle had had to sell his "old, battered Ambassador" (S&SA, 98), this did not prevent Sandeep from spending "days and nights at the old house with his cousins".

The carefree bubble of the children's universe protects them from the jolts of family crises like the adverse fortunes of Sandeep's uncle's business (S&SA, 102):

> They lived in their own world which was half illusion, because it was founded so much on fantasy, and half real, palpably real, because its tissue was wholly made of sensations. When they would grow up, and their lives and the lives of the grown-ups would be retold, they would seem like fairy-tales and legends. Certainly, they suspected nothing. They roamed in a silent, self-created web of sounds, smells and colours.

Ritual and traditional ceremony also play an anchoring role in structuring identity. For Sandeep, the smells, the sounds and "the cool taste of the offerings" were more important than the belief or object of prayer, providing "the vivid entertainment of the instant" that procured magical release from "the irksome responsibility of the world" (S&SA, 37). While Sandeep's progressive, intellectual uncle Chhotomama is hospitalized after a heart attack, he realizes the therapeutically ritual value of family visitors (S&SA, 121):

> But suddenly the visitors started coming in, and he had no time to think, he was forced to forget. Being ill was a kind of entertainment, a communal ceremony; it involved such a lot of people.

After celebrating the festival of the goddess Saraswati in her prayer room at home, Chhotomama's wife saves some of the traditional offering made of milk and fruit for her husband in the hospital, "who did not believe in the gods and goddesses, but loved the rituals and the taste of the offerings" (S&SA, 126).

In *Afternoon Raag*, age-old custom and habit form a comforting shell for several characters. For example, R.K.Laxman's daily cartoons in the *Times of India* constitute a part of the narrator's father's morning routine, sometimes serving as a pivot of communion with his wife (AR, 56–57). This little detail enables the author to convey a regular experience shared by millions of Indians from varied horizons through the "wonderfully simple window" of the cartoonist. While commenting on the life style of an elderly Sindhi widow who lived on the same landing as his parents in suburban Bombay, the narrator of *Afternoon Raag* confides (AR, 53):

> One felt she would be leading exactly this life wherever she was, whether in her village or in New York. And yet in no way did she belong to the past.

The annual gathering at the Ganesh temple in central Bombay, in honour of the narrator's music guru's father's spiritual teacher, is an occasion when traditional family solidarity and the sense of community of a little Indian village are displayed in the heart of the sprawling metropolis, transcending even death (AR, 111, 113):

> This solidarity, which was a form of dependency, for the poorer relatives used this as an opportunity to ask favours of those who, like my guru, were doing better for themselves, became evident again, in all its formal comedy and transient but sincere show of love, during my guru's illness. (...)
> The fabric of an ancient hospitality, irrelevant courtesies, meaningless gestures of good will, all-important in the creation of the decorum of that village-life – and they owned little else but that decorum – this was eternal, non-individual, it would go on; and already, my guru was an outsider to it, he was leaving it behind. After he died, this life, as expected, continued cheerfully....

In *Freedom Song*, it is Bhaskar Biswas' arranged marriage to Sandhya Ghosh that serves as an illustration of the maintenance of ancient tradition with the sound of the wedding blast of the shehnai, described as "that unearthly ululation" (FS, 174) and the presence of Brahmin priests to consecrate "the pact with ancestry, caste and divinity". After three days of festivities spent mainly in eating, the couple returns to Bhaskar's family home and everyone goes back to their everyday routine (FS, 177).

This traditional family life is based on patriarchal conceptions where the women are reduced to the limited agency of wives and mothers within their homes.[3] The rare single or separated women characters are portrayed as marginalised or ignored – the most memorable examples appear in *Freedom Song* where the protagonist Khuku Purakayastha's schoolfriend Mini and her sister Shantidi remained spinsters and worked as school-teachers because their family could not afford the expenses their marriages would have entailed (FS, 122). Khuku's niece Beena Mitra who lives with her parents after separating from her husband, was forgotten by the rest of the family and relegated to the place of "a shadow" (FS, 118).

In contrast to these single women, Sandeep's Mamima in *A Strange & Sublime Address*, together with her maidservant Saraswati, were obliged to scuttle around the lord and master of the household every morning "like frightened birds" (S&SA, 15) before his departure to work. Things only increased in intensity after Sandeep's uncle sold his ancient Ambassador car since he had to use the public transport to reach his place of work. As the narrator remarks (S&SA, 99):

> Around him, Mamima and Saraswati performed their old desperate dance, which was a little more desperate now, and a little less like a dance.

In *Freedom Song*, we learn that the protagonist Khuku Biswas was obliged to interrupt her education after completing school because her family said "they could not afford it" (FS, 197). As a result, she stayed at home and learned how to play the harmonium, actually purchased for her brother Bhola (FS, 132, 197). Her marriage to Shib Purakayastha removed her from her immediate family circle. Since Shib said that it was her singing that had clinched his decision to marry her, looking back this alarmed Khuku: "What if she had not been able to sing?" (FS, 198). "What would have happened to Khuku if Shib had not married her?" (FS, 197). These "unanswerable, obsolete questions" underline the fragility of women's lives in post-Independence India.

Also, in all three of Amit Chaudhuri's novels, the ladies from the well-to-do, upper-class families he describes seem to spend much of their time in siestas, since these naps punctuate his texts at regular intervals, highlighting the lack of constructive occupation and the long, idle hours in their lives.

However, these apparently firm moorings of cultural identity reveal certain incoherences and instabilities that necessitate negotiation, adap-

tation and repositioning in a syncretic flux of transformation. This ambivalence is what Stuart Hall refers to as "the shock of the 'doubleness' of
similarity and difference" in relation to the developed West and metropolitan centres and within the decolonized country or in relation to other
decolonized countries. This is why "the boundaries of difference are continually repositioned in relation to different points of reference".[4] The
process of re-telling and re-imagining enables self-fashioning and a positing
of autonomy among the "complex, mixed-up products of diverse colonial
histories".[5] One instance of liberating re-telling of history is observable in
personal experiences and imaginings of the upheavals of partition and
Independence. In *A Strange & Sublime Address*, a visit to elderly relatives
to the south of Calcutta where the setting is semi-rural, makes Sandeep
remember his mother's elder brother Shonomama's allusions to his childhood in Sylhet "when India was one big piece and the British ruled us",
followed by a move to Shillong with its "mountains and waterfalls" (S&SA,
64). In *Freedom Song*, it is through Mini's recollections of her childhood
in Puran Lane in Sylhet that pre-partition days are evoked (FS, 119). After
their parents had both died, the redrawing of the borders took place (FS,
120–121):

> Then the upheaval came, and friends, brothers, teachers, magistrates, ser-
> vants, shopkeepers were all uprooted, as if released slowly, sadly, by the grav-
> ity that had tied them to the places they had known all their life, released
> from an old orbit. They had awaited it with more than apprehension; but
> when it came they hardly noticed it. (...) They'd lost their home; but there
> was the silent, incommunicable excitement of beginning anew in what was
> now their own country.

Thus Mini with her sister Shantidi and three brothers moved from Sylhet
to Shillong and later to Calcutta, like Khuku's family and Shib Purakayastha.

The contradiction between Nehru's and Gandhi's opposite approaches
to ritual and age-old custom is presented when Chhotomama refuses to
allow a nephew and his wife to touch his feet in the traditional greeting of
obeisance to elders, since Nehru's secular India was supposed to be "free
of ritual and religion" (S&SA, 66). However the nephew persists in a token
gesture towards "Gandhi's India of ceremony and custom". It is interesting to note that the refusal of tradition comes from the uncle, of the older
generation, while the desire to maintain tradition comes from the younger nephew!

Certain paradoxes also illustrate cross-overs and subversive negotiations of position. In *Afternoon Raag*, the venerable university city of Oxford is presented with its absence of any centre and its "disturbing perspective" that make it "continually strange". Through a series of frames and changing angles of view, the author conveys the mystery and ambivalence of the ancient, imposing façades with their unchanging, eternal air as opposed to the blurred transience of the different voices and lives of the students since they chatter and mill about only to break up and vanish, leaving behind them "the dignity and silence of the doorway and the world beyond it" (AR, 72–77). This duality between the permanent and the ephemeral is crystallized around "the frame of the doorway" that marks the separation between the inside and the outside for the passer-by. This corroborates the paradoxical experience of the student who is necessarily only "in transit" at Oxford, so that Oxford "never becomes one's own, or anyone else's" (AR, 74).

Another surprising contrast is visible in the friendship that developed between the student narrator and the character called Sharma, in *Afternoon Raag*. The very distance that separates them geographically, socially, temperamentally, academically and in age, seems to constitute the base on which the bond between them grows. Sharma's tales of his life in his village in North India fascinate the narrator and they end up sharing many experiences, including an admiration for the poetry of D.H. Lawrence (AR, 132)! This communion across differences can be seen as an example of a negotiated syncretism or the emergence of what Stuart Hall calls a "diaspora aesthetic".[6]

Another character who embodies a subversive paradox is Bhaskar Biswas in *Freedom Song*. For example, the nature of his dreams is in strong contrast with the nature of his down-to-earth mother's dreams, since Bhaskar is a committed militant of the Communist party in Bengal, making the effort to rise at dawn each morning in order to distribute copies of the Party's newspaper *Ganashakti* to Party supporters (FS, 12–14). So while his mother dreams pragmatically of weakening her son's attachment to radical politics through an arranged marriage, Bhaskar continues to harbour lofty dreams of revolution for the nation (FS, 164). His choice of career also seems to leave unresolved certain obvious contradictions: this supposedly militant upholder of Communist ideals, joins his father's factory, that produces cranes and mechanical spareparts, in a managerial capacity, negotiating commercial transactions with Marwari traders and representatives of small companies for the family business (FS, 142–143)!

Even stranger is his motivation behind this choice of entering the business world: precisely in order to escape from it, together with a lack of ambition and a desire to avoid challenges to his pride, which would inevitably arise in a job with any large company! Similarly, his acceptance of an arranged marriage with a girl he has barely met once, stems from an urge to avoid prolonging the "wearisome business" of wife-hunting, accompanied by a surprising wave of fatalism (FS, 163).

The ultimate meeting place of cultural heterogeneities is language, to which Amit Chaudhuri devotes much attention. The quoting of only a few examples will suffice to show the multiple uses to which he stretches language. Writing in English and not possessing the Bengali of his ancestors fluently, language constitutes a natural site for splitting, doubling, crossovers and repositionings in his novels. A wealth of original metaphors and comparisons enrich the texts throughout. *A Strange & Sublime Address* terminates with the three cousins setting out in quest of sighting the elusive kokil bird at the behest of the hospitalized Chhotomama. This order from their elder is described as follows (S&SA, 129):

> It sounded like a directive in a myth or a fable, the old king ordering his son to bring him the fruit of wisdom, or Hercules being set his most difficult and hopeless task.

This comparison with classical Antiquity and universal folklore gives the story's ending an initiatory quality.

In *Afternoon Raag*, the narrator's tribute to his mother's use of the spoken English she picked up while she spent a few years in London is a paean to postcolonial appropriations of the language of the colonizers (AR, 58):

> Like most Bengalis, she pronounces 'hurt' as 'heart' and 'ship' as 'sheep', for she belongs to a culture with a more spacious concept of time, which deliberately allows one to naively and clearly expand the vowels; and yet her speech is dotted with English proverbs, and delicate, un-Indian constructions like, 'It's a nice day, isn't it?' where most Indians would say, straightforwardly, 'It's a nice day, no?' Many of her sentences are plain translations from Bengali, and have a lovable, homely melody, while a few retain their English inflections, and are sweet and foreign as the sound of whistling.

Emblematic, poetic images seem to stud the texts. In *Freedom Song*, as bombs explode in Bombay and India is rocked by violence in the aftermath of the Babri Masjid episode, a banal sight of birds rising into the air seems underscored by an unsettling note (FS, 160):

There, near Mini's house, near the sweet shop with its heavy smell and the decrepit landlords' houses, birds rose almost peacefully into the air.
Thus they would rise habitually from this most ancient part of Calcutta, shriek, and then return a few moments later to balconies and cornices.

This brings us to the extraordinary musical sensibility captured in *Afternoon Raag*, observable in particular in the eponymous epigraph in homage to the memory of Pandit Govind Prasad Jaipurwale (1941–1988) (AR, viii–x), embellished with architectural and cosmic tropes, as also in the lyrical evocation of the system of raags of Indian classical music (AR, 107–108). Appropriately, this musical presentation culminates in the hybrid interdependence of the raags:

> No raag is so pure that it does not remind one of another raag, that it is not, in some elementary way, a variation or version of a raag sung at some other time of day, or some other season. For instance, does not the heat and blaze of Shudh Sarang resemble, in its structure and shape, the watery gravity and plumbings of Megh? The seasons and hours have no absolute existence, but are defined by each other.

To conclude, Amit Chaudhuri, in the three novels studied here, seems to achieve the artistic feat of straddling the double axis of postcolonial identity, giving equal importance to the pole of continuity with the past and the enforced separations and open interrogations that are turned towards the future. He thus contributes towards consolidating India's self-creation by anchoring his prose in concrete sense experience and exploring her unstable multiplicities in his unique poetic vein. The overall bittersweet impression his reader is left with goes beyond a yearning for lost origins, and encompasses open-ended repositionings in the on-going challenge of existence.

Florence D'Souza
University of Lille III

Works cited

Chaudhuri Amit, *A Strange & Sublime Address*, London: Minerva, 1992 (first published in 1991 by William Heinemann Ltd.)

———. *Afternoon Raag*, London: Minerva, 1994 (first published in 1993 by William Heinemann Ltd.)

———. *Freedom Song*, London: Picador, 1998.

Notes

1. In Patrick Williams & Laura Chrisman (eds.), *Colonial Discourse & post-Colonial Theory, A Reader* New York: Columbia University Press, 1994, pp. 392– 403.

2. Amit Chaudhuri, *A Strange & Sublime Address*, London: Minerva, 1992 (first published in 1991 by William Heinemann Ltd.) henceforth referred to as (S&SA); *Afternoon Raag*, Minerva, London, 1994 (first published in 1993, by William Heinemann Ltd.) henceforth referred to as (AR); *Freedom Song*, London: Picador, 1998, henceforth referred to as (FS).

3. See Ania Loomba, *Colonialism/Postcolonialism*, The New Critical Idiom, London & New York: Routledge, 1998, pp. 218–221.

4. Stuart Hall, art. cit., p. 396.

5. Ania Loomba, op. cit., p. 182, 190.

6. Stuart Hall, art. cit., p. 402.

9

Personal Dilemmas and The Politics of Identity in Jean Arasanayagam's *All is Burning*

The tiny island of Sri Lanka whose pristine and scenic beauty has often been likened to that of the Garden of Eden is today the theatre of un-precedented violence. Caught in the crossfire of ethno-religious and eco-nomic rivalries, the civilian population is being slowly initiated into the cold strategy of survival. The short stories presented in the anthology of Jean Arasanayagam (née Solomons, a Sri Lankan writer of Dutch Bur-gher origin) represent critical moments in the lives of individuals, be they young or old, male or female, Tamil or Sinhalese, Eastern or West-ern, rich or poor, respectable or tainted, in times of both war and peace. Poised between homesickness and wonder, memory and forgetting, they dream of a glorious return and keep perpetually moving and mutating.

"At the end of the 20th century to be a citizen is to be an alien" remarks Julia Kristeva in her oft-quoted essay on the "Lonely New World". The war between belonging and exile is perhaps the most urgent and existential question that we are all obliged to solve in the postcolonial[1] and globalized era. According to Edward Said, "it is one of the characteristics of the age to have produced more refugees, migrants, displaced persons and exiles than ever before in history, most of them as an accompaniment to and ... as after thoughts of great post-colonial and imperial conflicts".[2] In India, however, exile is a familiar literary figure. Unlike the Homeric hero Ulysses who chooses exile, the Indian epic heroes both in the *Mahabharata* and in the *Ramayana* are compelled to undergo the trial of exile before they fulfil their destined roles on the face of the earth. It is as if exile is always already a reincarnatory journey. The founding myth of Sri Lanka is, in fact, a variation on the theme of exile.[3] A Bengali princess falls a prey to wanderlust and escapes to the region of Gujarat. Kidnapped by the bandit

leader Sinha, she becomes his mistress and bears him two children, Sinhabahu and Sinhasivali. Disenchanted with her nomadic life, the princess
comes back to her native land. Sinha seeks vengeance. It is his own son,
Sinhabahu, who slays him in order to win the reward promised by his grandfather, the king. Meanwhile, the king had died, but remorse stricken Sinhabahu prefers to relinquish the throne and err. Nevertheless, he founds the
city of Sinhapura and takes for wife his own sister. A son, Vijayabahu, is
born of this incestuous union. Having inherited the streak of unruliness, he
causes havoc among the population. His angry father puts Vijaya and his
companions in a ship and delivers them to the mercy of the ocean. They
land in Sri Lanka where the tribal queen Kuveni welcomes him. Thanks
to her unflinching love, he manages to murder her own folk and establish
the Sinhala (meaning Children of the lion.[4]) kingdom. Soon the exiled hero
is faced with another dilemma. Should he let the mixed brood of Kuveni
accede to the throne? He vilely abandons her and preserves his Aryan
heritage by importing a brand new bride from the kingdom of Madura.
Thus Kuveni finds herself exiled in her own land betraying her own kith
and kin before being betrayed by the man she loved. She is killed literally
by her own people and symbolically by her husband. This founding myth –
so primitive in its unfolding – including parricide and incest is stunningly
modern with instances of female revolt, self-imposed exile, banishment
and return, cross cultural encounters and transformed identities.

Readers from the West have constructed a Ceylon of their minds
based on the accounts of authors like Robert Knox, John Milton, Leonard
Woolf and D.H. Lawrence. They usually associate Ceylon with both seren-
dipity and the Garden of Eden. Recent Sri Lankan writing[5] in English by
celebrated authors like Michael Ondaatje, Romesh Gunesekara, Yasmine
Gooneratne, Carl Muller, Shyam Selvathurai and Chandani Lokugé, tend
to tell a different story – the slow but irretrievable transformation of the
lost paradise into a battle ground for ethno-religious and economic conflicts. Though the Sinhalese hostility towards the Tamils is nothing new,
the intensity of this hatred has divided the island into two. Jean Arasanayagam, née Solomons, a Sri Lankan writer of Dutch Burgher origin, trained
in Scotland, the United States and England, married to Thiyagarajah Arasanayagam, a poet, painter and playwright of Tamil origin has a special
sensitivity to explore the complex problematics of identity in postcolonial
Sri Lanka.

The profile of the post colonial exiles that we encounter, the socio-
political context that has lead to what Edward Said calls "their intransi-

gence and obdurate rebelliousness",[6] the mutation of the space in which
they live owing to the overlapping of territories and time leads to the rather
apocalyptic degeneration of the search for identity into a struggle for survival and the pertinence of Buddha's message to today's terror stricken
humanity.

The title *All is Burning* comes from the famous *Fire Sermon* of the
Buddha[7] which he pronounced at Gaya, when challenged by a Brahmin
who thought that he was superior to the Buddha in holiness.

> Bhikkus, all is burning. And what is all that is burning?
> Bhikkus, the eye is burning, visible forms are burning, visual consciousness is
> burning...
> Burning with what?
> Burning with the fire of lust, with the fire of hate, with the fire of delusion; I
> say it is burning with birth, ageing and death, with sorrows, with lamenta-
> tions, with pains, with griefs, with despairs".

Buddhism came to Sri Lanka in the 3rd century BC. It is Sri Lanka's official
religion today. But the irony is that after nearly two thousand three hundred years Buddha's words have come alive with a vengeance in Sri Lanka
where the Buddhists are burning the Tamil people and their properties.
To quote Jean Arasanayagam's own poem "Fire in the Village"

> Here too, the night is dark, thunder black, as the fire
> in the village spreads, it's best to escape while you can.

The ninth and eponymous story in the anthology depicts a lone and forlorn
mother, Alice, venturing into the darkness of the underworld to retrieve
the dead body of her future son-in-law in order to spare her daughter the
pain. All the young men in the village are massacred by Sinhalese police-
men or soldiers because they are Tamil[8] and suspected of subversive political activity in a village that periodically listens to Buddha's *Fire Sermon*
and wants to be liberated from the cycle of life altogether. The stark reality
of the picture of anonymous bodies of men huddled together seems to remind us of the paradoxical permanence of death and impermanence of
life on earth, a recurring theme in this collection and the meaninglessness
of any battle for self-affirmation.

However, we come across a simple yet operational definition of identity in the nineteenth short story entitled "Fear: Mediations in a Camp".
"One's needs had to create a space even minimal that would accommodate
the physical body (407)". Jean Arasanayagam touches on all the stages of

this temporal axis and the personal dilemmas peculiar to each stage mostly from the point of view of women's identity. I could discern the unconscious imprint of the traditional Tamil division of womanhood into a seven fold span – naive, intermediary, nubile, married, blooming, mature, post-meno-pausal – based on her knowledge of sex and fertility.[9] In "The Mutants", we are introduced to Zuleika, a young village girl abandoned by both her father and mother who makes an unhappy journey to Kandy where she is taken care of by an American lady belonging to the Seventh Day Adventist Church. Though the glimpse of another more ordered and protected way of life beckons her, she escapes and seeks refuge in another aunt's house. She draws the courage to do this from her Ninja turtles which protect her like guardian angels. The successful painting of a child's innocence, curiosity and joie de vivre set this story apart in a world filled with violence, death and destruction. The traditional and religious icons have been supplanted here by imaginary and secular ones. The contrast that the child makes between owls and turtles reveals her perception of the distance that separates the safety of her familiar moorings from the snares of city life.

The longing for the protected garden of childhood re-occurs in "Bali" where Janine, who has covered the full cycle from innocence to experience comes back to reminisce about her Ayah, Mungo. The bali tribals indulge in elaborate rituals to exorcise the evil within and in the minds of others. The Ayah is so attentive to Janine that she forbids the young girl to touch the bright and attractive white, red and yellow tropical flowers lying scattered after the ceremony lest she should be afflicted with sickness. The memory of the past accentuates the horror of the present, for human beings have become more monstrous than Riri Yakka, the great bali demon and the sacrificial blood of the birds has now been replaced by the blood of the virgin raped in the forest

The most poetic story in this collection, entitled "Elysium", celebrates the discovery of sexual identity by a young girl of sixteen. Occupying the disturbing space between adolescent day dreaming, an inculcated Christian culture that teaches her to resist temptation and an almost tribal environment which observes puberty rites that give her a heightened sense of her body, the narrator of this story remains a virgin and a nun and learns to sublimate her sexuality into sensuous poetry, even as the young man to whom she is drawn marries someone else. Three other short stories interweave the themes of young adult female identity and exile. "The Golden Apples of Hesperides" is set in Glasgow. The main characters are university students, many of them Scottish but a few British Council scholars on their Commonwealth fellowships. The young Sri Lankan poet who seems to be an alter ego of Jean herself, Marcia, develops a fondness for a forty year old Colombian student Domingos. The loneliness and transience of exile brings them close to a romance. "They were travellers in the same desert, thirsting for water, rest" (151). But Marcia's South Asian reserve and Domingo's South American ebullience do not melt. They share an eternal friendship, nothing more. Marcia arranges a farewell party on the eve of his departure and is in a dilemma whether to tell him how much she values him. When she makes up her mind in the morning and goes to his apartment, it is too late. She is left with the unforgettable memory of a shared repast. Let us note that all the religions of the world, be it the Hindu obligation of hospitality to the *paradesi* (literally transterritorial) or the Christian concept of *agape*, have foreseen a place for the exile. The charity of a shared meal constitutes an unsettling moment in the erring of an exile because it allows him to simply live and move on.

The predicament that awaits the heroine of "From Distant Ophir" is bitter. Sulochana has reached marriageable age and from her carefree self as a bachelor girl must now step into another dimension of her identity as a married woman. In spite of her being an English graduate and a teacher, she has been brought up in a culture where right from the beginning, with the onset of nubile womanhood and coming of age ceremonies, marriage is the desired end. Though in her heart of hearts she longs for the romantic "chance encounter, the magic alchemy of recognition" (124), she has to reconcile herself to the prospect of arranged proposals from prospective bridegrooms settled abroad – Commonwealth countries like the U.K., Canada and the West Indies or the Middle East. Caught between the traditions of the East and the possibilities offered by the West, she is unable to make up her mind on the suitable boy, unlike Vikram Seth's Lata! When the story ends, she is in her thirties and has not given up her provisionally perpetual quest for a mate from a distant and foreign land, with no intimations of what this glorified exile really means.

Exile can be both horizontal – a displacement in space or vertical – an exit from the meaning of existence.[10] *A Husband Like Shiva* is a study in contrast of more experienced women. One of the heroines, Radha comes from a high caste Vellala Tamil family. Though attracted to a poor bank clerk, Sivam, she rejects him and marries the bridegroom chosen by the family. Despite the fact that she willingly dons the mask of social conformity, a time comes when she realizes that in spite of a wealthy and comfortable life, a faithful husband and three well-doing sons, she is emotionally bankrupt. The other heroine, Sarada first plays the conventional game and marries the man she has not chosen. Later she meets an Italian sailor and elopes with him. After fathering a child, Luigi leaves her. Sarada is obliged to return from her Venetian exile and beg for alms in her native city where there is "no acceptance, no forgiveness" for this girl who took the risky alleyways of freedom. If the evolution of identity depends on making choices, both the choices seem to be equally deceptive.

To continue with the portrait of women's identities, we can take up "Fistful of Wind". Here Jean uses a first person narrative and the narrator resembles the seasoned author who offers us a short retrospective of her life. A teacher, who could have found better opportunities had she migrated but has been kept back by her attachment to her roots, visits what is called a cut-piece shop because she does not have enough money to buy clothes from expensive and fashionable stores. She realizes that buying such clothes would only amount to camouflaging her poverty. The cut-piece shop, which serves as a theatre for the *mise en scène* of the identity crisis, is a metaphor for the pathetic assimilation of the mercantile aspect of the Western culture by people who often have no inkling of its nobler aspects such as its arts and literature.

"Prayers to Kali" finishes the spectrum of moving and mutations with the picture of an old woman in anger. The narrator is a Tamil youth who has left his native Tamil village in the North, Navali, for the town of Katukelle, near Kandy. His method of ajusting to the new way of life is to visit the Hindu temple, which acts as a mediating space between his rural origins and urban leanings. His chance encounter with a Buddhist Sinhalese woman, who is worshipping the dark Hindu goddess, Kali, is edifying. Just as he had been compelled to move to the town in search of new economic opportunities, she had been forced by the changes in her horizon of expectations into worshipping more powerful alien Gods. This mother of eight sons and many daughters could not spend her old age in peace, as money from the Middle East sent by her daughters floods her household. Her idle sons-in law and numerous grandchildren exploit her and laugh at her moral uprightness. Obliged to work and be busy, she resents the onslaught of competitive, global culture and time on her slow rhythm and simple life and curses her descendants. Her temporary exile in the threshold of another religion helps her vent out her anger.

Jean Arasanayagam highlights the impact of the clash between the peace loving tradition and end of the century violence in two other striking short stories. The narrator of "I am an Innocent Man" is a school teacher who takes pains to dress in immaculate white. He is and wants to project the image of an innocent man, especially so because all around him, the dominant patterns of identity are "terrorist, militant, guerrilla or one of the Boys". One day as he is taking his bath, he is witness to an ethnic crossfire in which more than eighty-seven men die. Paralyzed by fear, he does not take part in what is going on either on the Tamil side to whose ethnic group he belongs or on the Government side to which he owes allegiance as a citizen. He is, however, suspected of being a survivor and a terrorist and questioned by the military officials and owes his release only to a superintendent friend who vouches for his trustworthiness. But the teacher has qualms: "And if you, in these circumstances, cannot speak the truth, aren't you betraying yourself too? What is it worth paying the price for safety when you see so many dying on both sides?" (39). Though his social identity has been preserved, his inner self is shattered.

In this context, exile has become not a choice but a necessity for many. Jean does not forget to depict all the three phases of exile – journey, sojourn and return – in her anthology. Prior to any exile is the loss of home. In "Time the Destroyer", Serena who inherits the family home after the death of her mother and brother realizes that she cannot live there. She does not want to sell the house or rent it, for she knows that it will be transformed into a luxury hotel for tourists. She decides to turn it into a home for orphans. In a way, exiles, emigrants and expatriates are orphans too, as they cannot lay claim either to their original culture or their assimilated culture. The most representative of contemporary Sri Lankan journeys is presented in the opening story entitled "The Journey". The narrator is a young Sinhalese migrant who ironically travels with the Tamil refugees from Sri Lanka via Moscow to Berlin and on to Saarbrucken. Forgetting their names by becoming mere numbers in the hands of the passers, shedding their meagre possessions and passports, facing cold, hunger and death, these refugees remind us of other journeys – of Buddha's towards illumination, of Indian migrants to Sri Lanka and of Jews escaping Nazi Germany. Thanks to their survival instinct, they safely reach Berlin, a city that seems to be reinventing its own identity after the fall of its wall.

If Sri Lankans migrate or seek political asylum in the West, some foreigners come to do business in Sri Lanka. This is the case of the Chinese entrepreneur Melwyn who has lost his name and language but is building a new identity as an industrial or those who operate lucrative prawn farms in the coastal villages or the foreign mercenaries who work for the Sri

Lankan army. "Fragments from a Journey" is a thinly veiled autobiographical piece in which Jean describes her Indian sojourn. Sri, the Hindu husband, has made a vow to go on a pilgrimage to the Meenakshi temple in
Madurai. His Christian wife and student daughter accompany him on this
trip, as travellers. Though the narrator Dewa's dress and colour does not
single her out as a foreigner, she feels alien and recalls her stay in the
West where she felt at home. She is aware that "looking back on the familiar past carries with it the regret of nostalgia" (255) and that an exile
ends either in a settlement or return.

What is the socio-political context that has lead to this population
drain in Sri Lanka? The most obvious reason, of course, is ethnic tension.
The post colonial history of Sri Lanka is one of impossible hybridity, unlike
Jean Arasanayagam's artistic style which fuses rich ethnographic details
with Buddhist philosophy and subtly incorporates Tamil and Sinhalese
words into English. The reinvention of the Tamil identity in the form of
the Tiger underscores this. The tiger is an animal that is at home in the
tropics as much as the lion (the lion is the emblem of Sri Lanka). In ancient Tamil literature, the archetypal mother speaks of her womb as the
tiger's cave, unconsciously comparing her son to a tiger's cub.[11] The tiger
is a symbol of valiance is Tamil Culture. The totemic animal of the Chola
kings of South India was the tiger which appeared in their flags. The Sinhalese majority has grown jealous of the enterprising Tamil community
that had managed to obtain key posts in the civil service thanks to their
anglicised culture and started to oppress them both by discriminatory measures such as disenfranchisement (of Indian born Tamils as against Sri
Lankan born Tamils), language requirement (Tamils had to learn Sinhalese to be able to work in the civil service), standardization (Tamil students
had to score higher marks to secure entrance to universities), resettle-
ment (to alter the composition of the population and the power balance)
and by coercion. More than the difficulties involved in a democratic power
sharing in a country which boasts of a ninety percent literacy rate, where
people have failed in the test of smooth transition, we also witness what
Samuel Huntington calls the clash of civilisations.[12] If elsewhere in the
world, Judaism and Islam, Hinduism and Islam, Christianity and Islam
are at loggerheads, in Sri Lanka the old rivalry between Hinduism and
Buddhism has taken on a bloody dimension, as Buddhists perceive themselves as passive and the Tamils as aggressive. But the root cause of this
misery seems to be the end of imperialism and the sense of loss suffered
by the population. In what appears to me as one of the truthful and key

passages of the novel, Jean Arasanayagam explains the fascination that the West and by extension abroad still exercises in the minds of Sri Lankans:

> Abroad was Elysium. Abroad was El Dorado. Abroad had become another country which could be anywhere on the map. Anyone who went there lived not in Germany, Canada, England but in Abroad. It was a country, exotic, mysterious, flowing with milk and honey and much sought after. 'In Abroad' was where the money was. Comfort. A higher standard of living... You were wealthier, more prosperous, more professionally qualified and educated if you lived and earned abroad. ... To be in abroad was to live in Xanadu.

The place left vacant by imperialism is occupied today by international capitalism. If as Rushdie says, "character isn't destiny anymore. Economics is destiny. Ideology is destiny. Bombs are destiny",[13] the god is money. The short stories presented in this anthology give us a glimpse of the mutation of people and their habitat which is by turns village, jungle and camps. Consumerism, sexual tourism, indulgence in drugs and terrorism have become the order of the day.

In the last and most distressing story, Jean Arasanayagam describes the predicament of a person caught between two languages, cultures and religions. As a Burgher woman, she is not considered as an enemy by the Sinhalese who want to take away the lives of her Tamil husband and children. While in the camp, her acceptance of the offer of milk by the Buddhist monks provokes disgust among the Tamils who wonder whether it is a poisoned gift. The picture of the refugees fighting for vital space to breathe, eat, sleep and wash under the threat of an armed attack seems to be an actualization of the innocent school teacher's nightmare in which he imagines a neglected prawn pond in which the prawns begin to war against one another and turn cannibalistic as the space that contained them shrinks. The prawn pond with its water clogged image represents the insular and therefore unstretchable nature of Sri Lankan territory. For the author, a path of self-discovery opens: "Civilization meant nothing here. Philosophies were absent. So was political theorizing. You delved deep into the hitherto undiscovered springs of your primeval psyche to find the source of pure and absolute energy" (393). She comes to the conclusion that she must relinquish her name and become everyman, everywoman. With this end of illusion comes nirvana, non-being. When one reaches this stage, one does not look upon others as brothers, nor does one look upon others as enemies. Buddhism's time honoured *neti-neti* formula is not only valid for Sri Lanka but the world over where nations are torn by ethno-religious conflicts and where humanity is in the grip of the invisible hand of the market forces. To the Nabokovian somebody, somewhere who is quietly setting out, buying a ticket to board a bus, a ship or a plane, one is tempted to quote Jean Arasanayagam[14]

> Once more to journey on a chartered course
> To reach which country?
> I have no country now but self.

Geetha Ganapathy-Doré
University of Paris XIII

Notes

1. Cf. Ania Loomba, *Colonialism/Postcolonialism* (London: Routledge, 1998) for an interesting discussion on the ideological battles surrounding this catchall term.

2. Edward Said, *Culture and Imperialism* (New York: Alfred Knopf, 1993), p. 332.

3. Shiv Naipaul, *An Unfinished Journey* (London: Abacus, 1986), pp. 95–99.

4. Carl Muller, *Children of the Lion* (New Delhi: Viking, 1997).

5. D.C.R.A. Goonetilleke, *The Penguin New Writing in Sri Lanka* (New Delhi: Penguin, 1992).

6. Edward Said, op. cit., loc. cit.

7. Maurice Percheron, *Le Bouddha et le bouddhisme* (Paris: Editions du Seuil, 1956).

8. Cf. *Sri Lanka, un pays déchiré* (Paris: Amnesty International, 1990).

9. These are known in Tamil as *Pedai, Pedumbai, Mangai, Madandai, Arivai, Therivai, Perilampen.*

10. For a more elaborate explanation of this idea, confer Fethi Ben Slama, *Une fiction troublante* (Paris: Editions de l'Aube, 1994).

11. See A.K. Ramanujan, *Poems of Love and War* (New York: Columbia University Press, 1985) for a translation of Sangam Tamil Poems.

12. Samuel Huntington, *The Clash of Civilizations and the Remaking of World Order* (New York: Simon and Shuster, 1996).

13. Salman Rushdie, *The Satanic Verses* (London: Viking, 1987), p. 432.

14. Jean Arasanayagam, *Reddended Water Flows Clear, Poems from Sri Lanka* (London: Forest Books, 1991).

Works Cited

Arasanayagam, Jean. *Reddended Water Flows Clear, Poems from Sri Lanka*. London Forest Books, 1991.

———. *All is Burning*. New Delhi: Penguin, 1995

Ben Slama, Fethi.*Une fiction troublante*. Paris: Editions de l'Aube, 1994.

Gooneratne, Yasmine. *The Pleasures of Conquest*. New Delhi: Penguin, 1995.

Goonetilleke, D.C.R.A. *The Penguin New Writing in Sri Lanka*, New Delhi: Penguin, 1992.

Gunesekera, Romesh. *Reef*. London: Granta, 1994.

Kristeva, Julia. *Etrangers à nous-mêmes*. Paris: Fayard, 1988.

Lokugé, Chandani. *If the Moon Smiled*. New Delhi: Penguin, 2000.

Loomba, Ania. *Colonialism/Postcolonialism*. London: Routledge, 1998.

Muller, Carl. *Children of the Lion*. New Delhi: Viking, 1997.

Naipaul, Shiv. *An Unfinished Journey*. London: Abacus, 1986.

Narayan Swamy, M.R. *Tigers of Sri Lanka*. 3d ed. Konark Publishers: 1995, Delhi.

Ondaatje, Michael. *Running in the Family*. Picador: London, 1984.

———. *Anil's Ghost*, Alfred A. Knopf, New York, 2000.

Percheron, Maurice. *Le bouddha et le bouddhisme*. Paris: Seuil, 1956.

Ramanujam, A.K. *Poems of Love and War*. New York: Columbia University Press, 1985.

Rushdie, Salman. *The Satanic Verses*. London: Viking, 1988.

Said, Edward. *Culture and Imperialism*. New York: Alfred A. Knopf, 1993.

Selvathurai, Shyam. *Funny Boy*. New Delhi.

10

"New Ways to be beautiful": The Search to Escape Identity in *The Moor's Last Sigh*

The postcolonial enterprise of which Rushdie is an emblematic and controversial figure is heavily committed to the rediscovery of the past and its
hidden narratives. In *The Moor's Last Sigh* he attaches himself to the am-
bitious project of the rewriting of the history of the Indian sub-continent
through the distorting lens of the present and from a new cultural perspective, that of the Portuguese, Spanish, Jewish and Moorish minorities
instead of that of the traditional British colonial or Hindu majorities.
The novel becomes a problematized space for various different discourses
or versions, competing for pre-eminence in a parody of official truth
which forces the reader to re-evaluate conventional notions of that truth
and his/her role in fabricating it.

Whereas post-colonial discourse usually centres around the need to rediscover lost or squashed identity, we will examine the way in which Rushdie
turns this premise on its head, showing how voluntary exile from identity
is the only means to redefine identity as an unfixed, constantly evolving
notion rather than a prison of pre-ordained meaning. Exile *is* identity in
Rushdie's world, but the most productive sort of identity, not just physical, geographical exile around which the book is organised, but mental,
intellectual exile from fixed truths. The *Moor's Last Sigh* becomes an un-
conventionally rebellious enterprise in escape as confrontation, as the hero
flees his family, his country and finally himself in order better to illustrate
the Rushdiean philosophy of "constant becoming" expressed on the first
page of *The Satanic Verses*, "To be born again, first you have to die…".[1]
In Rushdie's post-colonial world a multitude of possible truths vie with
the official version of history as an antidote to a dangerous oneness and
The Moor's Last Sigh becomes almost a parody of militant post-

colonialism in adopting the most marginal of marginal points of view and organising history around it, so that its artificial reductiveness will encourage the reader to glimpse the truth of multiplicity over which it has spread its successive layers. In Rushdie's (fictional) world, the only way to avoid dangerous reductiveness is for each individual to craft his life as if it were a work of art, exploring beauty without limits.

Defamiliarisation: Making strange in order to make anew, "The Naming of Parts"

The essential identification process necessary in any work of fiction by the naming of characters and the giving of a title to the book becomes under Rushdie's pen an exercise in defamiliarization and the first impression of the reader is one of confusion, as identification with the "I" of the narration, the expected "Moor"of the title, "a nowhere, no-community man",[2] seems increasingly compromised:

> I have lost count of the days that have passed since I fled the horrors of Vasco Miranda's mad fortress in the Andalusian mountain-village of Benengeli; ran from death under cover of darkness and left a message nailed to the door. [...] *Here I stand. Couldn't have done it differently.*
> (Here I sit, is more like it. In this dark wood -that is, upon this mount of olives, within this clump of trees [...]). (3; original italics)

The organising principle seems to be uncertainty, for the first page can only be fully understood in the light of the last and must be returned to and reinterpreted at the end, an end which is in its beginning so as to resist closure and crippling certainties, and whose eccentric trails of meaning will be renewed and revived by the inescapable circularity of Rushdie's creation.

As for the chronology of the book, Rushdie starts with the last branch on the family tree printed before chapter one and then plants us down in the middle, before going backwards, thereby establishing a worrying synchronicity in the place of the expected diachrony. Equally unsettling is the family chosen to serve as a chronicle for historical events (in Rushdie's world public and private are inextricably linked), and their multiple locations: Cabral Island in southern India, Bombay, that "super-epic motion picture of a city" (129), "the city of mixed-up, mongrel joy" (376), and, above all, the mysterious Andalusian village of Benengeli, the "village of uncertainty" (406). Thus the recent history of India is not told from a majority point of view, Hindu or Muslim, but from that of an eccentric minority, the Catholic/Portuguese/Jewish spice-merchant class of southern

India and its Malabar coast which yet partakes of a wider hybrid identity
by virtue of its hidden origins which are gradually revealed as the layers of
false community identity are stripped off to uncover a complex sense of alien
belonging, "*Outcasts*, peculiar Christians" (8; original italics), "Bunch of
English-medium misfits, the lot of you. Minority group members. Square-
peg freaks. *You don't belong here.* Country's as alien to you as if you were
what's-the-word *lunatics. Moon-men.* You read the wrong books, get on
the wrong side in every argument, think the wrong thoughts. Even your
bleddy dreams grow from foreign roots" (166; original italics). In identity
there is "id" i.e. the other, the strange, as well as the idea of similarity and
Rushdie organises the concept of identity around confrontation and interaction with other identities in order to discover one's own. Any acceptance
of pre-ordained meaning is a lie and a dangerous simplification which is
why multiplicity is posited as the book's starting point. The reader is left
with a difficultly identifiable whole made up of a multitude of parts, sym-
bolised by the image of the crowd of humanity in one of the book's numerous portraits, "the rapid rush of the composition drew him onwards,
away from the personal and into the throng, for beyond and around and
above and below and amongst the family was the crowd itself, the dense
crowd, the crowd without boundaries" (60). Thus Rushdie is able to show
that India is also made up of minorities, a fact which the book suggests is
not really taken into account by recent history, decided along the axis of
Hindu-Muslim opposition, "Christians, Portuguese and Jews; Chinese tiles
promoting godless views, pushy ladies, skirts-not-saris, Spanish shenani-
gans, Moorish crowns … can this really be India? *Bharat-mata, Hindustan-
hamara*, is this the place?" (87; original italics), asks the narrator rhetori-
cally, inviting the reader to participate in his re-imagining of cultural and
ethnic steroeytpes. This *is* the place, but not as we expected, for the eccentric becomes representative in order to contest the norm. The naming
of the different parts goes to make up the final whole, in fact before the
parts have been named, the whole cannot be defined, for all reality is
fragmentary in Rushdie's world.

"What's in a name?" asks the narrator at one point (84). Everything
and nothing one might reply. The name of the hero, "Moor" is a good
illustration of this. It means nothing on one level because it is the result of
whim; "Moor" is so-called because his first cry was a "moo" or possibly in
order to fit into the nursery-rhyme neatness of the family framework for
his sisters are named respectively Ina, Meeny, Minny! On another level it
could mean everything because, as the hero admits himself, "Our names

contain our fates"(70). Moor becomes an emblem not only of India's apparent contradiction, a contradiction which contributes to its richness, for, part Jewish, part Portuguese, part Moorish by his ancestry, he is a "real Bombay mix", a "highborn cross-breed" (3), "a jewholic anonymous, a cathjew nut, a stewpot, a mongrel cur" (104), but also of the necessity of the recognition of endless possibility as the only truth, in other words, as his name suggests, always more, the philosophy of excess indicated by the protosemanticism of his full name, "Moraes", that is to say, "more he is". Moor will undergo a process of *"atomisation"*, as he puts it (104; original italics), for it is only by exploding the false certainties of fixed identity that a newer, more authentic one, based on unresolvable contradictions, can come to the fore. The hero becomes the ultimate in defamiliarization for not only does he have a club for a right-hand but he ages twice as fast as normal, both factors preventing the reader from identifying with him and creating an extra dimension of unhoped for possibility, for he is "a magic child, a time-traveller" (219). His inescapable differentness is incompatible with the pinning down or pigeon-holing of his life-story as representative of a particular category, class, race, period. One must not forget either that historically, "moor" is a contested term for it includes Malays and Indian converts to Islam for trading purposes, thereby undermining any ethnically pure status it might be supposed to possess. At the same time "Moor" operates on a symbolic level as an icon of the political mutilation of India and its accelerated historical development and thus his strangeness illustrates a frightening and sad historical reality.

Resistance to interpretation has become a cliché over the last few years and is often applied in desperation to Rushdie's work, particularly, *The Satanic Verses*, but finally Rushdie's writing does not so much resist interpretation as multiply the possibilities of interpretation and thus of creation. His approach to language is based on preventing immediate understanding and identification which would constitute a dangerous process of simplification and manipulation of his public. Instead Rushdie confronts his readers with a topsy-turvy world of high-charged creativity situating his story in what he calls, "these back-to-front Jabberwocky days" (5), associating them democratically with the creation of meaning and substituting fertile confusion for narrative certainty. The deformity associated with "Moor", "some peculiar disorder" (240), seems to determine the way the book functions. The constant use of hyphens in order to separate things which should not be separated prevents immediate understanding and thus reductive classification, while the use of Indian words is often destined to force the Western reader to connect, as they are thrown into a sentence making it strange and then explained by a process of implication. Equally, the cultural and intertextual references and the different linguistic registers brought into play are so wide and varied that nothing but multiple identification can do justice to Rushdie's fictional hybrid. The critical distance imposed on the reader is part of a process of empowerment which will lead him to actively reconstruct a different version of reality from a maximum of points of view. Thus the first pages of the book, a veritable *tour de force* which surpass even those of *The Satanic Verses*, warn the reader of what to expect, setting up a courageous contract which has been the basis for Rushdie's fiction from *Grimus*[3] onwards, that is to say, the principle of uncertainty and democratic power-sharing with the reader, "So finally it is not for me to judge, but for you" (85). Posing as a nostalgic autobiographer telling his story in restrospect, the narrator starts back to front, "Now, therefore, it is meet to sing of endings" (4), confusing the reader by his refusal to assert incontrovertible reality, "of what was, and may be no longer" (*ibid.*), and yet laying claims to history, "Moraes Zogoiby expelled from his story, tumbled towards history" (5). All is contradictory subjectivity:

> A last sigh for a lost world,[4] a tear for its passing. Also, however, a last hurrah, a final scandalous skein of shaggy-dog yarns (words must suffice, video facility being unavailable) and a set of rowdy tunes for the wake. A Moor's tale, complete with sound and fury. You want? Well, even if you don't. And to begin with, pass the pepper.
> – *What's that you say?* – (4; original italics)

The narration seems based on personal ramblings, arbitary correspondances which turn out to be planned artificially to draw attention to the constructedness of the story, for example the mention of the pepper which will enable the narrator to introduce the Da Gama family around which the narration is centered. As one can see from the example just quoted, each word revels in endless polysemy ("skein", "yarn") flaunting a multitude of contradictory intertextual references (*Macbeth* and *Othello*, to name the two most obvious) and exploding semantically to reveal its under-the-surface multiplicity. The supposedly arbitrary connections between words foreground an artificial creation of links and signification destined to make the reader work. Metaphors are mixed or metonymised ("the scandalous skein of shaggy-dog yarns"), exacting from the reader a constant effort of substitution rather than imposing ready-made images. The project of defamiliarization is the basis for the escape from categorisation which is

Rushdie's main ambition for his work. Meaning is something to be fabricated democratically and should never be submitted to, but accommodated within the framework of multiplicity.

The way names usually function or are supposed to function, that is to say the way they are used to label, pigeon-hole, categorise people and are taken for granted, is turned on its head by Rushdie's art which makes them strange in order to show the hidden truths behind those labels. Thus not only does his "story" escape labelling but his "discourse" as well and the Rushdiean *récit* tirelessly resists identification, setting up endless possibilitiy as its goal, what is defined by one of the artists in the book as an "'Epico-Mythico-Tragico-Comico-Super-Sexy-High-Masala-Art' in which the unifying principle was Technicolor-Story-Line'" (148–149).

"The Hyperabundant Cavalcade"

The rejection of singleness and labels by a process of estrangement as a starting point leads to a literary construction of reality which can only be called deconstructive, for Rushdie will put different myths into conflict parading them before the reader in the "hyperabundant cavalcade" (84) of his fiction, lining them up for inspection in order for them to be compared to one another in a process of relativity, presenting layer upon layer of meaning. Thus different political, historical, personal and artistic truths become spaces for relativity, part of "the mythic-romantic mode in which history, family, politics and fantasy jostled each other like the great crowds at V.T. or Chuchgate Stations" (203–4), as the problem of interpretation is provocatively posed, for instance in the context of communal violence: "In the days after the destruction of the Babri Masjid, 'justly enraged Muslims'/'fanatical killers' (once again, use your blue pencil as your heart dictates) smashed up Hindu temples..." (365). The endless multiplication of possibilities stimulates the creative process in the mind of the reader and above all encourages him to identify only to distance himself subsequently. A real event, the kissing of a cricket star by a young girl during a test match, is turned into a picture by Aurora, the narrator's artist mother and subjected to different interpretations depending on the political affiliations of the viewers, "a state-of-India painting" (229), "a pornographic representation of a sexual assault by a Muslim sporstman on an innocent Hindi maiden" (232). Not only do different and conflicting realities collide in this episode, but it also highlights the difficulties of representation and the way art can modify reality depending on perception. Here lies the

difficulty of defining where reality stops and fiction begins, for from "the
'real' shy peck, done for a dare" (228), the kiss "was transformed into a
full-scale Western-movie clinch" (*ibid.*). Rushdie takes delight in placing
his reader on a see-saw between reality and fantasy until both are redefined
as interdependent in the creation of meaning, for as the artist Vasco Miranda advises Aurora, "The real is always hidden – isn't it? – inside a mi-
raculously burning bush! Life is fantastic! Paint that – you owe it to your
fantastic, unreal son" (174). As a fiction, *The Moor's Last Sigh* then, sets
up expectations of comprehension and definition through excess, and the
more excessive representation becomes, the more impossible it is to define
a single truth, as multitudes of truths grow out of the lie of single official
versions of history or reality. Thus Aurora's art is finally able to redefine
India with, "an alternative vision of India-as-mother, not Nargis's sentimental village-mother but a mother of cities, as heartless and lovable, brilliant and dark, multiple and lonely, mesmeric and repugnant, pregnant and
empty, truthful and deceitful as the beautiful, cruel, irresistible metropolis
itself" (204), for as Vasco Miranda affirms, "The truth is almost always
exceptional, freakish, improbable, and almost never normative" (331).

The artists in the book, of whom Vasco Miranda is one, and their art,
are constantly being recuperated by the authorities in power, so that the
reader is confronted with different versions of the same reality competing
for pre-eminence, but the most important element in their work is always
point of view:

> [...] it is easy to see in these canvases the tension between Vasco Miranda's
> playful influence, his fondness for imaginary worlds whose only natural law
> was his own sovereign whimsicality, and Abraham's dogmatic insistence on
> the importance at that historical juncture, of a clear-sighted naturalism that
> would help India describe herself to herself. The Aurora of these days [...]
> veered uneasily between revisionist mythological paintings and an uncom-
> fortable, even stilted return to the lizard-signed documentary pictures of her
> Chipkali work. It was easy for an artist to lose her identity at a time when so
> many thinkers believed that the poignancy and passion of the country's im-
> mense life could only be represented by a kind of selfless, dedicated – even
> partiotic – mimesis. (173)

Supposing, as Rushdie suggests, that the reality of identity were in the
conflicting whole made up of the different versions which like sideshows
in a carnival of possible reality flash past the readers eyes, creating a mosaic of "myriad worlds" (84). If art may be supposed to resemble life, what
if life were a story, and one were to see it as an individual work of art

crafted by a personal perception of reality? It would then be criminal to impose it on others as the one true reality. Rushdie pits the reductiveness of the official discourse on art, and thus on ways of seeing, against a constantly evolving and hybrid subjectivity which appears with brio on Aurora's canvas:

> [...] the Moor in his hybrid fortress, [...] a vision of *weaving*, or more accurately interweaving. In a way these were polemical pictures, in a way they were an attempt to create a romantic myth of the plural, hybrid nation; she was using Arab Spain to re-imagine India, and this land-sea-scape [...] was her metaphor [...] of the present, and the future, that she hoped would evolve. So, yes, there was a didacticism here, but what with the vivid surrealism of her images and the kingfisher brilliance of her colouring and the dynamic acceleration of her brush, it was easy not to feel preached at, to revel in the carnival without listening to the barker [...]. (227; original italics)

The role of the artist and the individual as artist, which the writer of the book also applies to himself, is to turn things around, positivising the negative, "making strengths of weaknesses" as it is put in *The Satanic Verses* (93), and summed up here by Vasco's philosophy of contraries, "hit-fortune [...] like hit-take, hit-alliance, hit-conception, hit-terious [...] Opposite of mis" (150). One's real self, one's real being, what is usually called "integrity" is part of a process of going out of oneself, of what the same Vasco Miranda might have been tempted to christen "outegrity". Recognising language and indeed any form of representation as a subjective tool which can be used to change reality for good or bad, is part of the recognition of one's responsibility as an individual who counts. It is this reality, perhaps the most important, of which Moor becomes aware when he joins the Hindu fundamentalist party as a way of rebelling against the identity imposed upon him by his parents, *"The names you have given me – outcast, outlaw, untouchable, disgusting, vile – I clasp to my bosom and make my own"* (295–296; original italics). It is the recognition of this fact of personal potential, positive and negative, which must be integrated into one's world view before the process of "re-dreaming" (337) can begin:

> He appeared to lose in these last pictures, his previous metaphorical role as a unifier of opposites, a standard-bearer of pluralism, ceasing to stand as a symbol – however approximate – of the new nation, and being transformed, instead, into a semi-allegorical figure of decay. Aurora had apparently decided that the ideas of impurity, cultural admixture and mélange which had been for most of her creative life, the closest things she had found to a notion of the Good, were in fact capable of distortion, and contained a potential for darkness as well as for light. This 'black Moor' was a new imagining of the

idea of the hybrid – a Baudelairean flower, it would not be too far-fetched to suggest, of evil. (303)

What the narrator identifies at one point as, "the willingness to permit the coexistence within oneself of conflicting impulses as the source of our full, gentle humaneness" (32), is the starting point for the creative reformulation of hidden realities such as the "invisible" poor of Bombay, dangerously neglected, who will swell the ranks of Hindu fundamentalism due to their discontent. Expressed by means of the *mise en abyme* of fiction in the discussion of the paintings done by the narrator's mother, art becomes a monument of empowerment through re-imagining:

> The 'Moor in exile' sequence [...] abandoned the notion of 'pure' painting itself. Almost every piece contained elements of collage [...]. When the Moor did reappear it was in a highly fabulated milieu [...]. But Aurora, for whom reportage had never been enough, had pushed her vision several stages further [...]. The Moor had entered the invisible world, the world of ghosts, of people who did not exist, and Aurora followed him into it, forcing it into visibility by the strength of her artistic will. (301–3)

Thus for the sterility and uselessness of high art, which is what of course the actual book, *The Moor's Last Sigh*, resists by its self-proclaimed status as a "blaring horn of plenty" (128), a lurid saga full of "the juiciest-bitchiest yarns, the most garish and lurid not-penny-but-paisa-dreadfuls" (128), is substituted the idea of art as a force for change, a force which must constantly seek to free itself of static certainties. As Aurora's radical and enlightened grandfather puts it, "These days the world is full of questions, and there are new ways to be beautiful" (17).

"Outegrity", or, as Rushdie expressed it in *Imaginary Homelands*, "opening the universe a little more",[5] opening up to the positive potential for otherness indicates the ambition of his fiction to feed out onto the outside world, onto the other, onto all that is else, onto all that is mixed. The redefinition of time and space which Aurora achieves in her paintings, surely a key to the definition of any work of art, and the search for a "many-headed beauty" (338), the conviction that "all is possible" (286), is a dangerous risk for anyone to take but it can be transformed into a strength, for it defies fate.

"The Consequence Was"

At one point the narrator mentions, "the bloody game of consequences our history has a way of becoming" (309) as if one thing led logically to the next. The flow of cause and effect can be interrupted by using the arbitrariness of individuality, the arbitrariness of self as creation, as a work of art, the "mutating, inconstant, shape-shifting realities of human-nature" (351). Moraes's fate incites him to deny fate, for the conviction that he will die sooner than expected makes his life all the more precious and significant. Does he not also deny the determinism of his name, "Zogoiby, the Unlucky" by effecting a lucky escape from the jaws of death at several junctures?. *The Moor's Last Sigh* shows us a world in which each individual is a player in the game of life, a game of chance, but also a game of choice and all the different versions of all these different individuals go to make up the fragmented mosaic of true history, as the floor tiles in the Cochin synagogue, books in miniature, "universes contained within the uniformity of twelve by twelve" (84) which show different pictures to different people, seem to prove. History is reduced to, or rather *increased to* the result of "strategies of conjecture" (220), "a miraculous composite of all the colours of the world" (227). Meaning and life, and the meaning of life, are games that people must play for the duration of their time on earth, an evolving story like history, "a story that took two-thousand years to tell" (119). Refusing this playfulness signifies running the risk of imposing the false truth, false solutions, false reductiveness, false identity which a society based on oneness may demand as a tribute from those who threaten its tyranny. Accused by fundamentalist Hindus of subversion, the artistic liberty of Aurora is compromised:

> She was required to speak ponderously of 'motives' when she had had only whims, to make moral statements where there had been only ('only') play, and feeling and the unfolding inexorable logic of brush and light. She was obliged to counter accusations of social irresponsibility by divers 'experts', and took to muttering bad-temperedly that, throughout history, efforts to make artists socially accountable had resulted in nullity: tractor art, court art, chocolate-box junk. (234)

Indeed, through Aurora, it is the whole creed of hybridity, of "unity in diversity" (412) which is under threat, the playing out of "the tragedy of multiplicity destroyed by singularity, the defeat of the Many by One" (408). To combat the deathly reductiveness of nationalism and assert the truth of difference, Aurora creates the ideal location for a "citizen of the world" (385), "Mooristan" (226), a,

> Place where worlds collide, flow in and out of each other, and washofy away. Place where an air-man can drowno in water, or else grow gills; where a water-creature can get drunk, but also chokeofy on air. One universe, one dimen-

sion, one country, one dream, bumpoi'ing into another, or being under, or on top of. Call it Palimpstine. And above it all, in the palace, you. (*ibid.*)

Thus at the centre of this imaginary world is the inspired individual, a "you" which refers equally to the hero, the reader, and indeed all humanity. The different watershed experiences which Moraes goes through as he "slips from one book of life into another" (285); suffering the death of his loved ones, betrayal, imprisonment, flight, seem to reiterate the creative philosophy expressed on the first page of *The Satanic Verses* : in order to die to oneself, one must lower the boundaries of the self so that they disappear, "In another version of the dream I would be able to peel away more than skin, I would float free of flesh, skin and bones, having become simply an intelligence or a feeling set loose in the world, at play in its fields, like a science-fiction glow which needed no physical form" (136). The main ingredient in the Rushdian masala of mobility and openness is, perhaps surprisingly, love; love which at times appears as an ideal, a creed, for it enhances man's creative possibilities and tears down boundaries. Thus the narrator claims to be telling a love story to emphasise the important liberating and empowering function of this emotion in constructing the individual as an independent but joined entity:

> I wanted to cling to the image of love as the blending of spirits, as mélange, as the triumph of the impure, mongrel, conjoining best of us over what there is in us of the solitary, the isolated, the austere, the dogmatic, the pure; of love as democracy, as the victory of the no-man-is-an-island, two's-company Many over the clean, mean aprtheiding Ones. [...] To love is to lose omnipotence and omniscience. [...] without that leap nobody comes to life. (289)

It is this sharing and positive renunciation which help us to grow as human beings, just as *The Moor's Last Sigh*, the book, grows out of the author's sacrifice of complete control and the desire for interaction with his readers. A creative attitude to life must be achieved, a world of the imagination which is yet real, and love is the best way of seeing life creatively in Rushdie's resolutely "open" universe.

A different future obviously depends on a different past and the ability to visualise the present critically, as Moor's family cook affirms optimistically, "We will cook the past and present also and from it tomorrow will come" (73). In order to rediscover and rewrite that past, distance and imaginative vision are required, "It is said that they have the power to show you the future, if you have eyes to see it" (396). The sacrifice of feeling is also demanded, the crucifixion of self which is the only route to real being, really existing, really feeling. Getting close to the truth of multiplicity takes a lifetime as Moraes's autobiography shows, and demands a constant struggle as the individual recreates himself imaginatively in relation to the tyranny of imposed reality. The Moor's Last Sigh, "his last breath, for a lost world" (4), becomes the icon of life in death, for, on the point of death, his breath gives life to a whole book, testifying to the amazing strength of a creator who, in front of the inevitability of death, is able to revel in creation. "Where there's life, there's hope", one might say! This is the ultimate empowering discourse, for he who has confidence in himself as a creative being, cannot be crushed by the truths of others. We must all become creators, for "In the end," as Moor affirms, "stories are what's left of us" (110).

Madelena Gonzalez
University of Avignon, France

Notes

1. Salman Rushdie, *The Satanic Verses*, Dover, Delaware: The Consortium, Inc., 1992, p. 3.
2. Salman Rushdie, *The Moor's Last Sigh*, London: Jonathan Cape, 1995, p. 336. Subsequent references are to this edition and will be cited in the text.
3. Salman Rushdie, *Grimus*, London: Victor Gollancz Ltd., 1975.
4. The sigh will last 434 pages!
5. Salman Rushdie, *Imaginary Homelands: Essays and Criticism,1981–1991*, London: Granta, 1991, p. 21.

Works Cited

Rushdie, Salman. *The Satanic Verses*. Dover, Delaware: The Consortium, Inc., 1992.

———. *Imaginary Homelands: Essays and Criticism 1981–1991*. London: Granta Books, 1992.

———. *The Moor's Last Sigh*. London: Jonathan Cape, 1995.

11

Otherness in Anita Desai's *Baumgartner's Bombay*

Baumgartner's Bombay is neither a novel of a place nor the novel of a hero. The identity of the protagonist is gradually deconstructed and Bombay, which is after all nothing but the place where the unwanted Baumgartner is exiled, is never described. The misleading title therefore fools the reader into expecting the opposite of what he will get. Relations to others, place, time and language, all the elements that make up the protagonist's identity play against him. Passivity and resignation in front of adversity turn him into an anti-hero. Memory and his own culture fail him. His final, and nearly sole, attempt to recover his past and culture is his last and tragic rejection.

Baumgartner's Bombay is the only novel in which Anita Desai comes so close to telling us about her family life, as her mother, a German born in Germany who suffered a complete exile in India during the Second World War.[1] Nevertheless, *Baumgartner's Bombay* is far from being an autobiographical novel although many autobiographical elements are woven into the story. In many ways, her protagonist is different from her mother. The main reason is that Anita Desai is interested in a certain type of character. In an interview published in 1982, she declared: "I am not interested in brilliant members of society, who manage to control their fate. I'm interested in the failures and the wrecks."[2] In *Baumgartner's Bombay*, her protagonist is one of those, totally unable to control his life or decide for himself. A series of events singles him out from other children first – from Christian ones, but also from the Jewish ones at the Jewish school – then from the German nation itself. Throughout the novel, Hugo Baumgartner is shown to be different, either rejected for being different, or standing deliberately aside, keeping himself to himself, a typical outcast. His inability to act or react turns him into a silent witness of pre-war violence in Nazi Germany.

From Singularity to Exile

Baumgartner's Bombay has elements of a *bildungsroman*, only inverted, and perverted, in that we are shown a protagonist whose psychological development is constantly shaken and who grows increasingly insecure as he becomes aware of his difference. Everything brands Baumgartner as different – the several references to his physical particularities, namely his nose and the colour of his skin, and many allusions to names given to him: the disparaging names Lotte and Gisela, the two German girls in Bombay, call him – 'turnip-nosed Jew' (96); 'a *Jiddischer* turnip.' (98) – names he and his Jewish family are given by their Aryan neighbours in pre-war Nazi Germany, the letters JUDE painted red on their shop-window, as a brand of dishonour; red, the colour of shame and guilt, the colour of sin and accusation.

According to Thomas Luckmann and Alan Dundes, a negative mirror image shapes a person's identity.

> [...] each individual acquires personal identity through his reflection from another individual: "reciprocal mirroring is an elementary condition for the formation of all personal identities... Beginning from childhood, in all societies the self is placed in social relations in which, by virtue of intersubjective mirroring, it is beginning to form a personal identity."[3]

Hugo's personal identity thus develops into a sense of not belonging and a sense of guilt which transpires through the boy's reactions – or rather lack of reaction, when he is handed a make-shift Christmas present at school – the glass globe at the top of the Christmas tree, a symbol of Christianity[4] –, when he stays at home rather than go out in order not to face the neighbours and their racist insults, when he and his mother are enjoying themselves while his wrecked, camp-returned father is alone and shivering at home, or when he is unable to save his mother from the Nazis. The letters JUDE painted on the shop window weigh him down and make him totally unable of taking initiatives till the end of the novel. Whatever action he undertakes is dictated to him by other characters. Even fleeing to India to escape persecution is not his decision.

Ironically, it is when he is seeking refuge in India to avoid being sent to one of the concentration camps that destroys his father's identity as a man, father, husband and shop-owner, and eventually kills him. The young Baumgartner is arrested in Calcutta and detained in several successive camps on account of his German nationality which makes him an enemy of British-ruled India when World War II breaks out. Baumgartner stands for 'the other kind', the outcast, the unwanted, the marginal. The arbitrariness of the two systems is made obvious by the criteria chosen for the selection of 'the accepted' or 'the rejected'. In Germany, Hugo is denied the right to be a German on account of his religion. In India, ironically, the British declare him German – 'German, born in Germany' (104) – and send him to an internment camp as an enemy, together with German Nazis, refusing any further explanation.

Even from the start, Baumgartner never really belongs anywhere. He and his mother do not match the teutonic type that is the rule around them. And ironically, for all that he is dark in Germany, he looks very pale and fair-skinned as soon as he sets foot in India. In fact, like a cameleon, he even changes colour and turns a bright red 'tomato' colour in India; but wherever he is, he is never the right colour; like a chameleon, wanting to pass unnoticed, but unlike a chameleon, always spotted and singled out.His unfamiliarity with the Jewish religion – which is supposedly his own culture – makes him the butt of the other Jewish children who laugh at his nose. The latter is a brand in his own flesh, a visible sign of his Jewishness, which ironically he cannot relate to.

Baumgartner's reaction to the growing anti-Jewish feeling is one of passivity and acceptance. He stays on even after his father dies from torture and after all his mother's friends have fled. He lets his mother sell their shop to Herr Pfuel, a gentleman from Hamburg. He doesn't react when he is pushed out of the family flat and he has to live with his mother, into the tiny backroom of the shop. The name on the shop is changed from 'Baumgartner' to 'Pfuel', 'a good, sound, Teutonic name' (50). Although Baumgartner is compared to a harmless and unobtrusive mouse,[5] his presence grows undesirable both in his country and in his own house. He is sent away to India – almost against his will. Forced to exile himself because of the Furher's plans, he is ironically saved by a protective decision of exile from one of the Furher's followers.

A Sense of Place?

Linguists agree that place "can be, and often is, an extremely meaningful component of individual identity."[6] By moving her protagonist about, Desai shows how flimsy and uncertain his sense of identity: as he never chooses to move; the decision always comes from another source. The episode of the cave in India is a repetition of the preceding scene, making a parallel with it. Finding a dark little cave, possibly a temple, in the Indian country-side, Baumgartner decides to explore it. Fright at the unknown makes him panick and rush out.

> [He] fell out on to the hillside as if ejected by whatever possessed or inhab-ited that temple. Indigestible, inedible Baumgartner. The god had spat him out. *Raus*, Baumgartner, out. Not fit for consumption, German or Hindu, hu-man or divine. [...]
> Go, Baumgartner. Out. He had not been found fit. Shabby, dirty white man, *firanghi*, unwanted. Raus, Baumgartner, *raus*. (190)

The episode of the cave can be seen as a regression to the womb, to the mother, to one's identity. The reader is made to understand that Baum-gartner is unable to face his own identity; the darkness of the cave stands for his inability to understand his own self; he doesn't know where he stands; he is in complete darkness, wishing to understand who he is, yet frightened to face the truth. For the protagonist, there doesn't seem to be a dilemma: being denied the right to belong in Germany, he is shown desperate to make a home for himself and his mother in India, whatever the difficulties.

> It seemed desperately important to belong and make a place for himself. He had to succeed in that if the dream of bringing his mother to India and mak-ing a home for her was to be turned into a reality.
> The news that came from Europe became rapidly more alarming, it was as if she, and therefore he, Baumgartner, were being pursued, run down to earth. She had to be made to leave, she had to be brought away, and then somehow he would have to make her accept India as her home. It was becoming clear to him that this was the only possibility, there was no other. It was why he plunged into it with such urgency. (93–94)

Desai places her character in a paradoxical and ironical position which puts things in perspective for the reader: undesirable in Germany because not considered a proper German, Baumgartner is also undesirable in India, for the opposite reason – that is, for being a German.

Ironically, the sense of belonging comes to Baumgartner when he is in the camp. In this enclosed space, the smallness becomes a mercy and the enclosure a protection against external aggression. Oddly enough, in this small, unnatural microcosm, the protagonist experiences a sense of belonging. The only reason why Hugo feels at home in the familiarity of the camp is because he has nowhere else to go and no one outside the camp he can relate to. The camp is reassuring in its smallness, its remote-ness and its familiarity. When the war ends, Baumgartner becomes 'unwanted' in the camp and is therefore set free – that is, pushed out of the camp, once again rejected.

His successive dwelling places are very apt comments on his identity and the downward spiral of exclusion in which he is caught. When he is in Germany, the cosy and richly furnished family home gradually loses its best pieces as the war approaches. Then he loses the ownership of it. When he arrives in India, Baumgartner goes from a cheap hotel to a cheaper hotel still. During the war, the detention camp replaces the hotel, and eventually, coming out of it, Baumgartner settles in a small flat in a tumbledown house, with poles propping up the crumbling walls outside. This last home is not a real home, as once again Baumgartner is asked to leave it and go away, as the building must be pulled down on account of the danger it represents.

> Monsoon after monsoon washed over Hira Niwas, leaving it more slimy, green, decayed and odorous [...] Sometimes a little plaster fell, occasionally a whole brick (204)

The further step down from this mere shelter – judged 'unsafe' (204) by the building corporation – would be a total loss of home. Baumgartner would not mind homelessness, were it not for his cats.

Baumgartner's last home mirrors his own physical and mental deterioration; he is emptied, devastated, like his empty cupboards. There is no food in the cupboards, neither has he any food for thought; oblivion is his lot, out of necessity, but also because it is more comfortable, less painful, easier on the mind.

Culture and Language – The Problem of Acculturation

In the process of integration, time plays a key role; it is both a positive element enabling a migrant to mix in and a negative element playing against him by blurring his memory. This dual aspect of time is exemplified in Baumgartner's language difficulties.Language is the first basic and immediate problem; Anita Desai's ironic images make it very clear. German is inadequate in India. English – the vehicular language – is a hazardous language as the choice of words and the accent cannot be entirely controlled. Anita Desai depicts several of such scenes very vividly, as when Baumgartner meets Chimanlal, on his second day in India:

> 'No, no, quite wrong, quite wrong,' he kept repeating as Baumgartner tried to question him, in his new and hesitant English, about the business the gentle-

man from Hamburg had assured him existed in Bombay. The man behind the
desk seemed puzzled at the mention of Hamburg, timber, shipping... every
word that Baumgartner managed to summon out of his new language, dragging it off his tongue with a reluctance bordering on paralysis, the bald, dark
man [...] shook his head at in mystified denial. [...]
Then he chanced to find the word 'Ex-port'. 'Ex-phott,' he said, and the fat,
puzzled, perspiring man seemed to roll himself up into a ball tight with excitement, and then explode out of his seat.
'Ex-pawt!' he gasped, clutching the side of his head. 'Ex-pawt. Of course, ex-
pawt.' [...]
He charged around the desk, grasped Baumgartner by the hand and pumped
it up and down, then slapped his shoulder for good measure, and began to
babble at such speed that Baumgartner gave up even trying to follow. (86)

Integration requires a language with which to communicate with others.
Learning the natives' language becomes a necessity, even if only to survive in the country.

According to William Francis Mackay, language is a reflection of the
process of acculturation.[7] Baumgartner has to deal with several languages
he doesn't know and has to cope as best he can:

Chimanlal [...] began to talk of business, of exports, of shipping, of trade in
what seemed to Baumgartner a bewildering combination of two or three languages. He replied in his own selection of two or three. (88)

And a few pages later:

He found he had to build a new language to suit these new conditions – German no longer sufficed, and English was elusive. Languages sprouted around
him like tropical foliage and he picked words from it without knowing if they
were English or Hindi or Bengali – they were simply words he needed: *chai,
khana, baraf, lao, jaldi, joota, chota peg, pani, kamra, soda, garee...* what was
this language he was wrestling out of the air, wrenching around to his own
purposes? He suspected it was not Indian, but India's, the India he was making out for himself. (92)

This profusion of words that Baumgartner picks up desperately, almost
compulsively, are quite representative of his desire to belong, his desire to
mix in and be accepted. However such profusion also creates confusion,
as the new language remains a tool – that is, something useful and even
vital – but never quite mastered. Till the end, even after a life-time in India,
Baumgartner's self-made vehicular language remains unfamiliar, even the
basic morning or afternoon greeting:

[He] mumbled 'Good morning, *salaam*', and went down the steps into the street with his bag, uncertain as ever of which language to employ. After fifty years, still uncertain. Baumgartner, *du Dummkopf*. (6)

Integration through language is shown to be difficult and incomplete, the foreign language remaining foreign, other, difficult to grasp in its nuances, never quite one's own. At the same time, the mother-tongue gradually loses its familiarity, its fluidity. It becomes awkward, stiff, unable to convey one's meaning satisfactorily.[8] As the mother-tongue gradually loses its quality, the acquired language gains fluency, up to a certain point which doesn't compensate for the loss of fluency in the mother-tongue. Language is a visible aspect of acculturation; it is the visible part of the iceberg. As language is slipping away from Baumgartner, so is his culture irremediably slipping away from him, while the Indian culture remains too different and difficult to understand. It only becomes less exotic and more familiar over the years, never integrated. The impossibility of returning to the pre-war Germany of his early childhood and his mother's disappearance sever him from his roots and deprive him of important elements of his identity. With his mother's death, he loses his religious identity, as she was the sole guardian of it. Her death reveals a gap, a failing in Baumgartner's culture and identity. He is a Jew who cannot relate his Jewishness to any specific customs.[9]

Knowing that he can never return to his mother country, he discovers that he has lots his German nationality and has become a citizen of India.:

He wrote to people, to addresses he remembered; he never had a reply; all of Germany might have been wiped off the face of the earth. That made him sort out the matter of his papers, his passport, his nationality, and found himself become an Indian citizen, the holder of an Indian passport. Holding it, he wondered if it meant that he would now never leave India and realised that, for all that it was a travel document, it did. (181)

Time, the essential element in the process of integration, acts as a destructive agent. Instead of contributing to a better integration, it destroys, in the protagonist, the wish to communicate with others. He is seen as a hermit, avoiding contact, outgrowing the habit of talking to strangers, however fleeting the meeting, for fear of having to talk about himself, his broken life and his puzzling identity: that of someone who stands in-between, is no longer what he used to be and not completely what he tries to become.

With time and geographical distance, memory fades but is never totally erased and a physical presence brings it all back. After 50 years of exile, Baumgartner is caught up by his past, by a culture he had run away from, when he is faced with a representative of the young generation of German Aryans. With his Teutonic looks, the boy embodies the so-called pure and perfect *race* that exiled Baumgartner. Yet he is depicted as a drug-addict, depraved, ill, the degenerated and pathetic descendent of the Furher's 'elite'. By taking the boy home to his flat, Baugartner tries to recover a long-forgotten part of his past and culture, which is refered to as 'blood'.

> only the blood knows.
> And that was stupid, stupid to talk of blood, thinking it was blood he had in common with this ruffian. It was not so. (152)

The reader is made to understand that the two characters have nothing in common; neither language as Baumgartner is shown to be irritated when pronouncing the word 'medicine' in the German way when addressing the young man; nor even Germany, which has been completely altered by the war. Yet it is this boy who embodies Germany, the mother-land. However, this feeling of sameness is only an illusion which lures the body and the heart whereas the mind 'knows better'. Blood, on the contrary, is shown to be a reality, only perverted, when the drug-addict murders his host and spills his blood. Blood, the symbol of life, the metaphor of kinship and group identity, is turned into the blood of death, finite in its rejection of 'the other'.

The central character is made physically present in the title of the novel by the use of a genitive connecting him to a place – Bombay. Similarly, Bombay, one of India's largest cities, is presented in relation to the character, thus foregrounding, right from the start, the problem of place and identity. Desai's title is deliberately misleading – Bombay is never described and is only occasionally present in the background merely to create the atmosphere of a cityscape. Baumgartner is only described in his inaction and is physically absent from the opening and closing pages. Anita Desai contrasts their presence in the title and their absence in the novel. By making them present in the title, she highlights their immateriality in the story. The character, central in the title, is only more obviously absent as a hero. He departs from traditional heroes in his lethargy, his constant escape from responsibility and his refusal to face reality like a responsible adult. He shies away from action when the female characters – two German expatriates – are so active in making a name and a place for themselves.

The name Baumgartner itself is a delusion. It refers to a tree and a gardener or a garden, thus implying a sense of place and belonging, a sense of continuity, whereas Hugo embodies exactly the opposite – he keeps moving, or being moved, from place to place, a figure of the archetypal Jew, always fleeing and never belonging anywhere. Maybe Hugo could be deciphered as the tree – growing, like a tree, from a fragile plant into a bigger one, adding new branches every year, so many new experiences and languages, and always standing in all weathers, until one day it is up-rooted by a strong gale. Unlike a tree, however, Hugo Baumgartner has no set place in which to take root. He could also be read as the gardener who tends plants. Yet, here again such reading is undermined since Hugo never tends anyone, apart from his family of stray cats who flock to him – the outcast tending other outcasts.[10] The only time he really takes care of someone, he does it against his will, and brings home the young Aryan German who will kill him. Germany – and India – could be seen as gardens and Baumgartner, the gardener. Thus the metaphor of the garden can be decoded as the impossibility of growing a tree outside its native land – whether Baumgartner-the-refugee, or Schwartz-the-drug-addict.

Desai's title is also misleading when she announces a hero, a place and a strong connection between the two, and she takes her reader by surprise by building her novel around a void – the void left by the transparent and elusive Baumgartner, the void left by the absence of the mother which is felt right to the end, as well as by the absence of a tangible place to relate to. The void is made almost physically palpable when missing periods of Baumgartner's long life are summed up in a few lines by the musing protagonist. The void underlines the fact that Baumgartner belongs nowhere and that his hesitant efforts to create a certain sense of belonging fall into the nothingness of oblivion.

Corinne Liotard
Professeur agrégé

Notes

1. See the interview with Anita Desai: "View from the outside", 1988.

2. See the interview with Anita Desai: "Creation born out of chaos", 1982.

3. Alan Dundes, quoting Thomas Luckmann (1979), in 'Defining Identity through Folklore', p. 238.

See also Thomas Luckmann in 'Remarks on Personal Identity: Inner, Social and Historical Time' (pp. 67–91). Ibid.
He explains: 'In face-to-face encounters, the (mediated) experience of one's self is built up in (immediate) experiences of others. [...] reciprocal mirroring in the 'here and now' of a concrete situation is an elementary condition for the development of personal identity', p. 74.

4. This refers to the climax in the scene following the description of the Christmas celebrations at the Christian school little Hugo goes to.

5. Terms of endearment in Hugo's mother's letters. 'Little mouse, Mäuschen', p. 3.

6. See for example Alan Dundes' article, 'Defining identity through Folklore'.

7. 'In the process of acculturation, almost all human activities may be involved; and although language is one of them, it is at the same time a reflection of all of them.' William Francis Mackey, 'Language and Acculturation', p. 8.

8. 'Gradually, the language was slipping away from him, now almost as unfamiliar as the feel and taste of English words or the small vocabulary of bastardised Hindustani he had picked up over the years.' (*B.'s B.*, p. 150).

9. 'He thought now that if he had been brought up as an orthodox Jew, he could have mourned her with ceremony; he would have followed the ancient customs, recited the ancient words of solace, and perhaps they would have helped to still the agony. But he was ignorant, and therefore helpless, held in the grid of an unexpressed sorrow. He had to allow the mournful blowing of conch shells and the chanting of Sanskrit prayers that drifted in through the windows at twilight suffice as a funeral ceremony for his mother.' (*B.'s B*, p. 165)

10. '[...] the cats that flocked to him in the alleys, knowing him to be the Madman of the Cats, the Billéwallah Pagal, or the sick and maimed ones he picked up from the streets and carried home to nurse, telling them they would have to leave when they were cured but never finding the heart to turn them out.' (*B's B*, p. 10).

Works cited

Desai, Anita. *Baumgartner's Bombay*, Penguin Books, 1989.

Dundes, Alan. 'Defining Identity through Folklore', in Jacobson-Widding, Anita (ed) *Identity, Personal and Socio-cultural: A Symposium...* Almqvist & Wiksell, Uppsala, 1983, pp. 235–261.

Luckmann, Thomas. 'Remarks on Personal Identity: Inner, Social and Historical Time', in Jacobson-Widding, Anita (ed) *Identity, Personal and Socio-cultural: A Symposium...* Almqvist & Wiksell, Uppsala, 1983, pp. 67–91.

Mackey, William Francis. 'Language and Acculturation', in Jacobson-Widding, Anita (ed) *Identity, Personal and Socio-cultural: A Symposium...* Almqvist & Wiksell, Uppsala, 1983, pp. 8–22.

"View from the outside", interview by John Cunningham, *The Guardian*, 29 June 1988.

"Creation born out of chaos", interview by Nazzem Khan, *The Guardian*, 4 November 1982.

Part III
AUSTRALIA AND NEW ZEALAND

12

New Zealand: Exile and Identity in a Transnational Age

It has been claimed that young New Zealand writers address a "true" contemporary New Zealand, exploding the myths of God's Own Country and showing that the nation can no longer pride itself on a society of equality and justice. An analysis of two books by young New Zealanders, *Left of Centre* by Maria Wickens, and *Not Her Real Name* by Emily Perkins, suggests a more complex relationship with national identity. The short stories in Emily Perkins's *Not Her Real Name* reflect a shapeless present, with no awareness that justice or equality might ever have existed in New Zealand's or in any other nation's past. If there is sense of disconnection, it is not disconnection from a meaningful nation state but from meaning itself.

To understand the "real" New Zealand of the 1990s, we are told, we need to get to grips with Generation X. This was a name used by Douglas Coupland in 1991 to describe young American adults with low pay, low status, and low future: since then, it has come to mean an art form as much as an age-group. Generation X artists are probably born later than 1968 and their writing, hard-hitting with an urban edge, is associated with a global popular culture propagated through television, popular rock albums, film and high-tech computer technology. Common topics are shareflatting, drugs, relationships, familial alienation, urban tribalism, frankness about sex and cynicism about power. In a review in Landfall, Sarah Quigley[1] acclaims Generation X writing in New Zealand and relates it to questions of national identity by saying that it looks a "true" 1990s New Zealand straight in the eye, exploding the myths of God's Own Country and showing that the nation can no longer pride itself on a society of equality and justice. And Mark Pirie, editor of an anthology of new young writing to be published by Otago University Press, says that "Our young writers are addressing the relevant social, cultural and political issues of the 1990s, and the problems of growing up in a market driven society."[2]

Let me try to put this in context. A "market driven society" is of course not unique to New Zealand: "the market" is sacrosanct in much of the world, along with a generation deemed to have special characteristics because of having grown up with it. Mark Davis writes from Australia:

> The present outbreak of generationalism is unlike previous outbreaks, in that it takes place against the background of the rise of economic rationalism, the increase in particular forms of youth demonisation...and the sheer numbers of baby-boomers in the population. Younger people have grown up in the shadow of a great demographic bulge, which foreshadows certain social problems.... Work patterns have changed: casual work has taken over from full-time work as the main area of employment growth. Families have changed: this is an era of single parents and "blended" families.... The dominant belief systems of the early to mid-twentieth century have changed. This is an age of discredited philosophies and institutions: the church, state family and even the sciences no longer have the authority they once did.... At the same time, economic insecurity has become endemic in most Western countries, producing its own kind of social nostalgia.... The idea of public culture has dwindled, with public institutions being privatised or corporatised and media ownership being concentrated in fewer and fewer hands. Economies have become globalised...and corporations downsized, making this quite a different world from that of even twenty years ago.[3]

A year-long research project in Britain confirms in the main that what Davis says about Australia is true also for a younger generation in Britain. Helen Wilkinson and Geoff Mulgan[4] studied the attitudes and experience of 18–34 year olds and concluded that there is a rejection of traditional restraints, frustration about work, convergence of values between younger men and women, a rejection of national identity and a serious disconnection from society.

Is the New Zealand version particularly acute? For some, yes. A sense of disconnection, of living in Someone Else's Country, is related to the rapid pace of change over the past fourteen years. From being a highly regulated and protected society that prided itself on its egalitarianism, New Zealand transformed itself into a fully-fledged free-market economy. The changes listed by Mark Davis happened particularly quickly in New Zealand, and contrasted markedly with what had gone before.

Jane Kelsey's book *The New Zealand Experiment*[5] has drawn attention to social dislocation seen to accrue from economic adjustment, and

in a full-page spread in the British Independent in 1994, Peter Walker
suggested that the New Zealand experiment ought to be taken as a warning of social collapse, citing as evidence statistics like the suicide rate for
young males, which at 38 per 100,000, was the highest in the industrialised
world.[6] In February 1997, electricity supplies in Auckland broke down,
and Will Hutton in The Observer in Britain used this as a warning of the
effects of over-enthusiastic privatisation with inadequate government
control. It is suspected that Mercury Energy, supplier of the city's electricity, had devoted undue attention to corporate profits at the expense
routine maintenance.[7] Darkness at the heart of privatisation in Auckland
would underline the importance of Generation X writing as Quigley and
others see it as political statement. If New Zealand really is near the brink
of collapse, you could understand that Generation X there has a particularly sharp axe to grind. There is an opposite version of a "real" New Zealand. Optimists would say that the economic reforms introduced rapidly
since 1984 are a measure of New Zealand's success in adapting to new
global realities, and an example for the rest of the world to follow. If there
are negative side-effects, it is argued that the changes were inevitable and
that if they had not been introduced, social deprivation would have been
even worse. A movement launched in the U.K. in 1997 called the New
Zealand Way claimed that with these changes New Zealand confidently
announces itself as a leading player on a competitive world stage, a Small
Country with a Big Attitude and an image of entrepreneurialism flourish-
ing in a clean, green land.

So are New Zealand's young artists looking a "real" New Zealand
straight in the eye, exposing the failures of the system of the last fourteen
years and the alienation it has caused, or is their relationship with the successful facade of the 1990s New Zealand rather more complex? I want to
consider this by looking at two books by young New Zealand writers: *Left
of Centre* by Maria Wickens[8] and *Not Her Real Name* by Emily Perkins.[9]
Left of Centre is about Marley, a deeply disturbed adolescent who begins
her story: "The summer I turned 17 they built a Kentucky Fried Chicken
outlet in Mudflats."[10] Her friends are either other deranged young people
almost permanently stoned on drink or drugs, or a former school teacher
who thinks that the best way to help her is by having an affair with her.
Eventually she faces the root cause of her problems which is that her father
had abused her, and she recovers sufficiently to take herself off overseas.

What of New Zealand in this novel? Despite Kentucky Fried Chicken
and the range of easily obtainable drugs, Mudflats where Marley lives is

related not so much to the problems of a globalised present, as to a disturbed past. Mudflats is a subversion of clean, green New Zealand, a town of malevolent undercurrents:

> In winter Mudflats is a cool green place. The temperament of our people is supposed to be cool too. Introspective. A town of outsiders. Men alone. Sometimes, though, dormant men erupt into violence. Quiet surly hermits blow away half a dozen of their neighbours with a semi-automatic. A drugged, mind-blown father kills seven family members with a baseball bat. A cool, green place of quiet madmen, perhaps.[11]

There doesn't seem to be any connection between the new market economy and the hidden malevolence in Mudflats and in Marley's father, the abuser. Instead, disturbance is related to an older violent tradition. Wickens has said that she was influenced in writing her novel by a sense of a seamy underside to New Zealand life that pre-dates the global market. For example, Ian Wedde's novel *Symmes Hole* (Penguin 1986) seeks to recover a submerged and threatening New Zealand identity that begins with the early whalers: their violence and ruthless exploitation of people and the environment is shown to set a paradigm that continues and merges imperceptibly into a present dominated by the ethos of the MacDonalds chain. Barbara Anderson (born 1926, so certainly not Generation X) starkly subverts the pastoral paradise myth by beginning her story about girls growing up in the country:

> All the girls could kill. Their father taught them. – Stand astride grip with the knees yank the head, knife in. Speed's the thing. They smell blood.[12]

Wickens acknowledges the influence of music she was hearing at the time of writing, of American movies and TV culture, and of subversive cult and pulp writers including Charles Bukowski and Hunter S. Thompson. If we juxtapose these influences with Wedde's turbulent whalers and Anderson's frenzied country girls, we might conclude that New Zealand's is a fruitful soil for the violence and moral nihilism of global pulp fiction to flourish in. There is certainly no detectable yearning in *Left of Centre* for a stable past, a golden age of New Zealand (or any other) stability: rather, through reference to Sylvia Plath's novel, *The Bell Jar*, a timely reminder of the suffocating sureties of the 50s. I remember the warnings we had at that time from writers like Whim Wham and M.K.Joseph about the strangling and smothering nature of welfarism, and the evils of spiritual vacuity and mental sloth in an egalitarian society.

Marley knows of no lost golden age, and if she's often nihilistic this isn't necessarily because of any economic or political system. There are shades of *Waiting for Godot* in the incident where she tries to make it easier for a suicidal acquaintance to actually get on and kill himself. At the end she heads off for Los Angeles hoping that she's "Flying straight into the heart of corruption, heady hedonistic fame, sex, drugs, rock and roll and tainted reality... How could I not have a good time?"[13] This underscores an ambivalence in the novel about the confusion and "tainted reality" besetting the younger generation. If absurdity is the human condition, if stability is only to be desired when you're too old to enjoy life, or if there's a sound practical reason for Marley's confusion – namely child abuse – the notion of this novel addressing the issues of the 1990s just doesn't stand up.

This is not the complete picture, however, because despite nods towards an absurdist universe and the expectation of savouring a "tainted" reality for a while yet, Marley does expect there to be an untainted reality somewhere. What form might this take? Her quest for some "answers" signals the failure of her society to provide any. She likes to stare at the Colonel Sanders sign outside Kentucky Fried Chicken and when Mr. Simons, her lover and former teacher, asks her why she explains: "I come here for inspiration... Don't you think the Colonel looks like, you know, he's wise. That he has some of the answers." Mr. Simons laughed for somewhat longer than I felt was polite... "maybe you should consider the possibility that the Colonel is an icon created by image makers?"[14] He goes on to ask whether it's peer pressure that makes her drink, while Marley, with an intuitive awareness of the dominance of image over individual agency in a market-driven society, reflects that some of her best friends are icons created by image makers. Her throw-away line is a serious point for those of us who are happy to theorise about images and to deconstruct them, but who are too old to know what it's like to grow up in a world of nothing but image. If we expect young writers to move on and "grow", we need to have some idea of how they are to emerge from this peculiarly image-ridden structure of feeling.

Not Her Real Name by Emily Perkins is a collection of short stories about young people who are nearly all alienated, lonely, and desperately seeking anything that will avoid tedium and disgust. The young woman in "the shared experience" wants a relationship. She thinks her peers are "all fatuous, self-obsessed, undirected, confused emotional retards. Whereas her boss, her managing director – she loves those words! – is nothing like that. He's young for his position – he must be driven, focused. And he's interesting, isn't he, and knowledgeable?".[15] Over dinner she nervously responds to his chatting about a proposed merger with a New York Company – exciting as long as they don't swamp us – while planning to get into bed with him. But when she succeeds she is disappointed: the best that can be said about it is that one day it might be a funny story to tell someone. She decides to give up her job: "No more girly office eyeshadow for her. No more dress code. No more being nice to stupid jerks and stupider cows just because they're more senior than her and make more money."[16]

No going back, she thinks, and she steals her boss's car and sets off, reviewing her options as she goes. Helen in "running around with you" has a small inheritance from her grandmother which is enough to live on while she decides what she really wants to do with her life: she does spend a lot of time in the library, photocopying chapters out of books she decides are interesting and staring into space. If asked, she is putting together some background material for a "screenplay – well possibly not a screenplay but at the moment I feel film is the right medium for what I have to say." She "doesn't want to be precious about it" but she'd "rather not discuss it. I'm hopelessly inarticulate about it" (self-deprecating smile). Meanwhile, her desk drawer becomes gratifyingly full with 'material'. She's thinking about investing in a box-file.[17] Rather than confronting a real life behind the facade, Helen has accommodated herself to living as a part of it. She convinces her boyfriend that she is a mystery woman with a tragic secret, and he never for a moment considers that there might be no more behind the mannerisms than another mannerism.

The most chilling story, and the most effective in pinpointing the potential horror of a world of image but no workable reality, is called "barking". It starts with Billy walking out of his drama class – his "stupid fuck drama class" where "we spend all this time looking for our centres or relaxing or rubbing each other."[18] His sister Carol is disturbed also: she's having treatment and her psychiatrist suggests that they must have both been abused as youngsters. Billy rejects this idea, and tries to find meaning in his own way. This is centred on a dream where he's in a cupboard with Carol and he feels good because, "you know, here I am and I've got Carol all to myself and it's kind of fun in the dark"[19] But this womb-like safety quickly turns to nightmare as he gets the idea they're stuck. They can't get out, and then Carol is not his sister but someone else who's laughing at him. He decides in his confusion that Karen, a girl he hasn't even met, is the one who will understand. "We're going to save each other from this shit-heap."[20] He breaks into her house and hides in her wardrobe, waiting for her to find him.

These stories reflect a shapeless present, with no awareness that justice or equity might ever have existed in New Zealand's or in any other nation's past. If there is a sense of disconnection, it is not disconnection from a meaningful nation-state but from meaning itself.

This is not the same as looking a real New Zealand straight in the eye, confronting its seamy underside. The relationship between these two Generation X productions and the state of the nation is much more complicated. There is some tendency to relish chaos, in print at least. Nor is globalisation necessarily a problem causing crises in identity. Arjun Appadurai suggests that globalisation means more opportunities for more fun, as electronic media and global popular culture provide more resources for self-imagining as an everyday social project than has ever been available in the past.[21] The sense of exuberance captured at times by both writers suggests that even if the world is an alienating and ungiving place, at least art is exciting. Mark Pirie confirms that the experience of modernity at large can be creatively invigorating: there is a growing ethnic and linguistic diversity within New Zealand, an increase in global travel among Xers, and a range of styles to choose from including some derived from the eclecticism of technology, television, film, popular music and pop culture.

Modernity can be fun. And to the extent that Wickens and Perkins do expose a seamy underside to New Zealand life, this is not necessarily detrimental to the nation's standing, nor is it the sort of revelation that must be felt to call for remedial action. If artists expose social dislocation, the ubiquity of market doctrines transforms degeneracy into a marketable commodity: The Small Country, Big Attitude slogan can be adapted to mean that New Zealand problems are bigger and better than anyone else's.

But the two books show that there is more to the experience of modernity at large than excitement and publishing opportunities. They show the destructive effects of market forces: people are transformed into signs that consume; individuals are reproduced as images. They also show that although this can be exhilarating, in the long run it is untenable. It didn't help Marley to be told that Colonel Sanders, whom she hopes has some wisdom, is an icon created by image makers: she accepts that public figures are icons but nevertheless would like to find one that makes some sense. Helen in "running around with you" is sick because she is an image, nothing more. The pathology of billy in "Barking" seems to be related to an inability to find anything he can believe in.

The New Zealand Experience might be seen as a warning to the rest of the world. The baby-boomers of the demographic bulge (and those of us even older than that) should look seriously at Generation X productions. Our golden age, if it ever existed, is certainly never going to return, and if things really are falling apart, it happened while we were looking away.

Ruth Brown
University of Sussex

Notes

1. Sarah Quigley, Reviews in <u>Landfall 192</u>, vol. 4, no. 2, November 1996, pp. 361–4.
2. Mark Pirie, "Reconstructing New Zealand Literature: Next Wave Writing in Aotearoa-New Zealand", <u>Kite 13</u>, The Newsletter of the Association of New Zealand Literature, University of Otago, December 1997, pp. 4–15, quotation on p. 13.
3. Mark Davis, *Gangland*, Allen and Unwin 1997, pp. 16–17.
4. Helen Wilkinson and Geoff Mulgan, *Freedom's Children*, Demos 1995.
5. Jane Kelsey, *The New Zealand Experiment*, Auckland University Press 1995.
6. Peter Walker, "What Happens When You Scrap the Welfare State", <u>Independent on Sunday</u>, 13 March 1994, p. 17.
7. Bill Hutton, "Darkness at the Heart of Privatisation", <u>The Observer</u>, 8 March 1998, p. 24.
8. Maria Wickens, *Left of Centre*, Secker and Warburg 1994.
9. Emily Perkins, *Not Her Real Name*, Picador 1996.
10. Left of Centre, p. 7.
11. ibid., p. 8.
12. Barbara Anderson, "The Girls", in *I Think We Should Go Into The Jungle*, Victoria University Press, 1989, p. 40.
13. *Left of Centre*, p. 190,
14. ibid., p. 43.
15. Emily Perkins, "the shared experience", in *Not Her Real Name*, p. 80.
16. ibid., p. 95.
17. Emily Perkins, "Running around with you", in *Not Her Real Name*, p. 235.
18. Emily Perkins, "Barking", in *Not Her Real Name*, p. 46.
19. ibid., p. 59.

20. ibid., p. 69

21. Arjun Appadurai, Modernity At Large: Cultural Dimensions of Globalization, University of Minnesota Press, 1996.

13

Katherine Mansfield: The Exile of The Mind

Although there is ample evidence in Mansfield's correspondence and fiction that nostalgia, and various configurations of loneliness and exile, form a significant aspect of her work, there is evidence too of a more broadly based, historical conception of 'exile'. The coinciding of her declining health and the First World War led her to draw parallels between the two, and led to her insistence on regeneration through the acceptance of suffering and contingency – an anticipation of existential thinking.

In the last year of her life, Mansfield wrote an important letter to Sarah Gertrude Millin. She had reviewed the young South African's novel, *The Dark River*, in the *Athenaeum* the year before, and a brief but warm correspondence followed. Millin, like the young Mansfield fifteen years before, was desperate to get to London, to the centre of the literary world. The older woman recalled her own earlier longing for the same thing:

I came to Europe to 'complete my education' and when my parents thought that tremendous task was over I went back to New Zealand. I hated it. It seemed to me a small petty world; I longed for 'my' kind of people and larger interests and so on. And after a struggle I did get out of the nest finally and came to London, at eighteen, *never* to return, said my disgusted heart. Since then I've lived in England, France, Italy, Bavaria. I've known literary society in plenty. But for the last four-five years I have been ill and have lived either in the S. of France or in a remote little chalet in Switzerland – always remote, always cut off, seeing hardly anybody.... It's only in those years I've really been able to work and always my thoughts and feelings go back to New Zealand – rediscovering it, finding beauty in it, re-living it. It's about my Aunt Fan who lived up the road I really want to write, and the man who sold goldfinches, and about a wet night on the wharf and Tarana Street in the Spring. Really, I am sure it does a writer no good to be transplanted – it does harm. One reaps the glittering top of the field but there are no sheaves to bind.[1]

There is no mistaking Mansfield's sense of personal disillusionment in that brief assessment of her writing life, or in her regret at what literary ambition of a particular kind – the colonial yearning for the metropolis – cost her in terms of immediacy and personal loss.

In speaking of Mansfield, it is easy enough to make a straightforward case for regarding exile, nostalgia, gender and writing as the cardinal biographical points. One also could quickly assemble a small anthology that underlines that constant motif of her writing – the isolated or solitary or abandoned woman, ill at ease among people who bring home to her the difference between herself and them. Her biography bears out how Mansfield herself quickly tired of wherever she happened to be living. Her letters are a vivid graph of excitement and inevitable disillusion, as she believes that to live somewhere else, will mean to live more happily. Her own country to begin with, then variously England, France, Italy, Switzerland, became places where hope is exhausted, although the immediacy and delight of her day to day responses prevent her from quite stalling on pessimism. However much critics and biographers are embarrassed by the fact, only Gurdjieff's Fontainebleau lived up to expectations. Although by then her expectations were few – to live without distress, to feel at home, as she said, 'among my own people, at last.' Yet one might easily enough demonstrate that most of Mansfield's adult life offers a prime exhibit for any critic who cares to descant on Derridean deferral, on a variant of Augustinian cliché, 'Lord, make me at home, but not yet.'

Mansfield offers considerable evidence that 'the do-you-remember life' as she called it, the emotional immediacy of nostalgia, was central to her finest fiction – rather as Nabokov, in his self-memorialising *Speak Memory*, insists on his right, beneath American skies, to yearn for one locality in Russia. One can point to such statements as her writing to a friend about *Prelude*, in imagery already anticipating 'At the Bay', and in a manner that locates her aesthetic ties with both impressionism and the techniques of cinema. She remembers Wellington, and that remembrance confirms how the story will be told: 'In the early morning there I always remember feeling that this little island has dipped back into the dark blue sea during the night only to arise again at beam of day, all hung with bright spangles and glittering drops. I tried to catch that moment with something of its sparkle and flavour. And just as on those mornings while milky mists rise and uncover some beauty, then smother it again and then again disclose it, I tried to lift that mist from my people and let them be seen, and then to hide them again.'[2]

One might read that paragraph in a number of ways, but however it is read there is the groundswell, so to speak, which is present in the writing of any exile, revisiting and refashioning the past in the hope of touching what Wordsworth, in another *Prelude*, called 'the vivifying virtue,' that rises from the wells of remembrance and lost time – those 'spots of time' he so celebrates, the forerunner of so many literary variations on epiphany. (*The Prelude*, 1805 text, XI, 258–260)

Yet a different emphasis is possible speaking on Mansfield and exile. There is a letter she wrote in February 1922, when she was immersed in Shakespeare, and particularly in *Antony and Cleopatra*. She remarks on how she begins 'to see those marvellous short stories asleep in an image, as it were. For instance:

> Like to a vagabond flag upon the stream
> Goes to and back, lackeying the varying tide
> To rot itself with motion.

'That is terrible', she goes on, 'it contains such a terribly deep psychological truth. That *rots* itself … And the idea of 'it' returning and returning, never swept out to sea finally. You may think you have done with it forever but comes a change of tide and there is that dark streak reappeared, and sickeningly rotten still. I understand that better than I care to. I mean – alas! – I have proof of it in my own being.'[3]

In fact she already had written the story that draws out that image. In 'The Man Without a Temperament', a reserved and slightly sinister Englishman looks after his consumptive wife in a French hotel. The woman is a figure of immobility in a supposed world of sunlight and youth, her husband emotionally inert. They are surrounded by a garden that 'lay open, motionless, as if exhausted, and a sweet, rich, rank smell filled the quivering air.' The story ends as the man, during the night, attends to his ill wife. As he sits by her bed, she turns the ring on his hand and asks him, 'Do you mind awfully being out here with me?' And so the story ends: 'He bends down. He kisses her. He tucks her in. He smooths the pillow. 'Rot!' he whispers.

Something like this, perhaps, is much closer to Mansfield's sense of exile – not so much the feeling that there is a country she will not return to, as a state of normality which she can no longer reach. One might follow it through in the almost hallucinatory images that persist in her notebooks and letters from the time of the First World War – the nexus of feeling and expression that makes her so distinctively a modernist figure.

For Mansfield felt, as did Freud, Eliot, and so many others, that the War
was not simply an episode in history. It was a fracturing of civilisation, a
point from which human nature must be differently perceived. Her irrita-
tion in 1919 with Virginia Woolf's novel *Night and Day* was exactly for
that – the fiction failed to concede how there was no going back to the
way the novel had once been, with its assumptions of steadiness, persistent values, stable personality. And so she wrote of Woolf's novel, 'it is a
lie in the soul – we have to take [the war] into account and find new expressions new moulds for our new thoughts & feelings.'[4] The War, indeed, was synonymous with rot. 'It's never out of my mind and everything
is poisoned by it. It's *here in* me the whole time, eating me away'.[5]

I have argued elsewhere that 'There is not a logical sequence to this
way of thinking, so much as a new focusing of reactions, a breaking of categories. If one was not also Europe and the War, then one was not cough-
ing, not ill, not wounded, not a living, dying, contemporary woman.'[6] The
War, as she said, is in all of us. What may have begun as a kind of mere
allegorical transfer became much more than that as her illness advanced.
One might even think perhaps of Kafka's story 'The Penal Colony', where
the bodies of criminals are deeply tattooed with their crimes, until the
sentence of one's life is literally the discourse one dies from. In what often
reads like an anticipation of existentialism, authenticity for Mansfield comes
down to confronting the dread of what we cannot evade. As she puts it in
October 1920, 'The little boat enters the dark fearful gulf and our only cry
is to escape – "put me on land again." But it's useless. Nobody listens. The
shadowy figure rows on. One ought to sit still and uncover one's eyes.'[7]

As Mansfield runs together her various responses to the War, her
own health, her quest for a philosophical stance, and the exploring contours of her fiction, talk about any one without implicating the others.
Consider how she spoke of her lungs as her 'wings', and how she writes in
her last poem, 'The Wounded Bird':

O waters, do not cover me!
O my wings – lift me – lift me.
I am not so dreadfully hurt.[8]

Consider, too, how she also jokingly called her lungs 'the battlefield'. This
is not the place to embark on a new reading of "The Fly", but it is impossible to read that late story without seeing that it is about health as well as
war, without the figure of 'the Boss' assuming the contours of her own
father as well as a traditional notion of divinity, the pitiable and brutal figure of a patriarchy that both causes and grieves over destruction. But that

story too is about *effort*, the drive to survive even when there is no chance
of success. The philosopher A.J. Ayer said that after the war of 1914–1918
mankind no longer moved *meaningfully* within history or even place, yet
the impulse to find meaning remained.[9] Fontainbleau was Mansfield's last
ditch stand to engage with reality on her own terms. Her vivid turning
against intellectualism in the last months of her life had a great deal to do
with what existentialism would call being 'properly historical' – how to
take on the role that gives meaning to time, that prevents temporality overwhelming one.

The momentary frisson, the grasping at life in vivid glimpses, the sense
of cultivated drift, were always deliberately sought in Mansfield's life. But
what to make of things when it became fairly clear that one was dying?
That one's wings would not, as the poem had hoped, 'lift me – lift me'?
Heidigger would advise that to isolate this recognition of one's own death
was itself an assertion of freedom, what he called 'the freedom to death.'
In reading the late Mansfield one may even be reminded of the words
Nikos Kazanzakis wrote for his own tomb: 'I hope for nothing. I fear
nothing. I am free.' Mansfield's way of putting it was to say, a fortnight
before her death, 'This place . . . has taken from me one thing after another (the things never were mine) until at this present moment all I know
really, really is that I am not annihilated'.[10] This refusal to be intimidated
is at the core of her last story, 'The Canary', written in July 1922, and is set
in a boarding house in Wellington. An old woman thinks about the death
of her pet bird, and her vague but insistent intuition that there *is* a meaning, if only one might get through to it. 'It is there, deep down, deep
down, part of one, like one's breathing.'

This note on Mansfield is called 'Exile of the Mind' – not a nostalgia
for a remembered past, although that is certainly there in the stories; but
more than that, the search for where reality is not so much acceptable, as
accepted. One might finish with another quotation, from another expatriate – Albert Camus, in 1937: 'Sur le chemin de Paris: cette fièvre qui bat
aux tempes, l'abandon singulier et soudain du monde et des hommes.
Lutter contre son corps. Sur mon banc, dans le vent, vidé et creusé par
l'intérieur, je pensais tout le temps à K. Mansfield, à cette longue histoire
tendre et douloureuse d'une lutte avec la maladie.[11]

Notes

1. To Sarah Gertrude Millin, March 1922, *Katherine Mansfield: Selected Letters*,
    ed. Vincent O'Sullivan (Oxford University Press, 1990) 257–8.

2. To Dorothy Brett, 11 October 1917, *The Collected Letters of Katherine Mansfield*, ed. Vincent O'Sullivan and Margaret Scott (Oxford, Clarendon Press, 1984), 1, 331

3. To J.M. Murry, 7 February 1922, *Katherine Mansfield: Selected Letters*, 241.

4. To J.M. Murry, 10 November 1919, *Collected Letters*, 3, 82.

5. To J.M. Murry, 3 February 1918, *Collected Letters*, 2, 54.

6. Vincent O'Sullivan, *Finding the Pattern, Solving the Problem* (Wellington: Victoria University Press, 1989) 12.

7. To J.M. Murry, 18 October 1920, *Collected Letters*, 4, 75.

8. *Poems of Katherine Mansfield*, ed. Vincent O'Sullivan (Auckland: Oxford University Press, 1988) 82.

9. A.J. Ayer, 'Some Aspects of Existentialism', quoted in Alasdair MacIntyre, 'Existentialism', *The Encyclopedia of Philosophy* (New York: 1967) 3, 153.

10. To J.M. Murry, 26 December 1922, *The Letters of Katherine Mansfield to John Middleton Murry*, ed. J.M. Murry (London: Constable 1951) 698.

11. Albert Camus, *Carnets: mai 1935-février 1942* (Paris: Gallimard) 59–60.

14

'Wrong Side of the Mirror': Exile in David Malouf's *The Conversations at Curlow Creek*

David Malouf's *The Conversations at Curlow Creek* addresses the topos of exile – a traditional one in Australian literature – in ways that are both conventional and subversive in terms of postcolonial narratives. The Irish protagonist's visit to Australia arouses in him a sense of alienation, of being out of place, even though he is a restless soul with no home anywhere. Unlike some colonists who will successfully adjust to the new land, Adair will go back to Europe, cured of his restlessness and ready to make a home in Ireland. Australia thus serves to effect a cure, by providing a mirror image of reality and allowing Europeans to project their neuroses and fantasies on it. It is therefore instrumentalized by colonists and visitors, and its alienness continues unabated.

Exile has been a major preoccupation in Australian literature, as one could expect since the non-indigenous inhabitants of a settler colony inevitably pine for the homeland they have left behind. They feel like strangers in the new land, like Topp the music master in Patrick White's *Voss*, who proclaimed: "It is no country of mine... except for the unfortunate accident of my being here."[1] After some two hundred years of colonisation the sense of exile remains quite sharp among white Australians–as witness Peter Carey who wrote "We're northern hemisphere people who have been *abandoned* in the south"[2]; Tim Winton, one of whose characters asks: "You think maybe *we don't belong here*, like we're out of our depth, *out of our country*?"[3] or again Les Murray, who asserted that

> ... It will be centuries
> before many men are truly at home in this country...[4]

Among Australia's novelists, it is no doubt David Malouf who has most consistently dealt with this theme. Acutely aware of his country's post-colonial condition, he has, in practically all of his fiction from *Johnno* (1975) to *Remembering Babylon* (1993), explored the sense of alienation which individuals as well as communities experience because they feel cut off from their roots, stranded in a strange and unfriendly land which they cannot call home and with which they have no spiritual affinity. But his novels also suggest that this estrangement can be overcome, perhaps less with the mere passing of time than through the wonders of the imagination. At the end of *An Imaginary Life*, this almost archetypal tale of exile, the poet Ovid, on the point of death, experiences an epiphany which reconciles him at last with his alien environment and abolishes the fracture which had tormented him since he was sent away from Rome:

> It is summer. It is spring. I am immeasurably, unbearably happy. I am three years old. I am sixty. I am six.
> I am there.[5]

In his latest novel, *The Conversations at Curlow Creek*,[6] Malouf returns once again to the topic, producing what would seem to be a straightforward tale of exile: the protagonist, Michael Adair, finds himself compelled to spend a period of time in the Australia of the 1820s – a time, of course, when the largely unexplored country felt stranger and more distant than it does today, and so a suitable background for a tale of exile – but his mind is very much on his native Ireland, to which he eventually returns. His sense of exile has a good deal to do with the strangeness of the raw colony and its vast distance from the familiar world he has left behind. But, Malouf seems to suggest, there is more to exile than this – it is never a mere matter of geography. There is a form of inner exile that can be experienced anywhere, even at home, and which amounts to a spiritual infirmity. Through the example of Adair, Malouf explores this painful condition and shows how, paradoxically perhaps, the experience of physical distance can help cure the soul.

Exile has a great deal to do with the sense of being out of place, trapped in a part of the world that is both unfamiliar and uncongenial, and Irishman Michael Adair, when first introduced, finds Australia as alien as he might find the surface of the moon: "My God, he had thought. What a place! He had never in all his life felt so far from the things that were closest to him, from any object that gave him back the comfortable assurance of being in a world of his own kind, a habitable place crowded with other lives – even the lives of ghosts" (5). Physical distance from home combines with psychological or spiritual distance from the homely to create an uncomfortable impression of *Uheimlichkeit*. Adair feels "as if he had been set down on a new planet rather than the far side of the old one" (106). The comparison of Australia with an alien planet emphasizes what lies at the heart of his sense of exile: the absence of recognisable, that is to say European, human inscriptions in the new land,[7] which makes him feel utterly alone, surrounded as he is by "the blackness of the night, which only deepened the silence and your sense of being lost in it, in fearful loneliness" (25).

Australia is a place unfit for (European) human beings, and thus in stark contrast with old Ireland, even though, according to former Prime Minister Paul Keating, "No country in the world is more like Ireland than Australia".[8] Not that Ireland is described as particularly cheerful, quite the opposite:

> A sorrowful land, with the fine rain thin as smoke blowing in from the Atlantic so that the taste of it was there on your lip, the smell of it in sheets that had been laid over a bush to dry. Salt and sorrow over the fields, a sad country; mournful, made human by the long sorrows it had endured, the sorrows yet to come (54).

The operative words here are *made human*. It is the sense of the long interaction between the land and human beings, rather than some intrinsic charm or beauty, which makes it homely, thereby allowing a character such as Carney to maintain he's been colder in Australia than in Ireland even though the latter is hardly famed for its hot climate.[9] Contrasting Australia with Ireland (or Britain) is part of the antipodean *topos* which informed early European visions of the Great South Land, presented as the very opposite of all that was proper and pleasant. "Sometimes, when the moon was just a sliver," Adair reflects while looking at the Australian night sky, "the fact of its being reversed down here gave you the odd sensation of being turned about, as if you had somehow got yourself on the wrong side of the mirror" (105). Australia and Ireland are poles apart, then, but there is also a sort of necessary connection between them, as Malouf suggests through the mouth of Carney, the runaway convict who is to be hanged in the morning. As he explains to Adair,

> I think sometimes that this place – you know, is a punishment on a man just in itself. Like as if they'd taken Ireland and turned it into a place that made things as hard as they ever could be in this world. I feel sometimes, as if maybe I've never really left it. Just got meself into a part of it, you know, that's meant for those that've gone wrong in life, taken a wrong turning...(50).

The notion that Australia might be "an Ireland that has gone bad" (51), that is, a kind of hell, is no less part of the traditional antipodean topos, and reflects the historical circumstances of the settlement, which was indeed meant to punish those whom the British regarded as criminals, and to stop them from returning home to annoy respectable folks. In the words of John White, surgeon with the First Fleet, Australia was "a country and place so forbidding and so hateful as only to merit execration and curses."[10]

At the same time, and paradoxically perhaps, the association of Australia with hell humanizes the former, just as Ireland was "made human by the long sorrows it had endured." Suffering, especially what Patrick White termed "death by torture in the country of the mind," is part of the process which turns an alien place into home, so that the notion of exile becomes far more ambiguous than it appeared to be at first sight. Although for Adair Australia is not a country because it has too few human associations it might yet become one: "It was a place that was still being made habitable. A venture, another example of the inextinguishable will of men and women to make room for themselves, some patch of the earth, however small, where they could stand up, feel the ground under their feet and say, This is mine, I have made it, I have made it mine..." (54). No matter how precarious the European imprint looks in the 1820s against the vastness of the untamed bush,[11] a beginning has been made, and already colonists are offered better prospects in Australia than they would have had at home.[12] Furthermore, some of them have thoroughly adapted to the new environment, turning into a new type of man which could be described as recognizably Australian, and so is a bit of a mystery to those born in the northern hemisphere. Thus Garrety, with his "easiness of conscience as well as nerve and muscle" (7), his "wry, laconic style" (9), and a scepticism about the existence of the soul which makes him sound like Henry Lawson's Mitchell. Most of all, he has acquired an extraordinary bushcraft which makes him entirely at home in Australia:

> He was as good a tracker as any black. Better, Langhurst thought, he was uncanny. He knew before Jonas did what sort of weather was on the way, could read every sign in the sky, every shift of the air, every movement of the clouds, as if, when he looked up, his black eyes narrowed, his mouth at work on a grass-stalk, there was some intimate connection between the clouds' purpose and his own light but restless spirit. He knew every print in the sand, whether it was scrub-turkey or one of the many kinds of pigeon, or one of the bush-feeders that for some reason had alighted a momenr and left the mark of its foot, honey-earer or shrike or wren; or a wallaby, and of what size and

weight, or one of the many smaller creatures that lived their own lives back in the brush. He could smell the different sorts of grasses, and tell at a hundred feet where a troop of kangaroo had passed, and how long ago, an hour or last night (22).

In such respects *The Conversations at Curlow Creek* conforms to the standard pattern (or perhaps clichés) which can be found in many novels of pioneering tracing the passage from the early pain of exile to an eventual sense of being at home in Australia. If this were all, Malouf's novel would have little claim to originality. But actually it goes beyong those (relative) simplicities to probe the ambiguities of exile and, conversely, of any sense of place, thereby complicating the linear pattern of change which seemed to prevail.

If Adair experiences Australia as a place of exile, it is not so much because he misses his Irish home as because he has in fact no place to call his own, not even in Ireland. From the outset he is described as uneasy, tormented by questions to which he has no answer, incapable of feeling at one with himself.[13] Thus, something in his nature compels him to spend his life in exile of one kind or another even while yearning for home:

> It was one of the many contradictions of Adair's existence that though he was by nature a man who would have liked nothing better than to see the sun rise and set each day on the same bit of turf, he had spent all the years of his manhood, thirteen to be precise, in one foreign army or another far from home – if by home one means not four walls and a roof, with a fire and a chair before it, but the place of one's earliest affection, where that handful of men and women may be found who alone in all the world know a little of your wants, your habits, the affairs that come nearest your heart, and who care for them (34).

The reason why he is so acutely aware of "his uneasy place in the world" (93) is to be found in his childhood: having lost his parents at a very early age, he was taken in by a friend of his mother's, who brought him up as if he was her own son. But in spite of Mama Aimée's love, Adair is nagged by a sense that he doesn't truly belong in that household, and this sense is complicated by his feelings of guilt towards Fergus, Mama's true son, whose birthright he thinks "he had somehow, innocently, unwittingly, stolen" (170). He has "an image of himself as cuckoo" (170) which prevents him from feeling truly at home at Ellersley, Mama Aimée's residence, in spite of his great attachment to the place and the people who live there, including the servants. This is why he'll keep on longing for home without being able to satisfy his longing.

His predicament is made worse by the very different outlook of the people who are dearest to him, Fergus and Virgilia. The former has the gift of feeling at home everywhere, as appears when he visits poor peasants: "In each of these households Fergus was welcomed as one of the family" (167). It is not simply that he is quite unselfconscious and pays no heed to the conventions which constrict those around him, and Adair in particular. Rather, he has an uncanny ability to look upon the world as if it was totally familiar while enjoying it as if it was totally new,[14] and thus to recover rather than discover things, as if they had always been his. As for Virgilia, she is endowed with a romantic imagination that makes the familiar dull and impels her to dream of faraway places, "to take flight from dusty reality and make their dull world yield up wonders" (67).

In the triangle that Adair forms with Virgilia and Fergus, he feels he is the odd man out – that his love for the former will not be requited because the latter is so much more attuned to her imagination. And so he is an exile at home, a feeling he externalises by becoming an exile abroad, by choosing to be a soldier and serving in various European wars, then by going all the way to Australia to find Fergus, who has disappeared and might have been seen in New South Wales. In a twist on the Orpheus myth, he goes all the way to hell in order to bring back Virgilia's loved one, but he fails in his mission since Fergus has encountered the most implacable and incurable form of exile, that is to say death.

The depiction of Australia in terms of hell is by no means proper to Malouf – it is in fact part of a well-established tradition in Australian writing,[15] and owes a good deal to the convict beginnings of the colony. Later, when the country disappointed the colonists' expectations, the paradise they had dreamed of turned, in their opinion, into a hell. One can see in this metamorphosis the process of othering through which colonists establish absolute distinctions between what is human and pleasant (their own world), and the colonial world which comes to epitomize all that is inhuman and unpleasant, thereby justifying the imperialist process. In the case of Australia, this othering was facilitated by the geographical opposition between the country and the British Isles, and Malouf duly refers to it as being "at the world's end" (180), again a familiar theme which runs through a good deal of Australian literature (though Malouf tones down the negative connotations which appeared in Keneally's phrases, "the world's worse end"[16] and "the world's wrong end"[17]).

In *The Conversations*, the theme of Australia-as-hell is built up in gradual fashion, beginning with descriptions emphasising what is unnerving about the country, such as the reference to "the blackness of the night, which only deepened the silence and your sense of being lost in it, in fearful loneliness" (25). Darkness pervades the main narrative, which takes place in the course of a single night. It is a disturbing kind of darkness, associated as it is with the Aborigines, because of their skin colour – with Jonas, who "could make himself invisible" (107) – and, more importantly perhaps, associated with suffering and retribution, as Carney suggests ("I think sometimes that this place – you know, is a punishment on a man just in itself" – 50). So Adair finds himself "usher[ed]... through into the underworld" (180). This image will recur towards the end of the novel, when Adair, on the eve of returning to Ireland, thinks of the new self which has emerged in him as a result of his Australian experience: "a self that has journeyed into the underworld and come back both more surely itself and changed..." (211). Orpheus then returns, empty-handed, but it is his rival, not his love, that is now gone, and Fergus's death opens new perspectives for him, not least the perspective of finding at long last his place in the world, and so of shedding for good his sense of exile: "He could scarcely contain his impatience now for dawn to come and their sailing-time. To be done at last with these years of moving from one place to another. To settle. To be at home" (211).

But, as we have seen, his years of exile cannot be regarded as the disruption of an otherwise settled life: they are the ordeal he had to go through so that he might find out where he truly belonged. More paradoxically perhaps, it is by establishing a permanent place for himself in Australia that he succeeds in exorcising the demons that drove him into exile. Strictly speaking, though, this permanent place does not belong to him but to his phantom double, O'Dare. He comes to understand the duality in his nature when, before embarking, he gazes at

> a sky he will exchange before long for the more familiar northern one, like a side of his soul that has been in recession here; not lost nor denied but out of sight for a time – and who can say that he might not have had to come all this way, and entered into some opposite dimension of himself, to know at last what it was? (203)

To find out about Fergus, Adair has become a police officer. He has hunted down a party of mostly Irish bushrangers (of whom Fergus was one), and presided over the execution of their last survivor, Carney. But the popular imagination has changed the story, and believes that he has allowed Carney to escape and has in fact joined him to roam the wilds of New South Wales. His acquaintance Saunders explains to him:

So you see, my friend, you do not quite get away. You leave here this shadow of yourself – not your real self, that would not serve – but this other more romantic, more outrageous self that fits the *story* and grows as it is passed on [...] Didn't you know that O'Dare was one of your names? The name of this other you that the story has knocked up? For all your stern dedication to duty, my dear fellow, which none of us doubts, you are really, deep down, of the devil's party – that is, an Irishman, after all. To your health, Mr O'Dare, folk hero! (204–205)

When the protagonist is first referred to as O'Dare by his troopers,[18] the reader already knows him as Adair, and assumes the troopers simply got his name slightly wrong – an insignificant mistake. But the protagonist's two names materialise the duality of his nature, which he expresses as early as in the opening page of the novel: "What is it in us, what is it in me, he thought, that we should be so divided against ourselves, wanting our life and at the same time afraid of it?" (1) Adair the soldier and trooper is a man at war with himself, and this, rather than the strangeness of Australia, is the source of his sense of exile. And it is precisely Australia, "a place that that has taken so much from him but has given him something too that he cannot measure yet, though more thanhe had expected" (213), which allows him to overcome this sense, offering him the prospect of fulfilment – not in the southern hemisphere, not as a pioneer in the new world, but back home, where he knows he belongs, and Virgilia is waiting for him: "He is free. There is, at last, just the two of them" (212).

The dichotomy home/alien land which underpins the sense of exile to be found in much postcolonial fiction is thus subverted in Malouf's *Conversations*. The two elements are not entirely separate, and in fact are not separable, as the novelist intimates almost from the beginning of the narrative. There is actually a sort of imaginary continuum between Ireland and Australia which makes the passage from one to the other something different from a plain uprooting, a frightful plunge into the unknown, the utterly alien. The protagonist senses this as, caught in the blackness of an Australian night, he thinks back to his Irish childhood: "'It's a long way off, eh?' a voice was saying. But it was not so far. Not far at all, Adair thought, his head rolled back against the wall. Close even. So close you could let the breath go from your body and step right back into it, instantly" (33). Neither time nor space form impassable gulfs in human existence, and one can sometimes return. A good deal depends on individual circumstances. Adair is sharply aware that he can go home while many other settlers, whether free men or convicts, are denied this possibility: "It struck

him now that the real difference between himself and these others was
that he could leave the place, and would leave it, but that they belonged
and would stick" (115). This would seem to set him apart, but going home
is not simply a matter of sailing back to the northern hemisphere: a home
has to be made.

Australia's role is not limited to doing away with Fergus and conjuring
up O'Dare. The protagonist has left a good deal of his self there "– of his
real self, of Adair –" (210), and in exchange he has received gifts. Apart
from the loaf of bread, these gifts would appear to be rather unsubstan-
tial, but they are essential to him: he has acquired a new self, and can now
appear before Virgilia "untrammelled and without intermediaries, in his
own form, as himself; the new self that something in this harsh land and
the events of these last months have created" (211).

Adair's new self is a unified one where the old one, as we've seen, was
deeply divided. It is as if he had been able to delegate to his phantom
inauthentic double, O'Dare, all the features which created tensions within
him, the dark wish "to annihilate the self with distance" (211) which had
turned him into something like the Wandering Jew. Australia has exor-
cized his wanderlust, and prepared him for the settled life to which he as-
pired but could not accept.

There is a good deal of ambiguity about the role of Australia in Malouf's tale of exile. While Adair admits it can provide a home for Europeans – a better home than Ireland, even – he never envisages settling
there (in fact, he turns down an opportunity to extend his visit and become something of an explorer – "I've done my bit, made my – contribu-
tion," he says (209). Adair is always conscious of himself as a visitor to
these strange shores, which keeps him apart from those who are there
for good. This is what prevents him from being entirely comfortable with
Saunders: "The slight tension between the two men has to do with the
fact that one is leaving and the other not" (203). The difference, Malouf
notes, is "decisive." There is a horrified side to Adair's reflections when
he considers what would become of him if he stayed in Australia:

> Life here, with its desperate routine and sparse amenities, its brutal plea-
> sures, might come in time to seem normal to him. Every shift of light would
> search his soul and ask mockingly, Are you still here then, Michael Adair,
> Michael Adair? Have you decided after all not to escape? (179)

The verb suggests Australia can only be a prison to Adair, as it is a grave
to Fergus and Carney. Life there would only be a travesty, hence Adair's

elation when about to be released: "he cannot resist the vigorous swing of his own soul upwards out of the dark" (212).

The metaphorical associations of Australia, in the above sentence and elsewhere, are basically negative. It is a place of darkness and suffering, an underworld, the wrong side of the mirror, the very opposite of a country that is fit for human beings. Nor is this an initial impression that will come, in the course of the narrative, to be replaced by a more sympathetic understanding – the negative metaphors persist to the very end. It is true that there are occasional indications that such unfavourable perceptions can be accounted for by the historical context: in the 1820s Europeans were barely learning how to come to terms with the strange new land, "a place that was still being made habitable" (54), and as civilisation took hold it could be expected to become more acceptable. But this is the merest of suggestions, and it remains unconfirmed by the narrative.

Australia is a repository of human illusions. Adair's persistent presence in the country under the guise of O'Dare is an illusion, as is the notion, entertained by a number of colonists, of "a golden city of escapees, an antipodean Cockayne run by riff-raff and runaway lords of misrule" (208). New countries no doubt need myths, but these are not particularly constructive ones. Australia plays strange tricks on men's minds, as Adair experiences when, in the middle of the bush, he has the vision of a lake teeming with fish and birdlife which turns out to be nothing but a mirage. This phantom vision of a plentiful Australia is closely connected with Adair's existential problems, his sense of being divided, of carrying a phantom self by his side.[19] It held out the promise of a solution to those problems: "It is a door in the darkness, a way out," Adair believes (176). But the dream vanishes, and there is in fact no escape – not yet anyway, not until he's reached the bitter end of his mission and served his time in the underworld, like a convict of another kind.

And when Adair is about to leave the country at the end of the narrative, one has the sense of his turning over a new leaf – the Australian episode of his life will soon be over and done with, not to be returned to. If the last few lines of the book show him chewing a piece of the loaf of bread he's been offered, "his saliva mixing with its sugars and driving new light into his heart, refreshing his mouth like common speech" (214), one feels that he will soon do what, in Malouf's first novel, Johnno was dreaming of doing, i.e. "shit this bitch of a country right out of [his] system."[20] The imagination here does not unify, bond the character with his new environment: on the contrary it divides, it separates the spurious (i.e. Australia, and the fantasies or illusions associated with it) from the real, which lies in the northern hemisphere. Adair does overcome his sense of exile in the end, but that doesn't make him less of a stranger to Australia – a country destined to remain forever the wrong side of the mirror.

Xavier Pons
Université de Toulouse-Le Mirail

Works Cited

Carey, Peter. *The Unusual Life of Tristan Smith*. London: Faber, 1994.

Edwards, John. *Keating – The Inside Story*. Ringwood: Viking, 1996.

Farmer, Beverley. *The Seal Woman*. St Lucia: UQP, 1992.

Frost, Alan. *Botany Bay Mirages*. Melbourne: MUP, 1994.

Gibson, Ross. *The Diminishing Paradise*. Sydney: Angus & Robertson, 1984.

Keneally, Thomas, *Bring Larks and Heroes*, Melbourne: Sun Books, 1968 [1967].

Lawson, Henry. "Up the Country", *Bulletin*, 9 July 1892.

Malouf, David. *Johnno*. St Lucia: UQP, 1975.

———. *An Imaginary Life*. Sydney: Picador, 1980 [1978].

———. *The Conversations at Curlow Creek*. London: Chatto & Windus, 1996.

Murray, Les. *Collected Poems*. London: Minerva, 1992 [1991].

White, Patrick. *Voss*. Ringwood: Penguin, 1960 [1957].

Winton, Tim. *Cloudstreet*. London: Picador, 1991.

Notes

1. Patrick White, *Voss* (Ringwood: Penguin, 1960 [1957]), 40.
2. Peter Carey, *The Unusual Life of Tristan Smith* (London: Faber, 1994), 117 (emphasis added).
3. Tim Winton, *Cloudstreet* (London: Picador, 1991), 231 (emphasis added).
4. Les Murray, "Noonday Axeman", in *Collected Poems* (London: Minerva, 1992 [1991]), 5.
5. D. Malouf, *An Imaginary Life* (Sydney: Picador, 1980 [1978]), 152.

6. D. Malouf, *The Conversations at Curlow Creek* (London: Chatto & Windus, 1996).

7. Malouf deliberately leaves out the Aborigines, save for passing references which suggest that in the eyes of his characters they don't really count as human beings (cf. p. 7: "They had been together, the little group of them, for just on three months... Before Jed Snelling was killed they had been four – the black who was with them, Jonas, did not count."). But in other novels, especially *Harland's Half-Acre* and *Remembering Babylon* he had emphasized their special affinity with the land.

8. Quoted in John Edwards, *Keating – The Inside Story* (Ringwood: Viking, 1996), 21.

9. cf. p. 119: "It's a different sort of cold – you know, to what I was used to. Up in the hills there, where we was hiding out, the nights got that cold it'd freeze the balls off you, it was like another hell. It's not the cold we was born to, you see. Back home – you know, in Ireland – I could go barefoot, sleep rough, it never bothered me."

10. quoted in Alan Frost, *Botany Bay Mirages* (Melbourne: MUP, 1994), 145.

11. cf. p. 53: "Men and women, small children too, were staggering over the land with great stooks in their arms, to lean them one against the other and make, in a place that had never known such a thing in all of previous time, a scene, busy, productive, that had at first glance the immemorial order of a landscape at home, till you raised your eyes and saw what a tiny patch of order it was in the surrounding bush and against the jagged wilderness of the mountains beyond."

12. cf. p. 54: 'Many of those families down there were ones whose menfolk, back home, would have had no prospect in all eternity of owning even an acre of land, and here they were offered hundreds if they had the strength to tear it out of the wilderness and plough and work it. That surely was something.'

13. p. 1: "What is it in us, what is it in me, he thought, that we should be so divided aginst ourselves...?"

14. cf. p. 76: "He... had his own way of going about things and of finding what it was in the world that shone out and demanded to be seen – thing they had not noticed till he touched them and took them up; and always as if their shape and colour were somehow already known to him; with the joy of recovery, as if his lighting upon them were a reassurance to him that he was in a world that was familiar."

15 cf. for instance Henry Lawson's "Up the Country", *Bulletin*, 9 July 1892. Cf. also Ross Gibson, *The Diminishing Paradise* (Sydney: Angus & Robertson, 1984).

16. Thomas Keneally, *Bring Larks and Heroes* (Melbourne: Sun Books, 1968 [1967]), p. 7.

17. ibid., p. 24.

18. cf. p. 24: 'Who's that? Who are you referrin' to? Him or mister bloody O'Dare?
    'Is that 'is name? O'Dare?'
    'That's it.'

    This short passage introduces a kind of ambiguity ('Him or mister bloody O'Dare?') which will later on reemerge as a duality within the protagonist's nature.

19. cf. his dream p. 175: "He was standing in clear sunlight at the edge of a vast sheet of water, so dazzling with salt and reflected light that he could not see the farther shore and had for a moment to shield his eyes against its blinding throb. He was aware of another presence, close at his side but slightly behind. He felt its heaviness there, but knew he must not turn his head to look or it would vanish, and with it the lake or inland sea and its wash of light, and he too, since he understood that the figure there at his side was himself, a more obscure, endangered self with a history that was his but had somehow been kept secret from him. The tenderness and concern he felt was for both of them."

20. cf. D. Malouf, *Johnno* (St Lucia: UQP, 1975), p. 98.

15
The Colonising Victim: Tim Winton's Irish Conceit

Tim Winton's novel *The Riders* is read in the context of the resurgence of nationalism in Australia. In *The Riders*, a new narrative of belonging is forged through an old ruse; the drawing into affinity of Ireland and Australia. Winton's representation of lines of consanguinity between Ireland and Australia has the intention of grounding Australian identity in Ireland and its history of colonisation and resistance. Borrowing Ireland's status as a victim of colonisation Winton occludes Australia's real history of colonisation. Winton's attempt to claim Ireland's colonial history and rebel tradition for Australia ends in reproducing an Ireland that has its antecedents in the English stage tradition.

Tim Winton's popular novel *The Riders*[1] is, ostensibly, a contemporary re-telling of the classic tale of a fool who loves too well. I have argued elsewhere[2] that grafted onto this classic tale of unrequited love, we find a more sinister love-story of mastery and misrecognition between nations, which leads the reader into the self-embrace of Australian nationalism. I have suggested we need to read *The Riders* within the context of the resurgence of nationalism in Australia and of new narratives of nation that have arisen in response to the successful challenges of feminists, multiculturalists, non Anglo-Celtic and indigenous Australians to the hegemony of the nationalist narrative. This is not how Winton is read "at home" where *The Riders* was one of the most critically acclaimed, popularly received and successful books of 1994. In this paper I explore the conceit that Winton deploys of Ireland qua Australia and suggest that Winton's deployment of Ireland is central to the attempt made by the novel to reaffirm the legitimacy of white Australian narratives of nation and to revalorise nationalist narcissism.

The novel's central character, Scully, has lost his heart to a woman who demands of him the servitude of a Snag.[3] Scully concedes everything to

Jennifer, his love for her leading him to abandon Australia as she searches for a creative outlet in Europe, dragging him, and their daughter Billie, behind her. The novel begins at the end of this journey. On the eve of returning home to Australia, a week-end trip to Ireland ends with Scully left to restore a newly purchased derelict house in County Offaly, while Jennifer and their child Billie, return to Australia to sell their Australian home to enable them to re-settle in rural Ireland. But while Scully labours on his Irish farmhouse, Jennifer sells their home and makes off with the cash. She's had enough of Scully and his love-sick and hometown Australian ways. She wants European finesse, culture and civilisation and entry into its closed worlds is hampered by the big-fisted, battle scarred, working class and ostentatiously Australian Scully.

The greater part of the novel is taken up by the harrowing attempt by Scully to find Jennifer who has abandoned Billie to an air-hostess and disappeared mysteriously in Europe. Scully and Billie lumber through Europe in an ever-degenerating state, searching for Jennifer, and an answer to the enigma of her disappearance. Following Scully, lumbering through Europe in search of Jennifer, the reader is taken on a grand tour of relations between the Old World and the New. We witness Scully rubbing up against European mores and suffering the familiar Australian incapacity to make an Australian symbolic stand up in the antithetical symbolics of Europe. Scully doesn't defer, he's innocently democratic and non-hierarchical in his dealings with people, his friendliness is open-handed and generous, and his demeanour that of the big-bodied big-handed largesse of the Australian bush tradition.

In contrast, the Europeans of the novel are supercilious, arrogant and most importantly, they just 'don't get' Scully; his innate goodness has no place in their symbolic hierarchies. This grand tour of Europe draws the reader into an affirmation of the Old World 'Other' of Australian folklore; a world in which the French are unstintingly arrogant, the English mercilessly superior and all the Europeans inexplicably hostile in the face of Scully's *Australian* amicability and vulnerability. As the degenerate Alex Moore comments: "something terribly provincial in that kind of niceness." But this "niceness",[4] the reader is reminded, is a matter of national character, and to jettison it is to betray what is most worthy, most essential to the Australian 'Thing'…

In this opposition drawn between a European dissembling and an Australian authenticity, Winton is entering an old argument. As he has made clear in a number of public interviews, his intention is to lend his voice to what is referred to in Australia as "shaking off the cultural cringe": a phrase that refers to the perceived need for Australians to transcend the Eurocentrism of colonial relations; to establish a sphere in which Australian mores, aesthetics, intellectual, political and social quests are pursued independently of European judgements of value. When the reader experiences Scully's worldly innocence, his democratic orientation and his generosity of spirit, the hierarchies and snobbism of Europe are cast into relief. De Tocqueville's castigation of the new world as "swinging backwards and forwards without begetting new ideas", as preferring the useful to the beautiful, as persecuting minority tastes and as replacing excellence with mediocrity,[5] is rebuffed yet again by the intrinsic worthiness of Scully and, by extension, of the intrinsic value of the Australian 'Thing'.

In contemporary Australia the necessity of 'throwing off the cultural cringe' has the status of an unassailable political verity. In the present 'culture wars', the old intellectual elite accuses the new generation of intellectuals of a dependency on European theory while the new generation accuses the old of a dependency on American cultural intolerances and Anglo-American assumptions of what is and isn't knowledge. The charge, however, of 'cultural cringe', remains constant. Even Mark Davis, the current champion of the new generation, takes this requirement of 'throwing off the cultural cringe' as unassailable verity.[6] The popular enjoyment and identification with the rhetoric of 'throwing off the cultural cringe' is evident, for example, in the frisson of cultural enjoyment that greeted Australia's former Prime Minister, Paul Keating in 1994, when he touched the body of the Queen of England, declaring in a gesture all Australians equal to an English monarch.

Camouflaged by this imaginary encounter between a European gaze, and the perceived sin of complicity in this gaze, however, is a narrative that sustains an endless re-enactment of cultural narcissism and provides a political justification for the refusal of difference. What continues to escape commentary is the aggressive nationalist identification that underpins the rhetoric, an identification with an imaginary site cleared of foreign contamination, and in which Australianness, in its inherent goodness, can find a boundary. A limit in which self and other can finally be identified and where the ego can find its resting place. It is precisely this *impossibility*, in a culture defined by its imbrication with other cultural traditions, and by its usurpation of another culture's ground, that makes this drive for an autochtonous culture and for an independent identity so pressing and yet so impossible. Hence the repetition of the narrative in which the moment of recognition of an autochthonous identity is always in the cusp of the future and yet at the same time grounded in a mythic past. Winton's narrative belongs, in fact, to a long line of similar narratives that have staged this moment of recognition when an autochthonous Australian identity finally recognises and embraces itself. Russel Ward in the 1950s, P. R. Stevensen in the 1930s, or going back further to a writer such as Harris in the 1830s, all share with Winton the attempt to stage an indigenous white Australian character – cast in opposition to an effete, unnatural and dissembling Europe – as an ideal point of identification and self recognition for the Australian reader. Winton's popularity belongs here, in the affirmation he proffers to his reader of a familiar, goodly Australian, who makes a journey of self-discovery into the rightness of his belonging in Australia. An affirmation on the far side of feminism and multiculturalism, and on the far side of the surfacing of the stories of the Stolen Generation, and of a culturally orchestrated genocide. And this journey goes, curiously, via Ireland. In Winton's re-enactment of the gesture of throwing off the cultural cringe, we find Ireland called upon as buttress, as ally, and as homeland.

In the opening passage of *The Riders*, the reader is taken on a surreptitious journey. Staring into the fire burning in the ancient hearth of his new home in County Offaly, Ireland, Scully, recalls the fires of his youth. He sits in a house "older than his nation," the task of clearing its mildew, refuse and decay before him, recalling the uprooted karri pines burning for days on the newly cleared land of his family farm in Australia. It is an image with an unavoidably mythic resonance that locates Scully within the mythos of the Australian colonial tradition. Cleared land, wood fires, we can smell the eucalyptus, see the billy boiling. But the context of the novel is post-feminist Australia, its fictional time beginning with the massacre at Enniskillen, Northern Ireland on the eleventh of November 1987, and Scully is a young man, not yet touching middle age.

In the fictional time of the novel, Scully's childhood memory would derive from the 1960s; if we pause to contextualise this fictional memory in real time a strange lapsus emerges. In real time most of the dairy farms of Western Australia had been carved from the rain forests, the karri trees cleared, by the 1920s and 1930s. By the 1960s most of these farms were bankrupt. Scully's journey in memory then, from a fire burning the refuse of old Ireland to the clearing fires of a new country travels by way of a curious anachronism which lends to the fictional Scully, a contempo-

rary Australian man living in the late twentieth century, a foothold, a belonging, to the mythos of colonial Australia. Perhaps we could bypass this
as a mere error were it not for the repetition of this journey in the second
passage of the novel where we are again taken on this same journey from
rural Ireland to colonial Australia.

In a passage that describes the quilted character of the Irish countryside and that gestures repeatedly to an archaic Irish past – the castle in
the corner of Scully's eye, the newspaper clippings underfoot of an un-
earthed bogman, the litter of ages of human habitation – Scully again remembers. This time his memory is of the only Irish song lie knows: *"The
wild colonial boy."* This song epitomises the mythic colonial figure of the
bushranger: a native son, who, carrying the stain of an Irish rebel tradition, defies the law. With this song the reader is again transported to colonial Australia, but the journey is no longer a simple transportation of the
contemporary Scully via old Ireland to a 19th century New Australia. In
The wild colonial boy, the Australian bushranger, Jack Doolin, is an Irish
son, born in Castlemaine: so Scully's memory carries Australia in all its
newness back into the fold of Ireland.

This journey from Ireland to Australia ends in a return in which affinity
is established through memories that begin from an encounter with difference. Reeling from the strangeness of Ireland, its foreign supermarkets,
its I.R.A bombings, its unfamiliar agedness, Scully is never the less in a
world that sings his song. "Our" songs are their songs, "our" Native sons
their Irish rebels; different but the same. And this song takes the reader
from contemporary Ireland to colonial Australia, gathering in passing the
mythos of the Irish nationalist tradition in a colonial re-enactment of Irish
rebellion which floats just outside the present, at the edge of Scully's memory.

In the very early pages of the *Riders*, then, Winton establishes a line
of continuity in which Australia, under the sign of Scully, fits within the
broader frame of an older nation. And as the narrative develops, so does
this surreptitious framing in which Australia is given a home away from
home. The novel begins and ends in Ireland. It is the safe haven from
which Scully ventures and to which he returns to alter the exigencies of
his sojourn in Europe; but Winton's Ireland is a strange rural Arcadia untouched by three hundred years of Irish/European dialogue; it belongs
more to the traditions of the past than to any contemporary Irish reality.
We could recognise Winton's Ireland in the nostalgic and sentimental Ire-

land of tourist brochures, or more uncannily we could find traces of it in the mid-nineteenth century novels of Charles Lever and Samuel Lover, or in other similar Anglo-Irish representations of Ireland as a rural pastoral peopled by garrulous, lovable and harmless Paddies. But WC could not find this Ireland – Scully's home away from home – in the works of contemporary Irish writers such as Deane, Healy, Montagne or Toibin. In contemporary Irish writing, the question of homeland is as troubled and unresolved as it remains in non-fictional Australia. As Timothy O'Leary writes of Denis Healy's *The Bend for Home*,[7] "the reader senses that for Healy home is something for which one always yearns but never reaches. The 'bend for home', the last turn in the road before home comes into view, is as close as one can get." [8]In *The Bend for Home*, Healy investigates the pull of nostalgia for a lost home, in this instance County Cavan. Nostalgia for home, Healy warns, "steals material from the same source as fiction, and then leaves the reality wanting." In Winton's Ireland we experience this act of theft; we are returned to a nostalgic rural Ireland replete with "local colour and charming gaelicisms",[9] but it is a homeland produced for an Australian readership where nostalgia stands in for reality and fiction itself is left wanting.

In *The Riders*, Ireland is never guilty of the sins of the old world. Old, but not of the old world, it floats, unattached and uncontaminated by European snobbism, inauthenticity and elitism. It is this structural opposition that gives the game away; Winton's Ireland is most pointedly an Ireland that belongs to a mythic, as opposed to a historical past.[10] As scholars such as Declan Kiberd point out, Europe has provided a conscious backdrop for most Irish cultural production since the seventeenth century and has been an important source for the regeneration of Irish cultural traditions.[11] Even Irish nationalists such as Padraig Pearse saw the development of Irish literature as requiring contact with the "European mind" in order to escape the limits of provincial Ireland. Beyond the realm of cultural production, Europe has provided Ireland with refuge (the Wild Geese), armies (1798) and the hope of political transformation (The European Union). But Winton's Ireland seems untouched by this history.

How different Winton's Irish fairies are from Seamus Deanes ghosts on the stair case. In *Reading in the Dark*,[12] magic is the form that truth takes when it can't be spoken, the ghosts on the stairs the real figments of an intolerable and unspoken truth. Winton's fairies however remain trapped in an Irish fairy circle, enigmatic figments from a mythic past. If they bear a message it is only that 'man' should not seek to know, should cease to question and should let the dead 'bury the dead.' Replete with haunted castle and fairies, Winton's Ireland hovers outside contemporary time, its contemporary realities screened by the gaze of an Australian imaginary in search of a homeland. Few today would attempt the stage Irish characters that Winton deploys nor attempt to sustain Ireland in this structural opposition to Europe. The question that needs to be posed is why does Winton require this imaginary Ireland, and how does it sustain his own deployment of an equally imaginary Australian homeland.

The answer to this question is to be found in the form of affinity Winton claims between Ireland and Australia; an affinity that requires that both Australia and Ireland share the status of colonial other, and this in turn requires that both Ireland and Australia are located in mythical time outside the unsettling demands of the present. Scully and the Irishman Pete-the-post, for example, share a bodily affinity. Scully's body defies European bourgeois standards of aesthetic conformity:

The broad nose with its pulpy scar down the left side from a fight on a lobster boat, the same stupid blue that caused his wonky eye. The eye worked well enough unless he was tired, but it wandered a little, giving him a mad look that sometimes unnerved strangers who saw the brillopad hair and the severely used face beneath it as ominous signs. Long ago he'd confronted the fact that he looked like an axe murderer, a sniffer of bicycle scats. He stuck out like a dunny in a desert. He frightened the French and caused the English to perspire. Amon Greeks he was no great shakes, but he'd yet to find out about the Irish.[13]

The French woman Marianne responds to this face: "Tell me about your face, your very sad eye. It makes me think of beasts you know." But in Ireland this face fails to register its difference. In lieu of a European horror at the bodily marks of an Australian labouring man's life – Scully finds affinity, recognition and welcome. The principle bearer of this Irish welcome is the local postman – Pete-the-post – whom we meet for the first time as: "long freckled shambles of a man unfolding himself like a worn piece of patio furniture ... beneath the postman's crumpled cap was a mop of red hair and two huge ears." These ears, like Scully's hair and wonky eye, refuse to keep quiet; signifying a shared Irish/Australian refusal to conform to European chic. These two bodies, moreover, share a position in the European gaze. Europe throughout the novel signifies an oppressive gaze – the gaze of the first world that perceives the colonised other, the Australian, as primitive, savage, unformed – and Ireland, as we know, is the savage of Europe. Claiming Australia as the object of this gaze Winton is demanding the shared status of Ireland as colonised; hence the recognition of affinity that greets Scully in Ireland. The Irish gaze seeing Scully recognises an odd but charming self. Thus Pete-the-post assures Scully that, even if Scully himself doesn't recognise it, his name signifies that lie is, at heart, Catholic Irish. And Scully admits to being desert Irish: a joke that nevertheless contextualises Scully in his claim on Irishness as a lost son, of a lost tribe, but nevertheless of the soil.

Similarly, Winton's Ireland and Winton's Australia share an affinity to nature. Throughout the novel, Scully's memory goes by way of eucalypts, beachscapes and high blue Australian skies, a journey home in which he is written into the landscape as its rightful occupant. Winton adumbrates again and again Scully's love of the land, the necessity for Scully of being in, and belonging to the Australian landscape. His disease in Europe is always premised on this ease at home, and home is always figured as landscape. What differentiates him from the Euro-centred Jennifer is this pull of the land, an irresistible force, that declares itself again and again in its clarity and brilliance, against the pale washed-out, prosthetic worlds of Europe. Sneja Gunew points out[14] that Australian nationalists deploy the land in its uniqueness as a rhetorical device through which to launch the claim of a unique cultural identity. Positioning the native son in a unique landscape and as the bearer of a unique identity, is an attempt to ground white-Australian claims to legitimacy in nature itself.

In the fictional world that Winton constructs, Ireland alone shares with Australia this affinity between culture and nature. And Ireland alone, possesses *landscape*. Thus Scully regards the castle below his Irish farmhouse:

He heaved himself over the wall and walked up into the field below the castle whose foundation seemed to be a great granite tor buried in the brow of the hill; the closer he came and the deeper into the shadow he walked, the clearer its size became. He saw it plainly now. Scully had long thought that architecture was what you had instead of landscape, a signal of loss, of imitation. Europe had it in spades because the land was long gone, the wildness was no longer even a memory. But this ... this was where architecture became landscape. It took scale and time, something strangely beyond the human.

In this passage, Winton is drawing an affinity between Australia and Ireland that establishes their shared difference from Europe. What Ireland and Australia "share" is – a relationship to nature, to landscape and the naturalness of their belonging to it. If the Irish have *landscape* rather than merely architecture, if they belong by nature to the soil, then by extension so does Scully. The Native son on a journey of recognition of the rightness of his belonging on the Australian soil sees his own affinity to land mirrored in the rightness of Catholic Ireland's belonging to the soil. Thus Australian claims to homeland take on the rightness, the unassailable virtue, of the Irish Catholic struggle against English colonisation.

The attempt to borrow a colonised status from Ireland is a constant conceit of Australian nationalism. This borrowed status of colonial victim is a central narrative, for example, in the discourse of Australia's new extreme right Party, Pauline Hanson's One Nation. In public rallies and speeches of One Nation, reference is frequently made to Pauline Hanson's red hair which serves as an identificatory tag to establish her affinity to the "fighting Irish." This rhetorical device anchors Hanson in the folk tradition of an Irish-Australian community, dispossessed and oppressed by an Anglo-Australian elite. Similarly, One Nation members frequently describe themselves as victims of the Irish famine, and provide stories of their attempts to reclaim their Irish land.[15] The impossibility of such attempts serves to delegitimise Aboriginal Australian's claims for land-rights and the legitimacy of recent legal rulings over Native Title in Australia. Ireland is thus called upon to establish the victim-status of One Nation members and to deny the history of cultural dispossession in Australia. As victims of dispossession, One Nation members are always positioned in narrative as innocent of any moral culpability in the dispossession of Aboriginal Australians, even while this dispossession is proceeding apace in contemporary Australia.

In *The Riders* we find a similar if more veiled narrative strategy. Scully's journey of recognition of the rightness of his belonging in Australia is framed by an Ireland which provides a home away from home. An ancient community that anchors Scully's new homeland in the primordial and organic belonging of Irish Catholics to the land and in the heroic anti-colonial rebel tradition. In this conceit Europe and England must be figured as colonial oppressors – of Australia – and the Irish rebel tradition re-enacted long after its eclipse in Ireland, in order to occlude the central fact that Australians were not victims of colonisation but colonisers. As victims of dispossession, of famine, of the crown – and of a contemporary Eurocentrism – they are positioned elsewhere than at the scene of the crime.

Recognising this conceit, we approach the necessity of Winton's construction of a mythical rural Ireland that floats outside of contemporary history. This Ireland is defined by its provincialism and peopled by Paddies that are recognisably those of English making and that belong on an English stage. In Winton's pastorale everything that issues from the mouths of these Irishmen fulfills some charming idyll: "Jaysus," Pete-the-post's first words of introduction, "I thought it was the truth all along ... would you be Mr. F.M. Scully now... You're the Australians then ... by God your as famous as Seamus around here already." These Irishmen speak in the parodies of the English stage tradition; and in this tradition they are garrulous, friendly, effeminate, their emotions ever on display, uncontrived, unmarred by the complexities, the snobbism and the inauthenticies of modernity. They have nothing in common with the often terse, bitterly black and sardonic world that emerges in Irish representations of rural Ireland, but much in common with an English colonial gaze and its deployment of the "Paddy."

Ireland, it would seem, is the sacrifice that must be made in order to establish a homeland that will lend its colonial status to a colonising people. This Ireland must hover outside of real time, just as Scully hovers in mythical time between colonisation and the present because real time has stories of its own. In Ireland these are the stories of the underside of the rebel tradition, the horror bred from hatred of the other, the petty rivalries and snobbism of rural Ireland, the bitter aftermath of colonial rule and of religions fundamentalism. In Australia they are the stories that are now surfacing of the Stolen Generation; the stories of a state-sanctioned destruction of Aboriginal families and Aboriginal culture; and of the legal recognition of the illegality of *terra nullius*. It is these stories that continue to unsettle white-Australian belonging to the land and that nationalists seek to occlude. In *the Riders*, we see an English colonial gaze called upon in order to continue this tradition of occlusion and, in the tradition of this colonial gaze, reality and fiction are left wanting.

Jennifer Rutherford
Macquarie University, Sydney

Notes

1. Tim Winton, *The Riders*, Macmillan, Sydney, 1994.

2. See, *The Gauche Intruder; A Genealogy of the White Australian Imaginary*, forthcoming, Melbourne University Press.

3. A sensitive new age guy.

4. *The Riders*, p. 163.

5. Tocqueville, A. (de), *Democracy in America*, vol. 11, trans. H. Reeve, Knopf, New York, 1953, p. 56

6. Mark Davis makes the point that the new generation, those supposedly guilty of importing French theory, do so in a way that 'writes back' – developing distinctive, pragmatic versions of 'critical theory'. While I agree with Davis' analysis, it is worth recognising how even in his defence of the so called young generation one finds the delineation of an authentic posture to an externally existing body of knowledge. It is a posture that has a great deal to do with defence of an imaginary place qua nation and less to do with an authentic rapport to ideas that might, or might not have something to say. See, Davis, M, *gangland: cultural elites and the new generationalism*, Allen and Unwin, Sydney, 1997.

7. Healy, D., *The Bend for Home*, Harvill Press, London, 1997

8. O'Leary, T., 'Great Hatred, Little Room,' review essay forthcorning, *The Australians Review of Books*, August, 1988.

9. O'Leary, T., ibid.

10. One only has to consider the snobbism of rural Ireland portrayed by John Montague to realise one is fully in the realm of myth. See Montague, J, 'Sugarbush, I love you so' in, *A Love Present*, Wolfhound Press, Dublin, 1997.

11. Kiberd, D., 'Irish literature and Irish history', in R. F. Foster ed, *The Oxford History of Ireland*, Oxford University Press, Oxford, 1992.

12. Deane, S. *Reading in the Dark*, Vintage, London, 1997.

13. "The Riders", p. 9.

14. Gunew, S., "Denaturalizing cultural nationalisms:. multicultural readings of 'Australia'," in Bhabha, H., *Nation and Narration*, Routledge, London, 1990.

15. Based on interviews carried out by the author with One Nation members in Victoria, New South Wales and Queensland, 1997–98.

16

Nineteenth-century Labouring Class Emigrants to New Zealand: Colonists, Colonials, 'New Chums'

From the late 1830s to the turn of the 1880s, various waves of assisted emigration were organised to populate the New Zealand colony and make its waste lands viable. Several questions will be raised: how did emigrants who received free (one way) passages react to their new circumstances, facing a highly disconcerting environment, caught in the dwarfing task of planting human nuclei in the least known place on earth? How much/little of their Britishness did they retain? What specific qualities and attitudes typified the new Zealand 'new chum'? The author, by reviewing a range of reactions (as expressed through letters, diaries, etc.) will conclude that emigrating 'down-under' meant a rejection of deference and servility, a newly acquired sense of worth, a priority given to vitality, buoyancy, optimism, boldness, vigour, practicality and enterprise, an attachment to materialism and competition, an acceptance of (material) success as the only measure of an individual's value, an openness to physical, professional and social mobility in a context entailing loneliness, individualism and masterlessness. The question of the democratic leanings of this colonial world, not classless but organised along different lines from those of the Old World will be tackled.

England's condition in the early 19th century, well-known as it is, can be summarised as follows: its post agricultural revolution economy combined with its full blast industrial metamorphoses had generated an unprecedented population boom, urban growth, accompanied by a large scale drift from the land, unemployment, deskilling of part of its working population, the creation of a waged urban proletariat, resulting in the burgeoning of hideous slums where promiscuity, violence, filth, precariousness prevailed, sporadically 'spiced' by riots, such as the Luddite ones or Chartist agitation, which themselves led to savage repression, so greatly dreaded was the havoc the new mobs might wreak upon that otherwise so utterly prosperous country. Emigration to the colonies had entered the minds of politicians and utilitarian philanthropists as early as the late 18th century as a panacea for relieving the distress of the redundant workforce: the ethos of expansion was, by the turn of the 19th century, powerfully at work, there were already myriads of settlements invested by British interests, including New Zealand's closest neighbour, Australia.

Yet, as a place of settlement, New Zealand did not naturally present itself as appropriate for it was facing major difficulties. Though discovered in 1769 by James Cook who charted it with great accuracy, the place remained in European eyes an extremely remote place, two dots at the bottom of the world, vaguely associated with Australia yet with specific and rather nasty features, full of swamps and of cannibals. Then how did New Zealand come to be accepted as a suitable place for British permanent settlement? As sociologist Claudia Bell puts it[1] New Zealand had been discovered by Abel Tasman (that is of course excluding its Maori inhabitants), given English names by James Cook and had to be 'invented' by British settlers agencies on whose backs lay the task of changing public ignorance into productive curiosity leading to colonisation.

Two phases can be noticed, both resting on the overriding desire to make New Zealand attractive to settlers: first Edward Gibbon Wakefield and his conception of "systematic colonisation" meant as planting antipodal micro-Englands on New Zealand soil by selecting the right migrants who would reproduce perfect segments of pre-industrial England, that is rural communities where wealthy landowners (having purchased land from England) would have their land tilled by labourers who, only in the long run, would themselves acquire their own tract of land – this system was applied, rather unsuccessfully, until the late 1840s; then, from the 1850s to the 1880s,[2] the vigorous actions initiated by the provincial governments soon replaced by a central body, in particular by the large-scale schemes of assisted emigration Colonial Treasurer Vogel set into action in 1870, who wanted to drag the lagging, chaotic, erratic economy of the colony into an organised, planned society endowed with workable infrastructures and a population sufficient to the colony's growth and well-being. These two men, one might say, "had a dream", and their dreams bore similarities: Wakefield wanted to create an ideal society away from the evils of the old world, its miasmic vapours, 'satanic mills' and thundering famished mobs, Vogel (a former emigrant himself), wanted to make the country he had come to love a place of progress and of contentment. Obviously the legend of an ideal society existed well before the European discovery of New Zealand but, somehow, this country came to fit especially well as is currently being argued by leading historians like James Belich or Miles Fairburn, into the Utopian/Arcadian mould: a land (which Cook had already described in similar terms) of pristine beauty, of sublime ruggedness, of natural abundance (trees, land, food)[3] though yet under the form of chaos waiting to be ordered. It was then rather easy to make use of her natural assets by exaggerating them, hence the strategy, used by Wakefield's New Zealand Company and by the agencies appointed from New Zealand, consisting in making New Zealand desirable. To do so, potential settlers had to be found, wooed, persuaded, in other words the colonisers launched a "colonising crusade"[4] in which imaging and imagining New Zealand became the two sides of the same colonising coin.

All in all, and to simplify, the European population of New Zealand grew from some 1000 people (mostly adventurers who were not living there permanently) in 1830 to half a million in 1880 (a vast majority of them being permanent residents), that is a 500,000% increase, as James Belich notes ... During those five decades, a country was being born: what Belich calls the "proto-people" were deliberately led, by individual and government action, toward some kind of national unity.

Imaging New Zealand was then central to that creation. Though prompted by differing motives, Wakefield and the provinces, later the central government, seem strangely to show a continuous line, that of propaganda, though centrifugal and British-based at first, then centripetal in its second phase because orchestrated from New Zealand; both strategies having one aim, peopling, the dreamer of dreams like Wakefield and the politician like Vogel turned necessarily into publicists. In both cases, the New Zealand Company and the numerous agents sent to London by the New Zealand governments resorted to systematic campaigning. In the wake of Cook's explorations, there was a craze and a craving for visual representations, in painting watercolours, engravings), later in postcards (thanks to photography), of faraway lands: the Victorian audience doted on exotic natives and scenery as well as on pioneering life. Soon, the Imperial Exhibitions were to give them the possibility to approach these magical places turned by the power of their representation into true imperial icons, celebrating military might and agricultural ingeniosity. Printed material was of course the main medium: Wakefield and his friends published widely any kind of literature that might promote the cause, travel books, journals, handbooks, pamphlets, articles, novels likely to entice the potential emigrant. From the 1840s to the 1870s, the recruiting agents (often clergymen or teachers paid on commission or private consultants working for fees) in England organised lecture tours, pictorial displays (such as in Leicester Square in 1830s, or the Angas paintings exhibition at Piccadilly in 1849–51 or the Chevalier Crystal Palace exhibit in 1871) all chosen because they offered vast panoramas of a boundless yet untamed land. Arguments were consistent in stressing that emigrating was at the same time "sure gamble and safe adventure",[5] that soon the exotic that might appear repellent to some would be turned into familiar scenery, with a little effort, the pioneer would make the wilderness flower and would know how to acclimatise British plants and animals to civilise the wastelands offered to him.[6]

Simultaneously, the recruiters agreed on the absolute necessity of selecting the right settlers: in their minds, the ideal coloniser who would receive a free passage to his new land, should be young, healthy, a manual worker (preferably craftsmen like carpenters, hairdressers, agricultural labourers), there should be a balance of sexes, emigrants should in any case be decent folks, or even victims of sudden misfortune, capable of achievement, desiring a promotion to the respectability which England was denying them, but certainly not the unfit, the disreputable, the undeserving poor, the workhouse scum, the felon: in that, New Zealand was very strongly designed to be the anti-Australia, so frightfully glutted with convicts. A significant feature of the way the colonisers viewed emigration was that they did not favour chain migration: they preferred to recruit after their own criteria rather than trusting to the advice of already settled people or families who may have wished to recommend members of their own kinship network. In fact less than a quarter of the emigrants were chosen because they belonged to the extended family of the pioneers; besides there was a clear reluctance to transport whole villages (the way it had been done in Canada for example) only in very rare cases were hamlets from Scotland for example transplanted to New Zealand hinterland sites.

The outcome of this deliberate selection was mixed: a quick (grossly simplified) survey of the occupational mix of the settlers show that about 1/4 were skilled craftsmen, 1/4 agricultural and pastoral labourers, the rest consisting of tradespeople and servants.[7] What of the moneyed would-be emigrants then? Obviously they were hard to lure: Wakefield did manage to attract a number of baronets, high clergymen military men, doctors, etc.,[8] yet his dream was doomed to turn sour, some even say that it was stillborn. His conviction that labourers were necessary to provide the hands indispensable to creating workable estates met with an impossibility: while there was so much land ready for the taking, the assisted migrants soon realised they would not be happy to work somebody else's land and that they too were entitled to free-holding, though on a small scale, hence the fact that they were not long in clamouring for cheap land. However much Wakefield believed in his dream and in how it should be systematically implemented, one can see that, to echo Shakespeare, "though this be method, yet there is madness in it"

If New Zealand was to be a working man's paradise, it had to "unlock the land", to offer land at very low prices, in contradiction to Wakefield's deep beliefs. A clamour was heard among the newcomers to whom the prospect of becoming waged labourers did not appeal "to unlock the land" and, to answer it, the provinces offered land on incredibly favourable terms: for example, between 1855 and 1870, the province of Canterbury leased sheep runs at one penny an acre, and Otago sold 10 acre small holdings for 10 shillings.[9] Later, Vogel's policy of borrowing overseas in order to fund massive immigration in charge of building roads, bridges, railways, etc, could only be successfully applied through the granting, in return for public work, of tracts of land, in fact very densely forested, which the pioneer had the task, if he wanted to survive, to clear and turn into arable land. Added to that were opportunities to get cheap leases and loans meant to help the aspiring farmer to break into what was called the "Backblocks", that is mostly the forested areas of the North Island, the Taranaki Great Bush or Hawke's Bay for example, the only remaining wastelands not yet taken by the early settlers who had acquired the best grassy plains: there the forest was so dense one could easily 'get bushed', that is to say lost within a small radius without ever being found by those living even at a small distance; there the soil was very heavy, huge trees like the totara and the rimu were unknown to the English settlers, would not burn and had to be felled – an activity known as 'bush whacking'. There did the pioneer spirit breathe. Men had to use local materials like fern trees, flax, to survive on damper (unleavened bread) and on tea made of the local manuka – nicknamed tea-tree –, boiled on the billy, before he could reasonably expect, after some years of backbreaking toil, to build a modest house (the raupa or cob cottage so dear to the national folklore).

Not all of them succeeded: some gave up, either returning to the 'towns' or, if they could afford it, to England or to some other colonies, most of them, though, stayed on, which raises the often asked question: did they have particular qualities? Attempting to answer the question implies touching upon the very much hackneyed and stereotyped analysis of their story as a British success story. It is true that most of them were of English stock and that they had come to recreate an ideal England, a rural Olde Worlde where work and nature shaped man; judging from the many written testimonies they have left us,[10] it can be said that, as Britons and Christians, they accepted the notion that they had a mission, to subdue the wilderness, to "take up the White Man's Burden", wrapped up in their Britishness as in a cloak which they put on wherever they went.[11] Since theirs was a chosen place (so they had been told by the propagandists) and a promised land, they seemed to have made theirs, though with a far more secular echo, the belief in a "manifest destiny". The providential Victorian ideology of British destiny seems to have permeated their might and made possible a dynamic combination of religions and secular creeds. It is often said that the work of the pioneers, seen from all its angles, both by the actors and the later observers, is "a history written in advance",[12] yet another tale of the British march of Progress. Besides, a survey of their geographic origins proves telling: 62% of them were English or Welsh, 10% were Scots, 12% were Protestant Irish, further to a strong predilection, on the part of the recruiters, for people of genuine Anglo-Saxon stock, a definition elastic enough to comprise some Germans and Scandinavians (some 3500 of the latter were transported in the 1870s to the Backblocks on special works) who after all, in eugenic terms, might be considered as belonging to the superior race, but rigid enough to exclude the Catholic Irish (toward whom the recruiters did not turn their eyes as they preferred to recruit in Ulster) regarded as too impetuous and not manly enough, let alone the fact that Irish emigration was very much perceived as an excretion of that God-forsaken island and that few of the emigrants wanted to be seen as or associated with excrements.[13] The British writer Trollope, after visiting New Zealand, noted[14] that the New Zealand settler epitomized the imperialistic impetus: at work in New Zealand was found British resilience and indomitability, here could the quintessential John Bull, i.e. the yeoman, the small farmer prove his "mettle" (to borrow again from Shakespeare).

The penniless man found himself competing with the wealthy and the well-educated and, most important of all, found that he was in most cases, fitter then the man of learning and refinement whose knowledge barred him from adaptation to the new challenges of the Bush. Moreover, pioneering life made him feel useful and even needed: he was no longer one among the thousands of paupers of industrial England, no longer made redundant by a system that, in Victorian mentalities, still considered that being a worker was synonymous with being poor. First of all, his wages were better than in England, his skills were in great demand (carpenters, bakers, servants for example were in chronic shortage) hence the feeling that his was a happy lot,[15] with work and wages in satisfactory supply, a 'working man's paradise' as the phrase went, where a great number of class distinctions were discarded or rather transformed by the new environment where a man deserved his gentility.[16] New Zealand also appeared to the settlers as a safer place: here was a contented population who should not fear the ominous threat of an uneasy class, that ever pending dread of social unrest which plagued the daily lives of so many Victorians. Furthermore, emigrating to New Zealand meant moving away from that most hideous social disease, the poor relief and its workhouses.[17]

That the settlers should have felt slightly smug and secure and contented did not preclude a sense of being in a somewhat weird situation: never did they forget, their letters and diaries are there to show it, that they had not quite recovered from the trauma of leaving England, their family and familiar background, never to see them again, for most of them: many testimonies tell the tearing feeling at seeing one's meagre belongings (furniture for example) hoisted onto the ship bound to the antipodes and many are the confessions in which settlers related the strangeness of their new circumstances, living in almost total seclusion, in the midst of an alien, disconcerting, hostile landscape which gave them no references as to seasons and to all that was associated to them in England: unknown trees, evergreens, inverted seasons, with that utmost heresy, celebrating Christmas in full summer, the lack of celebrations linked to village life (like harvesting festivals for example), the longing for familiar beloved smells like haymaking or even making jams in autumn.[18] This uneasiness came spontaneously to be expressed by an attachment to England, referred to as' Home'.

As a consequence, another spontaneous reaction was to try and reproduce Britain: not only did painters depict a Zeelandia strongly redolent of the hedged, smooth countryside of Albion, settlers themselves were not long in recreating their familiar settings, planting imported British trees, nurturing British gardens while they were in no rational need to do so.[19]

The last question to be asked is to what extent did the pioneer find that he was becoming a new man? This is where the mentioning and discussion of a particular though controversial word might be interesting: during the pioneer period, newcomers were, affectionately, called 'new chums'. While elsewhere the word chum is known to mean close friend, in New Zealand,[20] it seemed to have lost this meaning to signify a freshly-arrived, non-colonial born fellow, still very much awkward because lacking in colonial experience and, as such, the laughing stock of those already settled.[21] There are other words, borrowed from Australian colonial folk-lore, such as the 'cockatoo' or the 'cow-cockie' applying to the small dairy farmer, the emblematic settler who makes a success of his life, though on a modest scale, yet the phrase 'new chum' seems to be endowed with par-ticular significance in New Zealand where it seems to convey no allusion to any kind of special friendship: on the contrary, the 'new chum' becomes in fact his own chum thanks to the new perception he has of himself. First of all, he prides himself in having made the decision to emigrate: he has had the pluck to emigrate, which makes him feel superior to the stay-at-homes who have accepted their lot. Secondly, one salient aspect of his ex-istence is that he is living in a Frontier society, in the process of conquer-ing the Bush, hence an ever-changing small world, a community which cannot be static but is necessarily mobile, socially, economically, geographi-cally, ecologically. Nomadism was accepted as being perfectly normal and good.

This mobility entailed several consequences: the pioneer knew that he could leave and find employment everywhere, thus that he could afford to demand good wages because his employer needed him, he therefore felt very deeply that he was entitled to behave like a free man, the stigma of servility would have been attached to him in England being removed here, and that he could reasonably claim to be masterless.[22] His mobility caused him to be alone most of the time: he may have got married, possibly started a family, purchased a little farm, that would not stop him from working in the wilderness, from changing jobs (examples are known of people having had such different occupations as bakers, railway workers, publicans, gold-diggers, carpenters, etc.), from selling his farm to buy another one, bigger and more remote because, basically, the Pioneer valued his loneliness, partly imposed, sometimes dreaded, often chosen if not cherished.

The extreme dispersion which characterised this stage of development helped create a highly atomised society in which the pioneer himself pur-sued isolation, very much alter the fashion of the American pioneers. Like his American counterpart, the New Zealand pioneer shunned human so-ciety because, as Turner explained in his well-known thesis, frontier life

generates anti-social behaviours. As Miles Fairburn has pointed out, he had
no desire to reproduce his former English neighbourhood (severed as he
was from his family connections left in England) he accepted no norms,[23]
no sense of conformity – what could one possibly conform to in the wilderness? – and no sense of what was acceptable or reprehensible since there
was nobody anyway to approve or disapprove of his doings, he might therefore think it natural to behave in ways deemed treacherous in Europe,
breaching promises or not reimbursing debts for example. His quest for
isolation prompted him to look for extreme situations where he could flee
areas that were to him already too populated, in the pursuit of the belief
that the grass is greener the farther you go, sometimes reaching a state of
near madness due to extreme solitude: settlers' testimonies tell of cases of
men living recluse-like in utterly out-of-reach places referred to as being
'bush ratty', 'gone silly' or 'hatters', meaning insane. It is therefore no
wonder that such a way of life should have given birth to the literary stereotype, though created some 50 years later by John Mulgan in his – only –
novel *Man Alone*, of the loner who rejects society as much as he is rejected by it.

     A side-glance at Australia and at its colonial process allows further
comment: the Australian Bush is well-known for having generated a close-
knit community of itinerant workers united by a very powerful sense of
'mateship', heightened into a worship, responsible for the strong unionisation that was to mark the last decades of the century: there is no such
equivalent meaning of the word in New Zealand where it never came to
signify more than a person you work with (a workmate) but not particularly like or want to keep in touch with. Somehow in New Zealand the
practise of isolation and the realities of social atomisation seem to have
been incompatible with the creation of a class-consciousness and of re-
grouping of interests, at last in the pioneer period.[24]

     Last but not least in the depiction of the new chum is his basic attach-
ment to the land: the land found him a pauper and made him a man, the
land supplied him with some substitutes for his missing environment, both
physical and emotional, the land has come to signify much more than mere
acres of soil. It is a reference, a means of identification (by owning and
tilling it and making it fructify) in a context where he has no kin, no close
neighbour, no bosom friend. Together with his family cell – (which is per-
force his only ally, employer and employee –, the land is his anchorage.
Such a strong relation with the land accounts for a typical attitude which
was to cast a long shadow over the collective psyche, the resolute opposi-

tion between town and country, 'townies' versus country people, in which the latter are perceived as the real New Zealanders whose stuff is made up of earth, so to speak, the inheritors of the old archetypal Englishman who worked on the land before the dawn of the industrial era.

If colonisation is to be seen as a full circle process, then the New Zealand case is an excellent example of how the colonizing loop was looped. Conceived by the recruiters as a rural folk Utopia resembling England of Old, New Zealand eventually came to fill the mould of its dreamers, fitting into the typical geography of Utopia, an island nowhere and faraway, and therefore into the necessarily imprecise time situation of an utopian universe and more particularly the nostalgia of the past.

Like all utopian visions, utopian New Zealand never existed. Its new chums did, however, and live on today...

Francine Tolron
Université d'Avignon et des Pays de Vaucluse

Notes

1. In *Inventing New Zealand, Everyday Myths of New Zealand Identity*.

2. New Zealand was made into a self-governing colony in 1852.

3. As explored at length by Miles Fairburn.

4. Belich, pp. 279–87.

5. Belich, p. 311.

6. The 1850s saw the flowering of such idealizing literature, with the publishing in London, of propaganda books by T. Cholomondeley, R.Taylor, or C. Hursthouse.

7. From *Statistics New Zealand*, 1870.

8. In particular in the settlement of Canterbury: Anglican in its conception, it was to become the most wealthy colony due to the introduction of sheep rearing, pastoralism often leading to affluence. As such, it will not feature in this article concentrating upon the pioneering class.

9. See Simpson, T., p. 120.

10. An exhaustive list is impossible to draw here. A convenient overview can nonetheless be found in *Life in a Young Colony, Selection from Early New Zealand Writing*, edited by Hankin, C.A.

11. As Belich puts it, p. 297.

12. Belich, p. 279.

13. See Belich and Fairburn.

14. Antony Trollope was to write in *Australia and New Zealand* (1873): "The New Zealander among John Bulls is the most John Bullish (...), he is more English than any Englishman as he follows the same pursuits (...) but with less of misery, less of want, and a more general pariciparion in the gifts which God has given to the country", p. 632.

15. A highly significant detail, though not quite a detail when one considers that so many British workers lived below the breadline, is the contentment they felt at having food in abundance: their letters home all testify to their relish at having milk, butter, mutton and large roasts of beef on the family table; some even noted that they lived like gentlemen, fishing, hunting, riding, without being gentlemen.

16. Alfred Fell, a settler, noted that in New Zealand, "there are no gentlemen, (...) all are workers" (quoted in Belich, p. 321).

17. Significantly, the colony was very slow in establishing a system of assistance to he old and the needy, only when it had reached a postpioneer stage (in 1898) did it turn to state as provider of welfare for those left behind.

18. The collection of early women pioneers' writings (edited by Drumond, A.) entitled *Married and Gone to New Zealand* provides a comprehensive selection of such miscellaneous and yet very telling remarks.

19. A.Trollope (op cit) noted: "New Zealand is especially English, the land is divided into English-looking fields, with English grasses and English hedges". William Swainson wrote of the neighbourhood of Auckland: "Owing to the neat and uncolonial style of cultivation, and to the absence of trees having a foreign appearance, it presents the appearance of a home-like English landscape" (in *Auckland, the Capital City of New Zealand and the Country Adjacent*, London: Smith & Co, 1853).

20. The same word, in Australia, may not have had such strong significance.

21. A. Bathgate, an emigrant to Otago in the 1860s, notes: "A person coming from England may perhaps suppose that he should be the teacher, not the taught (...) but he is surprised to find that he is looked on as immature, and perhaps patronised somewhat, for wanting 'colonial experience' (...) this phrase means a good deal (...), a man possessed with this quality has acquired a degree of infallibility to be gained nowhere else out of the colonies" (in *Colonial Experiences*, Glasgow: James Maclehose, 1874).

22. There exists a multitude of statements and observations made by settlers which support this point of view, among which the following ones have been chosen because they are well-known and representative:

A servant" does not consider to be of an order of things different from your order (...) the badge of servitude is not heavy upon her" (A. Trollope, op cit, p. 44).
"There is a great deal of independence in bearing and manner, especially among the servants (...). The look of the immigrants appears to alter soon after they reach the colony (...). I like to see the upright gait, healthy look, the decent clothes (...) instead of the half-starved, depressed, too often cringing servility of the mass of our English population" (in Lady Barker, *Station Life in New Zealand*, p. 17 and 32).

23. The anonymous writer 'Hopeful' observed, in a letter to her brother: "There is little of the *home* feeling so strong and prevalent at home – no attachment to place, locality, or friends as in England (...) how many a man and woman at home among the humblest classes boasts of having known all the ins and outs of the qsuire's family for generations past (...) the history of the parish church (...); these associations are part of the air they breathe, (they) have every incentive to respect themselves and be respected by the class and neighbourhood where they have been so long known. But there are no associations or memories of that kind in the Colonies, therefore there is not the same check and restraint" (in *'Taken In': Being a Sketch of New Zealand Life*, London: W.H. Allen & Co, 1887).

24. The pioneer period is here strongly distinguished from the next phase, covering the 1890s, when unionisation was warmly encouraged by the Liberal government.

Works Cited

Barker, (Lady), *J., Station Life in New Zealand* (first published 1870) Auckland: Random Century, 1991.

Belich, J., *Making Peoples, a History of the New Zealanders from Polynesian Settlement to the End of the Nineteenth Century*, Auckland: Allen Lane-Penguin, 1996.

Burns, P., *Fatal Success, a History of the New Zealand Company*, Auckland: Heinemann Reed, 1989.

Drummond, A. (ed), *Married and Gone to New Zealand*, Auckland: Paul's Book Arcade, 1960.

Fairburn, M., *The Ideal Society and its Enemies, the Foundations of Modern New Zealand 1850–1900*, Auckland: Auckland University Press, 1989.

Hankin, C. (ed), *A., Life in a Young Colony, Selections from Early New Zealand Writing*, Christchurch: Whitcoulls, 1981.

Hewett, E., *Looking Back or Personal Reminiscences by the Widow of a New Zealand Pioneer Settler* first published 1910), Hamilton: Rice Print, 1978.

"Hopeful", *'Taken in'; Being a Sketch of New Zealand Life*, London: Allen & Co, 1887.

Simpson, T, *The Immigrants: the great migration from Britain to New Zealand, 1830–1890*, Auckland: Godwit, 1997.

Turner, F.J., *The Frontier in American Society*, New York: Dover Publications, 1996.

17

"Multiple Exposures": Spatial Dilemma of Postmodern Artistic Identity in the Fiction of Janette Turner Hospital

Janette Turner Hospital's recent novels gather up two major preoccupations of her nomadic Australian, American or Canadian characters in search of a sense of heritage, and a sense of geographical belonging, that of history, and that of space. The diachronic and the synchronic planes of reflection are indeed the bases for two competing models of knowledge and artistic action at work in Turner Hospital's recent fiction: that of the depth-model and that of the surface-model, to purloin a helpful binary opposition from Fredric Jameson. These two models correspond roughly to modern and postmodern modes of knowledge and aesthetic praxis, and seem to coexist uneasily in her novels.

The Australian novelist David Malouf was asked whether he believed Australian culture included a specific experience of space. In reply he mentioned instead an experience of time: that of being woken in deep of night by callers telephoning from European daytime. Malouf's reply, far from avoiding the question, directly addresses the question of contemporary Australian experiences of space by placing the issue in a global context. Australia, rather than being the land when any news from Europe is already six months old upon arrival, as one character observes in Malouf's most recent tale of the early years of white settlement, is intimately linked to the rest of the world (Malouf, 204). The "tyranny of distance" is eradicated by the communications technology of the satellite telephone link, only to be replaced by the temporal confusion revealed in the inevitable bewildered enquiry: "What time is it there?" Australia's place within shrinking planetary dimensions produces temporal rifts of an unexpected sort.

Precisely this experience of intercontinental telephone calls is a frequently recurring feature of fiction by the Australian-Canadian author
Janette Turner Hospital, such that it attains an emblematic value within
her novels indicative of the deep contradiction generating the narratives.
In her fictions, Australia is no longer a place on its own, but merely one of
several sites where the action occurs, thus generating a divided consciousness and a pluralisation of structures of meaning. In the closing pages of
Charades (1988), the young protagonist rings her step-mother in Queensland from Boston, Massachusetts, driven by a sudden intuition regarding
her real mother's identity. The conversation triggers the daughter's decision to return "home" to a substitute family accepted despite the absence
of "blood" relationships. At the end of *The Last Magician* (1992), two
phone calls, from the narrator Lucy in Queensland and her best friend
Catherine in London, and between Catherine and her ex-lover Charlie in
New York, illustrate the same tension: that it is indeed a phone call from
Charlie is only presumed, as the caller utters no word, and the communication between the two women heralds a return to a Queensland charged
with the painful memory of vanished loved ones. In *Oyster* (1996), this
global communication and the potential ruptures it might bring with it are
abruptly reversed in the opal town of Outer Maroo by the virtual impossibility of contacting the outside world by telephone; when contact is made
by dissident member of the small mining community, it signals the apocalyptic collapse of the siege-mentality basis of social identity in the township.

Janet Turner Hospital insists on the tension between shrinkage of spatial dimensions and the accompanying disruption of previously accustomed
modes of presence and fixity which is a hallmark of modern global society;
in particular, her work dramatises versions of Australian identity based on
scattered domiciles and divided cultural loyalties. Her early novels, she
has said, are "about people constantly obsessed with places other than
where they are at the moment... Even on a pragmatic level, when one has
family in Australia, one is always aware of the two different time schemes:
here and there. It affects my perception of things all the time" (Brydon,
21).

Martin Albrow claims that the increasing proximity of formerly discrete cultures and societies in the new global geography has produced
a collective identity crisis, where citizens of the global village ask themselves: "Who am I, where am I, where do I belong and to whom?" (Beck
182). Similarly, Fredric Jameson speaks of a loss of the capacity for "cogni-

tive mapping", that is, of the capacity of our minds to map the global, multinational, communication networks in which we find ourselves caught up as individual subjects, only vaguely sensed as "this latest evolutionary mutation of late capitalism towards 'something else' which is no longer family or neighbourhood, city or state, nor even nation, but as abstract and nonsituated as the placelessness of a room in an international chain of hotels or the anonymous space of airport terminals that all run together in your mind" (Jameson, 44, 116). In series of recent publications, Paul Virilio has described a culture in which dramatically increased mobility of transport, linked with a revolution in the media by virtue of which the technology of representation operates at constantly increasing speed, such that distances are cancelled out, places erased – in a process characterised not only by communicational possibilities opened up by the ubiquity of Internet connections, but also the coercive potential inherent in military technology and surveillance (*Vitesse et politique: Essai de dromologie* [1977], *L'Espace critique* [1984], *Esthétique de la disparition* [1980/1994]). Ulrich Beck has drawn attention to the increasing heterogeneity of the "transnational" communities created in the wake of revolutions in transport and communication, the resistance of localities to total assimilation in global entities such as multinational concerns; dense networks of international contacts also ensure that received notions of identity, meaning and values are levered open by contact with other cultures (something that every expatriate has experienced in trying to negotiate the pitfalls of intercultural codes, even between the various linguistic communities of the English-speaking world) (Beck 1997). It is thus increasingly urgent to deal with textual, and in particular literary manifestations of postmodern shifts of spatial sense. In Janette Turner Hospital's fiction this process is foregrounded under the sign of difference and plurality, going beyond the traditional geographical parameters of the nation-state. The overlap between the spatial mobility of the writer, with its corresponding complications of national or cultural identity and geographical multiplicity can of course be placed in the context of current debates touching upon the rapidly changing spatial paradigms of Australian identities, particularly regarding relationships with trading partners and international neighbours in the Pacific region and the issue of Aboriginal land claims.

Jurij Lotman has asserted that a narrative event is generated by a character's transgression of the boundaries of a semantic field, a observation which may be particularly pertinent in relation to Turner Hospital (Lotman 350). Roughly the same thought is articulated by her: "The arrival of any foreigner changes the map" – with the significant addition: "and foreigners spell the beginning of the end" (O 11). Turner Hospital's narratives signal attempts to rearticulate space, to re-plot the reference points of increasingly mobile (inter)national identities which disturb the spatial certainties of an earlier era. Significantly, Australia is always open to the outside world in these novels, always linked to other places whence the characters come or where they yearn to be. Her narratives register often disturbing and unwelcome changes in the topography of Australian identity. Both *Charades* and *The Last Magician* evoke the anglocentric, xenophobic Australia of the 1950s and 1960, where "all good little Australians" in the world of academia and letters would be "rewarded with Oxford", and when the schoolboy Charlie Chang's confident announcement, "I was born in North Queensland, Mr Brady. I'm a true blue Aussie" could earn him the teacher's retort, "Because a man's born in a stable, that doesn't make him a horse" (*Charades*, hereafter C 139/*The Last Magician*, hereafter LM 43). In *Oyster*, at the end of the 1990s, the graziers and Outback town-dwellers of Outer Maroo are instilled with a siege mentality which harks back to the times before Feminism, Republicanism, Aboriginal land-rights and the coming of "foreigners".

Janette Turner Hospital's fiction signals the demise of a form of Australian identity based upon a determination to "bash the difference out" (LM 77) – but whose decline is not without numerous rear-guard skirmishes and a degree of resistance: in the Outback town at the end of the 1990s, a Greek-Australian visitor realises that: "It's *difference* that Australians hate... Melbourne or Athens, they're much the same to people out here" (O 118). The multinational, multicultural composition of Turner Hospital's narratives constitutes a sharp rejoinder to this aggressive parochialism.

Spatial Confusion

Shifts in spatial references points, whether geographic, subjective or linguistic, generate confusion and insecurity. In Turner Hospital's fiction, the paradigmatic expression of this confusion is that of losing one's way. Her most recent novel, *Oyster*, can be seen to determine this theme retrospectively when the narrator Jess, a surveyor in an earlier life, describes the confusion of the motorist searching for Outer Maroo: "Somewhere far ahead, according to his map, are the dotted lines of the South Australian and Northern Territory borders, but he can see no sign of these poignant ideas of order. They leave no trace on the land... The translation of these markings from map to landscape is a psychic skill, in the exercise of which earnest map-readers may go astray and may wander into Outer Maroo." Significantly, the *only* travellers who find the Outback opal town are those who have lost their way (O 5, 6).

Reading Janette Turner Hospital's decidedly postmodernist fiction, which scrambles dream and reality, swaps various time planes and rocks from one fictional place to another, the reader gains the impression of total abandon of stable narrative orientation, of generalised spatial confusion. But a modicum of order can be introduced into the experience of disorientation which characterises these novels. A distinction can be made between spatial confusion caused by perception of contradictory aspects of reality, and spatial confusion produced by the contradictory character of artistic *representations* of that reality. The frequent feeling of *vertigo* which so often assails Turner Hospital's characters, designating the intensely physical experience of a loss of fixed spatial coordinates, stems from two quite distinct sources.

The first variety of vertigo is precipitated by her characters' abrupt awareness of the contiguity of radically incompatible or conflicting social spheres, contradictory worlds which nevertheless share common borders. The photographer Charlie Chang descends into the quarry, a massive open-cut pit which plunges hundreds of meters deep beneath the impoverished inner-city Sydney suburb of Redfern, and extends into a complex of underground tunnels and passages running under the city. He is overcome by "dizziness. He has to crawl back, he has to lean against the cliff face" (LM 93). The quarry gives concrete form to the social injustice of an Australian society of the near future, and at the same time, the threat which this underworld presents to the privileged ruling classes.

A second form of vertigo is provoked by the work of art. In *Charades*, disorderly verbal narratives convey the chaotic form in which events are perceived and registered in human memory. Young Charade, listening to her Aunt Kay's erratic account of the improbable sighting of Charade's long since vanished father, cries: "'Wait, that's a switchback jump. I can't... How did we get to Toronto?' ... 'Aunt Kay, don't do this to me. We're in the refectory with my father, and then suddenly you're – '" (C 156–7). Charade's own lacunary syntax points up the inability of verbal language to deal with the acceleration of the narrative and the consequent spatial rifts that are thus opened up. Lucy, an older Lucia, experiences a new form of vertigo upon seeing one of Charlie Chang's postmodern arthouse films, a "mutational collage" of Queensland rain-forest, Salgado photos of Mexican open-cut mines and paintings from the Vatican. The voice-over commentary shocks her: "It is unmistakeably Charlie's voice. It reaches me from outside of time, it echoes, it causes vertigo and pain... The lens catches the braided water where it twists into a whorl around two boulders. I am looking into the eye of the whirlpool... Now, as though swaying or drunk, I seem to lose my footing or perspective... very clever, Charlie, though you're making me lose my sense of balance" (LM 58). Charlie's film juxtaposes places geographically separate, and peoples them with persons long since vanished, persons who never met in reality; the connections made deeply disturb Lucy's sense of order and reality. The narrator of *Oyster* is aware of the same potential of narrative topsy-turvy, warning the reader that "the facts may seem to float loose in a sequence of their own devising, much as a bunch of helium-filled ballons, their strings all reached from the same hand at the same moment in time... will certainly not reach you in a cluster... Some will veer north or south and never reach you at all. Some will spin on contrary winds and come back to you, days later, from further on" (O 6–7). In this novel it is not only the characters who are confronted with bewildering narratives; the reader too is explicitly identified as being caught in the same dilemma. The very idea of vertigo as an aberrant experience suggests that the *desire* for spatial order is deep-seated, rooted in a physical sense of orientation long before becoming affective or psychological. That characters such as Charade express dismay at the odd twists and turns of her Aunt Kate's story, that the narrator of *Oyster* believes it necessary to warn the reader of impending narrative dispersion, speak for the strong urge, in Turner Hospital's narratives, to put things in their right place, to understand the world.

The Hermeneutic Drive

The forms of vertigo provoked by spatial dislocation in these novels presume a spatial order in representations of the world, but paradoxically, testify to the illusory character of that order: the moment of giddiness arises from the discovery that assumptions of spatial fixity are inadequate versions of reality because partial, in the double sense of *biased*, on the one hand, and of *incomplete*, on the other. Jess, for instance, claims that linear narrative is based on an occlusion of the narrator's view point; if a different viewpoint is chosen, the linear progression which will emerge will be very different: "I do know that time does not run in a straight line, and never has. It is a capillary system, mapped outwards from whichever pulse point the observer occupies… To put this another way, stepping into a story or constructing a map are much the same thing" (O 47). As John Berger has said, "It is scarcely possible any longer to tell a straight story unfolding in time. And this is because we are too aware of what is continually traversing the storyline *laterally*" (quoted in Soja, 22).

This collapsing of linear narratives into dispersed localised places where versions of reality are constructed perhaps accounts for the frequent switching between first, second and third-person narrative in Turner Hospital's fictions. Yet the idea that apparent linear order is a mere facade to be torn away to reveal an underlying spatial dispersion nonetheless implies the assumption that this underlying disorder also has a governing logic, if one not immediately apparent. The inadequacy of maps to describe the situation of Outer Maroo actually transpires to be motivated by an illegal economic order: Outer Maroo has been erased from the maps so that outsiders will not investigate the shady opal deals taking place there (O 64). It is for this reason, then, that Turner Hospital's novels are inhabited by a powerful hermeneutic drive despite their apparent vitiation of such a paradigm.

The quest which drives the plots of Turner Hospital's fictions ("I'm looking for someone" Charade announces to Koenig at their first meeting [C 4]; Lucy is searching for Gabriel, Catherine for Charlie, Charlie for Cat, Mercy goes searching for Brian, Sarah and Nick are searching for their children Amy and Angelo respectively – and the author too describes herself as an "urgent quester" [Hamelin, 106]) is a search for a single, stable place. Lucy is tormented by the problem of determining an originary chronological site where a linear narrative can be anchored and thus made to offer up a logical explanation of subsequent events: "I cannot start there" she says, thinking of Cedar Creek Falls, where Cat's bones were discovered (LM 3). The same search for origins drives Gabriel's similarly spatialised investigation of the underside of Sydney wealth and power. It is the haunting enigma of his parents' estrangement which propels a second version of quest in Turner Hospital's fiction, the question of "how to read meaning in appearances", which Deborah Bowen sees as the author's "fundamental concern" (Bowen, 184). Gabriel's effort to uncover the reality behind appearances leads him into a wider-ranging interrogation of "something lurking beneath his father's dogma: heresy perhaps; a countertruth; a lie" which in turn becomes a dangerous investigation into the covet "backroom-back-stairs-off-the-record" activities of Sydney's respectable ruling classes; when his investigations into business concerns become too penetrating, he himself vanishes into the obscurity which conceals the criminal activities of the rich (LM 265–6). The vertical metaphors of interpretative depth are ubiquitous: "Gabriel mapped the quarry", "the city's *underside*", the literal underside of the illegal operations of the likes of judge His Honour Robinson Gray, just as the underground opal mines of Oyster's Reef are the literal underside of Andrew Godwin's and Dukke Prophet's shady financial dealing with American hamburger concerns, Singapore jewel wholesalers and arms traders (LM 265, 199; my emphasis). Lucy as temporary prostitute and erstwhile quarry-dweller claims to have "always wanted to mail my own notes from underground. I want to see the nether side of our cities and send back word" (LM 19). Finally, the search for chronological origins or the reality behind appearances takes on an ethical as well as an interpretative character. Says Lucy: "You do actually meet people who make you want to keep on looking" – "Looking for what?" – "Oh you know, *goodness*, *meaning*, crap like that. One throw in a hundred" (LM 33). This assertion of "redemptive" meaning, as Charlotte Clutterbuck has noticed, is the apex of the paradoxical prominence of search in narratives which otherwise display purely contingent, constantly shifting spatial parameters (Clutterbuck, 121).

These narratives do not dispute the reality of the historical events which generate their narratives or their narration. In *Charades*, the disappearance of Verity Ashkenazy's parents in the concentration camps, which indirectly leads to Charade being abandoned by her parents Verity and Nicholas; in *The Last Magician*, the death of Willy, the rape of Cat and Charlie and Catherine after Cat's trial, and the subsequent presumed murder of Cat; in *Oyster*, the arrival of Oyster in Outer Maroo and the destruction of his religious clan – these are the traumatic events out of which the narratives flow, and without which narrative would not be initiated. But their traumatic force, generating pain and guilt, is such that they can never be related with any semblance of factual objectivity. Such events can only ever be told from several mutually exclusive narratives vantage-points, and often at several removes.

Thus the hermeneutic urge has an extraordinarily problematic position in the fiction of Turner Hospital. It presupposes the capacity of narrative to offer up identity, truth, unambiguous chains of causal connection, and distinct separation of time and place at which and in which events "take place". But this urge is embedded in a narrative whose voices are multiple, dispersed, contradictory, and which never tire of pointing this out to the reader. To foreground such narrative relativity and plurality clearly strips away the facade of fallacious objectivity, but it may also vitiate the possibility of any reliable place from which a critique of illusion and ideology may be launched. Kate Temby claims of *The Last Magician*, "the novel's self-conscious questioning and metafictional narrative form subvert the possibility of its providing a comprehensive or effective critique of oppressive power structures" (Temby, 47). The erosion of singular spatiality in her fiction also furnishes a new and unexpected variety of truth guarantee. The resolution of this contradiction can perhaps be achieved, though never completely, her texts suggest, by playing off the spatial disruptions of narrative art against the spatial disruptions of social reality.

Spatial Interpretation

Most forms of identity are structured by an exclusive either/or: A = Non-B. Janette Turner Hospital resists such dualistic constructions of truth. Professor Koenig, for instance, is fascinated by the idea that two mutually contradictory theories can both be right, and consequently comes to the paradoxical conclusion that he was, on the one hand, never married to his elusive ex-wife, and on the hand, will never cease to married to her (C 94, 210); likewise, Bea say to Charades, at the end of the novel: "Verity's your mother. But me and Nicholas made you, that's the truth" (C 285). The wealthy citizens of Sydney delude themselves that their comfortable neighbourhoods are safely sealed off from the threatening world of the quarry, and implement such wishful thinking by a ruthless politics of "triage". But in reality, Lucy claims:, "The quarry is leaking into the city, and the city is slipping quarrywards. Everyone knows this, but everyone denies it. The quarry is growing, imperceptibly, relentlessly, inch by inch". Dualistic social order is based upon the officially sanctioned violence of "containment"; the mutual contamination of these two opposed terms cannot however be halted (LM 89–90). These versions of truth based on binary oppositions are replaced in Turner Hospital's fiction by less reductive triangular structures.

Charlie's obsessive photography expands the dual subject-object gaze into a third dimension as the original moment of perception is re-run and subject to scrutiny: Charlie claims to take photos ("So I'll see what I've seen." LM 36). Lucy's narrative opens with a similar example of self-reflection: "In the middle of the journey, I came to myself in a dark wood where the straight way was lost... *Ah, how hard a thing it is to tell of that wood*" (LM 3). Her self-recognition, self-recollection is provoked by the mediating influence of Charlie's film, and reinforced by the emphatic secondary mediation of Dante's epic, and by more discrete mediation of her own problematic attempt at narrative. Whether the doubling of the self by virtue of the mediating instance (listener in the case of narrative, or photograph in the case of visual art) the same effect ensues: with the creation of self-reflexivity, distance, a new form of self-knowledge is produced.

Not only self-knowledge, but also knowledge of others, can be gained in this way. Both Charlie in *The Last Magician* and Jess in *Oyster* are silent characters whose reserve provokes others to "colonise silence with their unburdenings" ("Silence, Charlie said, seduces"), "a wall or a boulder, or perhaps as a rock cavern in the breakaways, hollow, receptive, capable of the infinite absorption of sound, a black hole that gave nothing back" (LM 83, O 165). Faced with an apparently impassive silence, the garrulous reveal themselves. The listener is at once intercalary surface (like Koenig for Charades) and careful observer. A more active form of production of knowledge, and another clear example of triangular structures of knowledge, is that utilised by Charlie with his enigmatic Chinese riddles, or equally, his photographic collages.

These conundrums oblige the hearers or spectators to create a meaning out of the rebus with which they are confronted, a meaning is of their own making. The riddle-teller or artist can then read off the meaning produced out of the interaction between art, spectator and artist-observer. Charlie's photo-montages offer various potential meanings which are not directly stated, but which the spectator must assemble her – or himself: "There is no order, no sequence... The sequence is determined by the viewer, a magician of sorts, who must shuffle the crossed destinies and read the cards. Meaning is in the eye of the beholder..." (LM 243). Accordingly, a New York neighbour in the same apartment building feels himself publicly exposed by one of Charlie's photo exhibitions which unwittingly features the children he has sexually abused; similarly, Robinson Gray tacitly admits guilt when confronted by Lucy's juxtaposition of photos of Gabriel, of Sheba with Cat's hair clip, and of herself at Cedar Creek Falls. "So you know", says Gray, producing, by his own implicit confession, the potential knowledge to be gained from the photos' mute contiguity and suggestion of causal connection (LM 233, 339). The references to Hamlet in this novel are no coincidence, pointing as they do towards indices of guilt (LM, 32, 71).

Charlie's collage art produces knowledge by a process of combination and juxtaposition (one thinks of Nietzsche's "Denken ist ein Herausheben" [Nietzsche, 30]). The description of Charlie's flat might equally well apply to the artworks it contains: "Space. That is what the apartment celebrates: the mysterious quality of space, and the way it draws attention to single objects placed judiciously within it, and the way these isolated objects, in turn, give space a form" (LM 46). Both the relations within the artwork, and between artwork and spectator are productive of knowledge. Here, knowledge is not an inert pre-existent entity to be absorbed in the way one might learn facts or dates or vocabulary, but is produced in ways that cannot be predicted or controlled by contingent interactions and relationships. Charlie's collages exemplify a form of spatial knowledge based on relations of contiguity, rather than the relations of identity inherent in "objective" knowledge (see Pred). The collage method is thus entirely contextual, both in the possible relations asserted by the mute juxtaposition of images, and by the specific, local place of production of knowledge. Robinson Gray's "So you know" proves nothing, it is not a form of objective knowledge; it is far more subjective, or better, intersubjective. It is no coincidence that Turner Hospital cites Werner Heisenberg – "What we observe is not nature itself, but nature exposed to our method of questioning" (C 288) – for the mode of triadic knowledge which her fiction dramatises is productive, local, contingent and always inherently social.

Janette Turner Hospital's fictional artworks offer a riposte to the pessimism of a critic such as Peter Zima, who claims that Brechtian *Verfremdung*, as an exemplary form of the cognitive-critical role played by art in the era of modernism, has today lost the stable site from which it could unmask ideology: all that is left to it is to cater to aesthetic enjoyment or to figure as "provocation without truth content" (Zima, 255). Her fiction points to a way out of this bleak alternative. Accepting that there is no "outside" of textuality, or of the power mechanisms of late capitalism, for that matter, Turner Hospital creates a new form of the "critical distance" upon which, according to Fredric Jameson, left cultural politics has traditionally depended and which seems to have been abolished in the cultural space of postmodernism (Jameson, 48; see also Chambers, xi–xx). Turner Hospital herself comments upon the situation of her narrators *in media res* ("Letter to a New York Editor", 562) or as Lucy says, "the way the teller inserts herself into the tale" (LM 71). She renews aesthetic critical distance by installing a refraction of disparate vantage-points within the shifting and multiple outlooks of contemporary culture. It is a mode of knowledge which, like her novels, offers no final answers, no dialectical closure or resolution of contradictions, but rather an open-ended dialogue and experimentation: a mode of knowledge which is thus resolutely postmodern, following Hutcheon's anti-dialectical characterisation of the concept. (Hutcheon, x). As Lucy says, "All I can do is feel my way, advancing, retreating, positing theories, testing, rejecting, going in circles and always covering new ground. Everything I say is provisional... I spin my webbed translations as I go" (LM 85) (see also Callahan, 74–76, 79–80).

To David Malouf's simile of confusing telephone conversations in which time and space are simultaneously telescoped and fragmented, Janette Turner replies with the concept of "multiple exposure." Felicity in *Borderline* describes, in a way which prefigures Charlie Chang of *The Last Magician*, "her night-time collages, a multiple exposure, a Perugino superimposed on a Bosch or a Munch" (*Borderline*, 35). An apparently singular visual artefact encompasses pluralised temporal and spatial relationships which are at once radically incommensurate and productive of meaning when taken up by an observer. Felicity's life itself has been "multiple-exposure life" (*Borderline*, 16) and the reader senses that this is the way in which Turner Hospital conceives her own nomadic existence, the creative process by which her novels are written, and the model she proposes for modes of social interaction in the new local-global society in which we now live.

Russell West
University of Lüneburg

Works Cited

Albertazzi, Silvia. "Beautiful Travellers: Some Notes on Postmodern Fiction", *Commonwealth Essays and Studies*, 11:2 (Spring 1989) 53–62.

Anzieu, Didier. *Une Peau pour la pensée: Entretiens avec Gilbert Tarrab*. Paris: Clancier-Guérard, 1986.

Beck, Ulrich. *Risikogesellschaft. Auf dem Weg in eine andere Moderne*. Frankfurt/Main: Suhrkamp, 1986.

———. *Was ist Globalisierung?* Frankfurt/Main: Suhrkamp, 1997.

Bowen, Deborah. "Borderline Magic: Janette Turner Hospital and Transfiguration by Photography", *Studies in Canadian Literature/Etudes en littérature canadienne*, 16:2 (1991), 182–96.

Brydon, Diana. "The Stone's Memory: An Interview with Janette Turner Hospital", *Commonwealth Novel in English*, (Spring 1991), 14–23.

Callahan, David. "Acting in the Public Sphere and the Politics of Memory in Janette Turner Hospital", *Tulsa Studies in Women's Literature*, 15:1 (1996), 73–81.

Carter, Paul. *Living in a New Country: History, Travelling and Language*. London: Faber, 1992.

Carter, Paul. *The Lie of the Land*. London: Faber, 1996.

———. *The Road to Botany Bay: An Essay in Spatial History*. London: Faber, 1988.

Chambers, Ross. *Room for Maneuver: Reading (the) Oppositional (in) Narrative*. Chicago: Chicago University Press, 1991.

Clutterbuck, Charlotte. "A Shared Depository of Wisdom: Connection and Redemption in *The Tiger in the Tiger Pit* and *Possession*", *Southerly*, 52:3 (June 1993), 121–29.

Cowley, Julian. "'Violent Times': Janette Turner Hospital's Art of Memory and the History of the Present", in *Image and Power: Women and Fiction in the Twentieth Century*, Ed. Sarah Sceats and Gail Cunningham. London: Longman, 1996, 173–83.

Drew, Philip. *The Coast Dwellers: A Radical Reappraisal of Australian Identity*. Ringwood: Penguin, 1994.

Gillet, Sue. "Charades: Searching for Father Time: memory and the Uncertainty Principle", *New Literatures Review*, 21 (Summer 1991), 68–81.

Hamelin, Christine. "'Novelist as Urgent Quester': An Interview with Janette Turner Hospital", *Australian and New Zealand Studies in Canada*, 9 (June 1993), 106–11.

Harvey, David. *The Condition of Postmodernity: An Enquiry into the Origins of Cultural Change*. Oxford: Basil Blackwell, 1989.

Huggan, Graham. "Orientalism Reconfirmed? Stereotypes of East-West Encounters in Janette Turner Hospital's *The Ivory Swing* and Yvon Rivard's *Les Silences du corbeau*", *Canadian Literature* 16:2 (1991) 182–96.

Hutcheon, Linda. *A Poetics of Postmodernism: History, Theory, Fiction*. London: Routledge, 1988.

Jameson, Fredric. *Postmodernism, or, The Cultural Logic of Late Capitalism*. London/New York: Verso, 1992.

Lotman, Jurij M. *Die Struktur des künstlerischen Textes*, Trans. Rainer Grübel, Walter Kroll and Hans-Ebehard Seidel. Frankfurt/Main: Suhrkamp, 1973.

Malouf, David. *The Conversations at Curlew Creek*. London: Chatto and Windus, 1997.

Muecke, Stephen, with Paddy Roe and Krim Benterrak. *Reading the Country: Introduction to Nomadology*. Fremantle: Fremantle Arts Centre Press, 1984.

Nietzsche, Freidrich. *Die nachgelassenen Fragmente: Eine Auswahl*, Ed. Günter Wohlfart. Stuttgart: Reclam, 1996.

Pons, Xavier. "History and Her Story: The Deconstruction and Reconstruction of the Past in Janette Turner Hospital's *Charades*", *Caliban*, 29 (1992), 145–55.

Pred, Allan. "Re-Presenting the Extended Present Moment of Danger: A Meditation on Hypermodernity, Identity and the Montage Form", in *Space and Social Theory: Interpreting Modernity and Postmodernity*, Ed. Georges Benko and Ulf Strohmeyer. Oxford: Blackwell, 1997, 117–40.

Schenkel, Elmar. *Sense of Place: Regionalität und Raumbewußtsein in der neueren britischen Lyrik*. Tübingen: Niemeyer, 1993.

Soja, Edward W. *Postmodern Geographies: The Reassertion of Space in Critical Social Theory*. London: Verso, 1989.

Temby, Kate. "Gender, power and postmodernism in *The Last Magician*", *Westerly*, 40:3 (Spring 1995), 47–55.

Turner Hospital, Janette. "Letter to a New York Editor", *Meanjin*, 47:3 (Spring 1988), 562.

———. *Borderline*. London: Virago, 1990.

———. *Charades*. London: Virago, 1983.

———. *Oyster*. London: Virago, 1996.

———. *The Last Magician*. London: Virago, 1992.

Virilio, Paul. *Esthétique de la disparition* [1980]. Paris: Livre de poche/Biblio essais, 1994.

———. *L'Espace critique*. Paris: Christian Bourgeois, 1984.

———. *Vitesse et politique: Essai de dromologie*. Paris: Galilée, 1977.

Zima, Peter V. *Modern/Postmoderne: Gesellschaft, Philosophie, Literatur*. Tübingen/ Basel: Francke/UTB, 1997.

Part IV
NORTH AMERICA

18

Demons and Martyrs

This essay deals with the historical evolution of Quebec's English-speaking minority, and the community's changing relationship with the francophone majority. Beginning with the conquest of La Nouvelle-France by British soldiers in 1759, it analyzes the changing reality and perceptions of the English-speaking population. A historical and personal perspective is given, the essay weaves the author's personal experiences as an artist and writer with the social reality of Montreal in the 1980s and 1990s.

Given the hegemony of the English language in the 21st century, it may be difficult to imagine cultural anxiety in an anglophone population. Yet the English-speaking minority of predominantly francophone Quebec is surely an example of a community suffering the strain of minority status, and a dwindling minority at that. The province of Quebec comprises less than a quarter of Canada's total population. Quebec is a minority within predominantly English-speaking Canada, with a population of seven million, with 1.2 million living in the city of Montreal. Within Montreal, specific neighbourhoods – the West Island, Westmount, Town of Mount Royal, Plateau Mont-Royal – are home of some 500,000 Montrealers whose mother tongue is English. Born in Canada, half of them have cultural roots in the British Isles, 10 per cent are Jewish, the rest hark back to Europe, Asia, the Central Caribbean and the United States. Fewer in number than the polyglot population of immigrant Montreal whose first language is neither English nor French, English-speaking Montrealers are a diverse and dispersed minority with stronger ties to profession and personal culture than to the political entity of Quebec. In an effort to get an analytical grip on this segment of the population, experts have lumped together and christened them "anglophones". It's a clumsy word, but a useful one, for whether they know it or not, regardless of when their ancestors arrived, what they believe, or when they will leave, these anglophones do share a 200-year history, or at least the burden of that history. In the eyes of francophone nationalists whose goal is to remove Quebec from the federation of Canada, they are a democratic block – rich, grim-faced NON voters responsible for the meager (50.57 per cent) victory of the status quo in the 1995 referendum on Quebec independence.

Regardless of their personal histories, Quebec anglophones carry the baggage of those conquering British who started the whole story with the conquest of la Nouvelle-France in 1759. In the iconography of national liberation, they are Demons, as surely as the forces they passively defeated are Martyrs. The Demonization of Quebec anglophones, how it happened and why, is an essential part of the Quebecois psyche. Where it will lead, how long the demons will burn, is a subject which has interested me from the moment I moved to Quebec following the first referendum on Quebec independence in 1980.

The oldest Anglo-Saxon names in the Montreal phone-book go back to the Fraser Highlanders, officers and soldiers who stayed on after they had helped General James Wolfe win the battle of the Plains of Abraham in 1759. Fresh from the din of Culloden, they took off their red coats, accepted free land, married *Canadiennes* and, in a generation or two, disappeared into francophone society. They and subsequent waves of British immigrants who chose assimilation, account for the Daniel Johnsons, Claude Ryans, the LaHaye/Leahys, Silvain/Sullivans, Nolin/Nolins, Martin/Martins and so many other anomalies among *les grands noms* of Quebec. Hard on the heels of the francophile Highlanders came a group of English-speakers for whom assimilation was never an option. From Scotland, England and New England, some one hundred merchants poured into the new colony to service the British Army, eager to pick up when most members of the French commercial class left for France. With excellent contacts and credit in England and the US, these camp followers soon became a powerful lobby. In the decade following the conquest, these merchants lobbied hard for a political and legal system favouring their business, and they lost.

Locally, their enemy was a high-born Scot, Sir Guy Carleton, Governor of Quebec, who spoke flawless French and chose his bride from the Court of Versailles. An aristocrat, Carleton loathed trade, and deeply admired the quasi-feudal calm of seigneurial life on the banks of the St-Laurent. With the help of his indefatigable connections in London, he bucked the pattern of British colonial policy with the Quebec Act of 1774, by which Parliament guaranteed the French language and civil code, the Roman

Catholic religion, and greatly extended the territory of Quebec, opening up the fur trade westward. No mention of an elected assembly, but then the bishops didn't mind. Behind this extraordinary legislation was the very real fear that 65,000 *Canadiens* might accept Benjamin Franklin's invitation to fight for liberty against the British. So, the looming American Revolution and Carleton's francophilia established the foundation of a civic structure within which *les Canadiens* could grow to become 6 million Quebecois in about 14 generations.

The anglo business class lost in 1774, but they prospered anyway, and they won big in 1867, being the main movers and shakers behind the fusion of five British colonies into the Dominion of Canada. Following the American Revolution, British North America was flooded with refugees, and immigration surpassed even the high birth rate of French Quebec. By 1867, Montreal was a predominantly English-speaking city, population 100,000, and firmly established as the most important commercial centre in North America after New York. With persistent encouragement from their priests, French-speaking Quebecers concentrated on farming, or left for the factories of New England. By 1900, the anglo business elite of Montreal controlled 70 per cent of the wealth in Canada. In addition to banks, railways, shipping lines, breweries, mills and factories, the McGills, McTavishes, Molsons, Redpaths, Aitkens, etc built impressive mansions, hospitals, schools, libraries, museums and galleries.

Their taste and values were conservative, colonial and London-obsessed. Today, when visitors to Montreal comment on its European flavour, they usually say something about the *joie de vivre*, and it is generally agreed that the flavour of Montreal is French. However, the anglo penchant for grand continental lookalikes in architecture, and their inherently conservative twitch, provided the impulse behind civic movements to preserve this past, and not tear it down as many other North American cities did. In terms of saving beautiful old buildings, it helps to have a fading economy, and that's also what happened to Montreal. By the end of World War I, as the source of money and trade shifted from Britain to the United States, Montreal's anglo business class proved rigid, unimaginative, helpless in the face of competition. Some recovered from the crash of 1929, but most often the new generation lived off Old Money, or moved to Toronto. While their dynamism waned, their mythic power soared, a creation of successive generations of nationalist leaders, ranging from the emotive conservative Premier Maurice Duplessis, to novelists, playwrights, historians, editorial writers, stand up comedians and chansonneurs. Period

TV series and even cartoons still carry the requisite token anglo: usually male, overweight, engaged in business, and speaking bad French.

Until the 1960s, the rural and agricultural parish remained the centre of French life and the focus of Quebec politics. English was the language of business and many, although by no means all, large businesses were owned by English-speaking males. In 1961, for the first time, the national census gathered data on wages, and headlines exploded with facts to back up what was popularly known: French-speaking Montrealers earned 66 per cent of what their English-speaking counterparts earned. Another figure was, I think, just as important but got far less publicity. For the 70 per cent of workers earning less than 5,000 dollars annually, i.e. most people, language made no difference. Thus we can see that the census data added to the stereotype of the rich anglo, but in fact, the truth was closer to a class problem – educated well-connected English-speaking males had the advantage. Clearly, the pact struck in 1774 had born results, though results which were to be hotly contested in the twentieth century. To modernists in Quebec, the rural society admired by Carleton and ruled by the Church had been excessively preserved, leaving too much room for English-speaking Quebecers to gain political and financial control. However, the cultural guarantees of the Quebec Act did ensure that a minority language not only survived but flourished.

In a modern economy, money talks. In a modern democracy, numbers count. In the 1960s, when Quebec embarked full force on a modernization campaign, this substantial French-speaking population base, concentrated in a central territory; was an essential element. Called the Quiet Revolution, an intense decade of changes had an impact on society on all levels. I will mention only one barometer, salaries. Using the same categories as quoted above, the average French-speaking wage earner now takes home about 90 per cent of the average English-speaker. This gap disappears altogether if you consider that the mean age of anglophones is higher, therefore they are at the high end of their earning power. The impact of the Quiet Revolution doesn't live by statistics alone, it is visible on the streets: Montreal today looks, sounds, runs in French. The burgeoning provincial civil service is entirely French; the language of business is by law French, and the language of public interaction is instinctively French. While shopping or walking along the street, I would never think to speak English to a stranger – even if it means conversing briefly with an anglo salesperson in French. The city's cultural life is overwhelmingly French, and its success with theatre, music, dance, cinema and even hockey players has earned international acclaim.

Where does this leave the anglo Demons? In reality, their financial and political clout is pretty well gone, their historical presence in Montreal diminished visibly by an ongoing campaign to remove their names from city streets. Still, despite a fading of real power, these financial and political titans hold a fierce mythical power over the soul of Quebec. They may be old or dead, but they are *les Anglais*, incarnations of ancient wounds and grandfathers of everyone who stands in the way of a purely French Quebec. For the anglo population as a whole, change has been radical. On the microcosmic level, a goodly number of actors I worked with in my theatre company have found lucrative work on French TV; one is playing an anglophone lawyer who speaks not so bad French, though he doesn't get the girl. Thirty years of social change and political crisis have had a sharp and two-fold impact on Quebec anglophones. A huge number have left the province, primarily for economic reasons.

The jobs are elsewhere. In the late 1990s, Montreal had the highest unemployment rate of any North American city and the lowest job creation rate. Nearly a fifth of its working-age population received a welfare cheque in 1996, and a quarter of households earned less than 10,000 dollars a year (40,000 FF). Often with families and contacts elsewhere, anglophones were understandably tempted to follow work. Still, brute political insecurity clearly accelerated the flow. In the five years after the 1976 election of the separatist Parti Quebecois, more than 100,000 anglos left, following corporate head offices, friends, and instinct. In almost every professional field, the centralizing, expansionary power of Toronto has bled Montreal. CBC radio and TV English service in 1999 was a fraction of what it was ten years earlier. The once-vital National Film Board operated mainly in French, if at all. A dozen theatre companies were founded and disappeared in that decade, unable to find audiences for edgy new work. Writers have moved to be near the publishing hub, and provincial arts funding favours francophone activity.

Demographers claim the anglophone population has "stabilized", which may be true in strict terms of numbers, but hardly indicates a vital community. Twenty per cent of the anglo population is 60 years or older, 41 per cent are under 25. Given that more than half of all university graduates leave the province, it seems likely that the anglophone population of Montreal will increasingly be dominated by old people and the mobile young, backed up by droves of out-of-province students; Montreal is a wonderfully cheap place to live. Rents are half the price of Toronto, and the bars are open late. But, where are the mortgagees? The theatre-goers? The networkers and social animals and workaholics who make it – sometimes – worth putting up with life in a busy Western city? It's a question few in the shrinking generation can avoid. The other major trend in contemporary anglo Quebec is somewhat more cheery, at least for anyone excited by life, who gets a rush from competing, coping, fighting and winning. There is clear evidence that the camp follower attitude is dead, and the Fraser Highlander spirit is alive and well.

In 1960, less than a quarter of English-speaking Montrealers could speak French. Today, 62 per cent are bilingual – a remarkable change in a remarkably short period of time. A few years ago, visitors complained that French-Canadians all spoke English and you couldn't practice your French on the streets of Montreal. Not true now. Only 34 per cent of francophone Montrealers speak English. Older people and the TV-soaked young are much more likely to know English than the 30 to 55-year-olds, because the school system invests slim resources into second-language teaching, and middle generations were actively discouraged from speaking English. In the anglophone communities, bilingualism is now considered a must, and anyone would be ashamed to admit failure. The tendency of English-speaking parents to send their kids to French schools has weakened their own system gravely, although there is a lot of political rhetoric around protecting the right to English-language education. In 1970, 5 per cent of students in the Protestant School Board of Greater Montreal were in the French-language stream, or French immersion. By 1999, more than 50 per cent were studying in French; and a further 20 per cent were in the French-language system, presumably because their parents felt they would be more fully socialized and learn a proper accent, ready to enter, invisible, into Quebec society.

On the evening of October 30, 1995, I gathered with a party of friends around a TV to watch the results of Quebec's second referendum on independence. Or at least that was the general idea behind the vote. The actual question was somewhat more complex than you'd expect for a Yes or No answer: "Do you agree that Quebec should become sovereign, after having made a formal offer to Canada for a new economic and political partnership, within the scope of the bill respecting the future of Quebec and of the agreement signed on June 12, 1995?" The question assumed familiarity with the complex political strategy underway, or at least hinted that such a strategy existed. Still, the complexity of the question did not deter voters. Ninety-four per cent of eligible voters turned out to cast a ballot, and the result was close: 50.57 per cent NON and 49.43 per cent OUI. A muted sigh of relief, but no cheers in the room. Then the Premier, Jacques Parizeau, came on TV and the sigh became a gasp. His bitterness was palpable. Business leaders and the ethnic vote beat the Quebecois, he said, repeatedly. A few days later he resigned. In fact, 54,000 votes made the difference, but it could have been any 54,000 votes. Leading Francophone businessmen had loudly denounced the OUI side, millions of French-speaking Quebecers voted Non, but Parizeau, in his moment of understandable bitterness, could not resist harking back to an ancient stereotype, could not resist invoking the Demons, those rich smug monolithic Anglais.

When the dust had settled, it soon became clear that the most shocking aspect of Parizeau's statement was its utter, brutal honesty. Without nuance or apology, he exposed the guiding assumption of the independence movement, *circa* 1995, that Quebec sovereignty is an ethnic movement whose enemies are other ethnics. Never once in the campaign did I hear a speech or read an editorial outlining why a bilingual citizen who chose as an adult to live in Quebec, and willingly sent her child to French schools, might feel better governed under the *fleur de lys*, as I had done. In fact, I can think of many good arguments why a Quebec anglo would vote for an independent Quebec. In a global economy, the 19th century nation state is not necessarily the most important boundary. Some kind of an association and dual passport would suit me fine. Still, Parizeau's statement clarified the options. I am not prepared to vote OUI as an act of charity, out of sympathy for victims, when I know very well that the long, tortured history of the Quebecois is far from a tale of brave slaves battling rich indifferent oppressors on their journey to a new unilingual Jerusalem.

Moreover, I suspect that what held the crucial 54,000 francophones back from voting OUI was their sense that it is impossible to give a positive answer to what is essentially a negative question. The demonization, and exclusion of *les autres* in contemporary Quebec may well be the natural gut reaction of a society which has raced from rural Catholic nonindustrial to urban, secular, neo-liberal in the space of barely more than one generation. But it is also evidence that this same society is nowhere ready for the burden of nation-statehood in the jungle of the late 20th century. Demonization is a potent psychic force. It propelled francophones out of civil lethargy and away from a primitive form of Catholicism which was often a hideous tool for social control. But the Quiet Revolution – which seemed pretty loud if you lived through it – has cast too many leading Quebecois minds into an equally primitive form of secular grudge-politics.

Old demons have been replaced by new. Independence still feels more like an exclusive religion than a political movement with the vision and irresistible power to sweep along citizens from all streetcorners. There will be another referendum; Parizeau's successor Lucien Bouchard has promised as much, and vowed that the next referendum will not be called until "winning conditions exist". If a third referendum does somehow succeed in getting a majority OUI vote, an independent Quebec will face, for the first time, the demands of pluralism. The fundamental aims of those who have devoted their lives to the cause include preservation of the French language inside a territory where French is the predominant language of communication, inside an economy which includes a middle-class and offers all citizens a standard of living not too far behind their neighbours. In the global context, with so many more fragile economies attracting brisk business, it is hard to believe the international economy would shrink from opportunities in newly declared, resource-rich country. An independent Quebec would have a substantial well-educated population of young bilingual anglophones ready to embark upon new economic and social challenges. Perhaps these young anglophones, forced by politics to realize that being bilingual is essential, will move into the jobs created by the international global economy. Will they, then, become the New Demons?

Marianne Ackerman
Canadian writer

19
Connecting Past to Present: Louisiana Cajuns and Their Sense of Belonging to An Acadian Diaspora

Many Cajuns claim an Acadian ancestry, despite the fact that their origin can be traced to the different immigrant groups which have settled in Louisiana (French, Acadian, Spanish, Irish, Black and White Creoles...). This sense of belonging appears through the enhancement of a "blood" filiation with the Acadians from the Canadian Maritime Provinces, of a common historic memory based on the "Grand Dérangement" experience (the expulsion of the Acadians by the British in 1755) and of the survival theme. The bond felt with the Canadian Acadians is also based on the sharing of common language and values, and even extends to the perception of a physical resemblance. The notion of an Acadian Diaspora has spread within the Louisiana French revival Movement, and has been fortified by the World Acadian Congresses (in 1994 in New Brunswick and in 1999 in Lafayette).

Cajun culture has many sources. The metaphor most often employed to illustrate this process of creolization is of culinary nature. The *gumbo* is a dish whose every ingredient has a different origin: the basic element, *roux*, is a French technique; *okra* is a vegetable imported from Africa; *filé* has an Native American origin; finally, rice and the other ingredients incorporated (seafood, poultry, pork or wild game) are local products. Cajun last names also show the diversity of this culture's origins. In addition to Acadian surnames (Leblanc, Broussard, Arceneaux...), names reveal a German (Hoffpauir, Shexnayder...), Spanish (Castille, Domingue, Romero...), Scottish (McGee), or White Creole (de La Houssaye, Fontenot...) origin. However, this cultural mix is not always enhanced by Cajuns who tend to increasingly emphasize their Acadian ancestry, thus making it the essential criterion of definition of the group's identity.

After examining the way by which the primacy of Acadian ancestry is expressed, we will see how the Cajuns' sense of belonging extends beyond Louisiana's geographical borders to a community which includes the Maritime Provinces of Canada. We will then attempt to establish the foundation of this ethnic consciousness through the examination of collective history. Finally, we will consider how Acadian identity interacts with American identity.

The Enhancement of Acadian Ancestry

Several factors have led Cajuns to emphasize Acadian ancestry in the definition of their identity. In its efforts to give a positive image of French Louisiana culture, CODOFIL (Council for the Development of French in Louisiana, located in Lafayette) favored the Cajuns' Acadian origin to the detriment of the cultural mix they derive from, thereby influencing their self-definition. Consequently, many Cajuns perceived it as a criterion of definition, whereas they had not taken it into consideration earlier. The Cajuns identification with Acadians is therefore widespread within the whole group, although those who do not refer to it come from the lower class.

The terms "Acadian" and "Cajun" are used as synonyms both inside and outside the group. It is demonstrated in their joint use in official labels: the tourist region called "Cajun country" echoes the official one called "Acadiana", the football team "Ragin' Cajuns" is part of "l'Université des Acadiens"; the state tour guide talks about "Acadians, or Cajuns". The three regional "Acadian cultural centers" have misleading names since the exhibit features Creoles as well. These designations show the persistent assimilation of Louisiana French culture with Cajuns and by extension with Acadians.

Most of the time, the use of "Acadian", without being exclusive, indicates a deliberate desire by the members of the group to draw attention to the importance of Acadian ancestry. Sometimes this emphasis results in making Acadian ancestry a *sine qua non* condition for belonging to the group, to the point where most Cajuns become usurpers. Being Cajun turns out to be the privilege of a restricted population defined by its historical roots, a definition based on a mythic view of the group.

Even though it seldom includes such restrictions, the definition of the group often conceals those who have contributed to the elaboration of Cajun culture, despite the recognition of non-Acadian persons as members of the group. Some consider that "Acadian blood" makes a "real" Cajun, including in this category those who come from intermarriages, while distinguishing them from a "pure" Cajun, who only has Acadian ancestors: one is considered more or less Cajun depending of the number of one's Acadian ancestors. The highlighting of this heritage does not exclude, however, the awareness of a mixed origin and the role of other groups in the constitution of Cajun culture. Many deliberately emphasize their Acadian descent while spontaneously mentioning their other origins. The emphasis indicates a sentimental choice which makes them see themselves as Acadian in spirit.[1]

The craze for genealogical searches is part of the increased interest in Cajun history. The ethnic revival led several Louisiana historians to document whole sections of their overlooked past.[2] This academic trend followed the Civil Rights Movement of the 1960s, which made many American minorities eager to research their origin. The immensely successful publication of *Roots* by Alex Haley in 1976 and the television show which followed contributed to sharpen Americans' interest for their historical and cultural heritage. In Louisiana, Father Donald Hébert wrote in 1974 a genealogical collection of Acadian ancestors which encouraged the population to trace their family ancestry. Available in all local libraries, it is still assiduously used by those who undertake such searches.

These searches are combined with an oral practice of genealogy, by which Cajuns carefully list every person they are related to, without necessarily going back very far. Upon meeting somebody for the first time, Cajuns routinely inquire about each other's name, origin and relatives. Searches beyond Louisiana borders deepen an already keen genealogical memory, omnipresent in social relationships. When I asked a woman from Acadian origin about her husband's identity, French on his father's side and Irish on his mother's side, she pointed out she did not consider herself more Cajun than him:

> We've both been raised with our grandparent's language, we both have the same lifestyle as our families had. (...) So we're basically Cajuns to the same degree.

This attachment to Acadian ancestors is expressed in the recent constitution of genealogical centers. The main one, in downtown St Martinville,[3] opened its doors in 1997. It offers the public an impressive multimedia center which makes tracing Acadian ancestry possible. It also gives access to the history of Acadians from 1604 to the present, as well as biographical notes on each identified Acadian exile who came to Louisiana. The creation of this research center and the information it gives communicate a growing interest in the search for Acadian ancestors and a desire to encourage the local population to take part in it. It seems as though Acadian ancestry is unanimously recognized as a criterion of definition by the local social elite, keen to develop this dimension in the members of the group's self-consciousness, despite the existence of an important social and cultural diversity.

It is interesting to point out that the persons who initiated these projects count few Acadian ancestors. One of them specified she had just one while giving me a passionate account of the Acadian exile. This awareness of a mixed origin does not affect in any way the sense of belonging to the Acadian community.

The Trauma of the *"Grand Dérangement"*

Acadians were the descendants of the first settlers from Northern Europe in the New World. They were French peasants, mainly from Poitou and its neighboring regions. In 1632, these immigrants crossed the Atlantic to settle in Acadia (present-day Nova Scotia). At this time, hostilities between France and England were constant and Acadia changed hands several times. It eventually became English with the Treaty of Utrecht in 1713. Steadfast in their neutrality, Acadians were left largely alone until 1755 when the Seven Years War started between the French and the English. Suspected of embracing the French cause, they were given an ultimatum to take an oath of allegiance to the British Crown. Upon the Acadians' refusal, the British military governor, Charles Lawrence, finally chose a radical solution – their deportation.

Among the 12 000 Acadians, 6 000 to 8 000 were imprisoned, then expelled and herded into boats in order to be dispersed in the English colonies. These expeditions were fatal to many prisoners, devastated by epidemics, cold and malnutrition. Groups were shipped to the Carolinas, Georgia, Massachusetts, Connecticut, Pennsylvania and New York. Many survivors, as well as those who had fled to Canada or to New Brunswick, moved back to Nova Scotia as early as the 1760's. There, they survived in misery before being able to resettle in the whole Maritimes after the war. Some returned to France, taking advantage of an agreement between English and France. Unable to adapt, they decided to leave for Louisiana in 1785. Others, in search of a welcoming land, took refuge in the French

West Indies, particularly in St Domingo, before heading to Louisiana which they reached in successive waves between 1764 and 1785.

The hardships suffered during this tragic episode, dubbed the "Grand Dérangement," laid the foundations of a common identity for Acadians. Even though not all of them experienced deportation, Acadians as a group share the memory of exile and persecution. This dispersal is associated with sites and characters endowed with an emblematic status. In Nova Scotia, Grand Pré, the historic site of the departure for many prisoners, and the church where the Acadians were imprisoned, have become potent markers. Acadians of the Maritimes rebuilt a commemorative church in 1922 at the same place where the original church had stood and have made it a National Historical Park. All Cajuns who have been to Grand Pré remember their visit with deep emotion.

Strongly connected with the heartbreak of the Acadians, whose families were separated as they were boarded on ships, the American poet Longfellow's heroine Evangeline is logically listed amongst the emblematic characters. The heroine's statue, dedicated in Grand Pré, since 1920 makes a pair with the one in St Martinville, as a sign of the twinning of both of these places of memory. The remembrance of the "Grand Dérangement" has become a main element of the official collective history both in the Maritime Provinces and in Louisiana. In Cajun Country, activist organizations and museums also play an important role. The film *Acadie Liberté* is screened at the Acadian Cultural Center in Lafayette and at meetings of ethnic associations. It carefully traces the course of the Acadians from France and extensively documents the deportation. Recently, a new museum was created in Abbeville, south of Lafayette, which is devoted to all Acadian settlements, including Prince Edward Island, Maryland and Nantes. The genealogical center in St Martinville is part of a project put together by the Acadian Memorial Foundation. It contains a mural representing the arrival of Acadians in Louisiana and a list of 3000 names of persons identified as Acadian refugees, as well as an eternal flame in tribute to the exiles who perished at sea.[4] Kinship by blood and memory of the deportation are then extolled, inviting Cajuns to think of themselves as Acadians.[5]

The expulsion of Acadians has left such a deep wound in memories that the terms to name it are borrowed from the deportation of Jews by the Nazis. References to the "holocaust", a "genocide", Halifax "concentration camps" are frequently used by Cajun activists. Some also compare the

"Grand Dérangement" with the "ethnic cleansing" in Kosovo and Rwanda. The celebration of the first Acadian World Congress in Moncton, marked the 390st anniversary of the foundation of Acadia. It called on to "the cousins of the great scattered Acadian family" and gathered more than 300 000 Acadians from the Maritime Provinces, Louisiana, France, and Quebec.[6] It awakened the Acadian awareness of musician Zachary Richard, who started to write songs in French again and created the cultural association *Action cadienne* (Cajun Action). Recently, a bilingual newsletter created by young activists was explicitly entitled *L'Acadjin*. The French spelling "cadjin" is sometimes used to name Cajuns. World Congresses planned every 4 years are in this regard an opportunity to instill and develop the notion of diaspora by regularly commemorating the "Grand Dérangement".[7]

Descent and history happen to be essential factors in the constitution of an ethnic identity. The objective link with the past matters little compared to the importance attached to it (Weber, 1922; Alba, 1990). Ethnicity then cannot be separated from a significant perception of descent and of a common history which unifies and extends it. This historical memory is grounded in the evocation of a past which makes the Acadians martyrs as well as rebellious and resistant human beings.

Surviving Adversity

Forged by the hardship endured throughout their history, survival is seen as a common value for all Acadians and defines their contemporary identity. The perseverance showed by Acadians throughout the centuries is constantly invoked to praise them as "survivors". As a result of their resistance, the independence of the group is constantly underlined. Folklorists and historians often present it as the Acadians' main characteristic (Brasseaux, 1987, Ancelet, 1991). In Acadia, their political independence kept them from giving up against British government threats, and also from joining the French cause. In Louisiana, their history was marked by economic independence and territorialism, combined with anticlericalism (Brasseaux, 1987).

Cajun activists not only emphasize the historic basis of resistance but also strive to embody it in their actions. Some elements symbolize the adoption of this attitude, such as the rooster, emblem of Cajun Action, or the language used by activists. Words (used in French) like "brave", "valorous", "proud" punctuate mail and brochures, while "Dear fighters", "Don't drop it" – from the local expression "Don't drop the potato", which means "Don't give up" – urge the members of the association to be perseverant and determined in their action. Among the group, oft-used attributes refer to independence and resistance as well: *"avoir la tête dure"* (to be hard-headed) defines a person who refuses to back down. *"Canaille"* refers to a mischievous, cunning person, who has more than one trick up his sleeve. It is often employed in a friendly way but can also express a certain duplicity.

As a symbol of Cajuns and consequently of "Cajun Country", the crawfish shares the same quality of "survivor". This omnivorous animal adapts to all environments. Similarly, Cajuns describe themselves as people who eat everything and enjoy joking about it. Pugnacious and fearless, the crawfish resists its attackers by brandishing its claws, just as Cajuns have resisted oppression, from the time of the "Grand Dérangement" until the banishment of French in schools at the beginning of the century.[8]

The perception of common values among Acadians from the Maritime Provinces and Cajuns testifies to the Acadian ability to survive. An essential factor is their faithfulness to Catholicism. Along with the attachment to land and family, Catholicism appears in historical studies as a key value of Acadians.[9] Acadians and Cajuns feel they are united by the same devotion, an affiliation symbolized by two eternal flames (one in St Martinville, the most recent in Erath). The ceremony held in St Martinville to light the flame took place on a Sunday and started with a procession led by the city's priest who blessed the flame, a "traditional element of the Catholic Church rituals".[10]

The feeling of sharing similar values is combined with genetic ties established within the Acadian population. The World Congress in Lafayette included a conference specifically devoted to this subject. The conference sought to « increase awareness of the unique genetic history of the Acadian people resulting from their story of survival ».[11] These bonds encouraged belief in the existence of physical resemblance between Cajuns and Acadians. During their stay in New Brunswick, many Cajuns were struck by such similarities, to the point that they referred to "doubles" or "doppelgangers" and had the disconcerting feeling never to have left Louisiana. The perception of common physical features, linked to the identification with Acadian ancestors, has encouraged those who funded one of the historical characters of the Memorial in St Martinville to physically represent their ancestor by posing for the artist.[12] As numerous as the

signs of the feeling of belonging to an Acadian diaspora are, as strong as
the desire to develop it further may appear, this self-awareness never comes
into conflict with the Cajuns' American identity.

The Duality of American Identity

The supporters of bilingual programs are far from willing to isolate themselves and strive to avoid any misunderstanding: they insist that these programs are an asset and not an obstacle to their integration in American
society. The oaths of allegiance which systematically open the meetings of
all Cajun cultural associations show their fidelity to the American social
contract. The members of these associations do not see any contradiction
in promoting Cajun culture while participating in festival parades with the
American flag on their float. During the Gulf War, one could read on the
floats signs proclaiming "We support our troops".

> I guess the best way to put it is that we're Americans, mais on est pas amé-
> ricains!,

Asserting their cultural specificity and enhancing it is even interpreted by
some Cajuns as an American feature. In a letter addressed to the Acadian
Memorial, a man wrote: "Thanks to your efforts, we can now be proud.
From now we are perceived as a society which has the true American spirit
of freedom".[13] The tribute to the deported Acadians and the celebration
of the survival of the Acadian community represented by the Memorial
are considered by Cajuns to be true American values. The fight for freedom and the struggle against oppression are proofs of their spirit of independence, which defines all Americans. Cajuns have developed a sense of
belonging to an Acadian community with the Acadians of the Maritime
Provinces of Canada. This feeling has significantly increased over the past
years, both caused and strengthened by Acadian World Congresses (the
next one will be held in 2004, in Nova Scotia).[14] This sense of belonging,
although increasingly widespread, is not shared by all Cajuns. Just like
other identity markers, this one is not unanimously adopted. Some never
refer to it, in particular those at the bottom of the social ladder, although
in itself it does not imply a strict and exclusive social division. Certain
groups favor it only in certain contexts, stressing the situational nature
of ethnic identity. Other groups like the Creoles, long overshadowed by
Cajuns in the local image of French Louisiana culture, claim their distinct
African descent against a uniform vision of French Louisianians. However, the sense of belonging to an Acadian diaspora represents an essential

element in the way Cajuns define themselves, as well as in the collective history of French Louisiana as a whole.

Sara Le Ménestrel
Centre National de la Recherche Scientifique

Works cited

Alba, Richard D., *Ethnic Identity: The Transformation of White America*, London: Yale University Press, 1990.

Ancelet, Barry et al., *Cajun Country*, Jackson: University of Mississippi Press, 1991.

Brasseaux, Carl A, *The Founding of New Acadia: The Beginnings of Acadian Life in Louisiana 1765–1803*, Baton Rouge: L.S.U. Press, 1987.

———. *Acadian to Cajun. Transformation of a People, 1803–1877*, Jackson: University Press of Mississippi, 1994.

Le Ménestrel, Sara, 1999, *La voie des Cadiens. Tourisme et identité en Louisiane*, Paris: Belin, collection Cultures américaines, 1999.

———. "Bienvenue au pays cadien. L'essor du tourisme culturel dans les petites villes franco-louisianaises", numéro spécial, "Tourisme en villes", *Espaces et sociétés*, n⁰ 100, p. 35–55, 2000

Mouton, Todd, "Going back to Acadie", *The Times of Acadiana*, 14, July 13, pp. 13–17, 1994.

Sollors, Werner, *Beyond Ethnicity. Consent and Descent in American Culture*, New York: Oxford Press, 1986.

Weber, Max, "Ethnic groups", in W. SOLLORS (ed.), *Theories of Ethnicity. A Classical Reader*, New York: New York University Press, pp. 52–66, 1996 [1922].

Notes

1. The official choice made by activists to use the French spelling "Cadien" for naming the group expresses even more clearly Acadian descent through reading, although the pronunciation sounds different (it is written "Cadien", but pronounced "Cadjin"). Also, categories offered by the Census reinforce the association of Cajuns with Acadians. French-Louisiana can identify themselves as "Acadian", "French" and/or "French Canadian", but not as "Cajun". This category gathers without distinction everyone who identifies with "Acadian" as well as those who preferred to use the term "Cajun".

2. Cf the work of the Center for Louisiana Studies of U. L.L (University of Louisiana in Lafayette), and of C. Brasseaux in particular.

3. A little community East of Lafayette.

4. The mural of the Memorial is twinned with the one situated rue des Acadiens, in Nantes, which represents the departure of Acadians refugees who left France in 1785 to settle in Louisiana. Both were painted by the same artist from Lafayette, Robert Dafford.

5. A Cajun lawyer from Lafayette, also present-day president of CODOFI, presented a petition to the Queen of England in January 1990 urging the government to officially recognize that Governor Lawrence had acted in contravention of British and international rules of the time.

6. 1994, *Programme préliminaire des conférences du Congrès mondial Acadien*, 2nd édition, p. 3.

7. During the Congress in Lafayette in 1999, a priest from New Brunswick giving a presentation at the Memorial exhorted the audience to "sow Acadia". Suiting the action to the word, he offered everybody small bottles of sand he had brought from his home.

8. A legend makes the crawfish the embodiment of Acadians by incorporating it to their historic memory: it would come from lobsters of Nova Scotia which, at the time of the deportation, swam to follow their companions. Exhausted by their trip, they arrived in Louisiana greatly diminished, turned into crawfish.

9. The present-day religious practices of Cajuns reveal the persistence of this devotion, characterized by a limited role accorded to the clergy. The Mardi Gras ritual celebrated in some rural communities of Cajun Country (different from the one in New Orleans or Lafayette), the king cake, the whitening of the tombs for All Saints Day, the abstaining of eating meat during Lent and Good Friday and its celebration through crawfish boil are proofs of the respect of the religious calendar.

10. 1995, program of ceremony of the lightening of the eternal flame.

11. 1999, Program of the conference, Lake Charles.

12. This feeling of sharing a common identity and values, revived by the World Congress, motivates Acadian touristic networks to target Louisiana as a favorite customer.

13. 1993, *Calling all Cajuns*, letter of information, St Martinville, Acadian Memorial Foundation.

14. Besides, interactions with the Acadians from the Maritimes Provinces at these gatherings have fueled the desire of Cajuns to improve their language skills. As a result, they increasingly take part in immersion programs, such as the one offered by University of Ste Anne in Nova Scotia. However, it is too early to evaluate the extent of this new trend.

20
Remembering Difference:
Living in Two Languages

The minority groups in a country often ask themselves the questions "Who are we? and "How can we keep and protect our culture?" The Franco-Americans in the state of Maine in the United States are no different from other minorities in their search for meaning as to what being Franco-American really signifies and how they can preserve their traditions. For the French Canadian immigrants in Maine the French language connects members of a community into an information sharing network with formidable collective powers.

Growing up in two linguistic spheres while having many advantages can also create problems of self-definition. For Franco-Americans who immigrated to the New England area in the United States, the answer to the complex question of cultural identity lies intertwined in the history and mix of the French and English languages, the Catholic religion, and the French-Canadian/Quebecois socio-cultural background. By examining the relationship of the two languages spoken by Franco-Americans and by studying how each reign over a particular realm of the speaker's existence is it perhaps possible to find solutions to the problem of collective identity. Romano Guardini in Pierre Jakez-Hélias' book *Le Cheval d'Orgueil* stated that "the language a man speaks is the world in which he lives and interacts; it belongs to him in a more profound and essential way than the earth and the things he calls his country."[1] (my translation)

The term *Franco-American* or *Franco* for short is used in this paper "solely to designate an American of French-Canadian or Acadian ancestry."[2] This definition is taken from Denis Ledoux in *Lives in Translation, An Anthology of Contemporary Franco-American Writings*. Ledoux also explains that strictly speaking *Franco-American* can designate any American of French-speaking ancestry: French of France or Belgian for example, but in New England it does not carry that connotation. The term itself came into use with an elite group of the French Canadians in the United States towards the end of the 1890's and gained wider acceptance in the 1920's.[3]

In an endeavor to find historical answers to questions raised about the fragmentation of language, I would like to examine a typical Franco-American community, Sanford, Maine, located in the southern part of the state and subsequently a contemporary poem by a Quebecois, Jean Morisset, in order to better understand how the separation of languages functions today. Gerald Brault in his book *The French-Canadian Heritage in New England* lists Sanford as a medium-sized town whose Franco-American population represents a high percentage of the total population.[4] Sanford is also representative in that the influence of the parish priest and the Catholic Church was very strong until the late 1960's, as in so many other towns such as this. A kind of circle of security was wrapped around the people, created through the use of the French language and the bonds of religion. The key figure in the preservation of these ties was the parish priest who, above all, wanted to keep his flock safely under the authority of the Catholic Church and away from what he perceived as the dangers of the Protestant Anglo-Saxon world. Sanford, thus, possesses the main features of many towns and cities settled by French Canadians.

The Franco-American immigrants who settled Sanford in the nineteenth century came to work in the booming shoe factories and textile mills. Most of them spoke little or no English. It was unnecessary to do so as "the move to the south depended as a rule on kinship ties and acquaintance networks developed in the parishes up home."[5] They created in New England what Morissonneau described as "the true network of migration, integrating the individual wherever he goes; it is in effect an invitation to go off without calamitous disruption, for one remains within the family, that is, among one's own, even in the homes of others."[6] Thus, with strong bonds safely in place the French-Canadian immigrant felt equally at ease in New England as he did in Quebec province. He was in *"le Québec d'en bas"*.

This concept was further fostered by *la survivance* a term coined in the nineteenth century. *La survivance* was the view that French-Canadians were duty bound to preserve their cultural identity. This notion implied they had to keep Catholicism alive in Canada, by maintaining their mother tongue and customs and by staying on the land.[7] Later on, this was applied in relation to the large numbers of emigrants to New England. The Quebecois elite felt this emigration could be an extension of French-Canadian influence. The very nature of *la survivance* itself applied to the United States created a contradictory space for the French-Canadians.

Acting and believing one was in one's own country while living in the United States could only serve to be disturbing in the long run. Since many of the immigrants spoke only French or felt more secure with their own kind they bought only from the French-Canadian merchants. They were fearful of the people of their host country, as many new immigrants are, but also of English, the very language which represented their oppressors in Canada. Steven Riel, a Franco-American poet, who writes in English, begins one of his poems with a quote from Adrienne Rich: "This is the oppressor's language yet I need it to talk to you."[8] Most of the French Canadians who came during the great waves of immigration to the United States, the period of 1865–1920, came for obvious economic reasons, but many were also trying to save money to pay off debts on their farms in Canada. Navigating the space between the two countries was easy from a practical standpoint also, since the railroads stopped in many of the towns, large and small in New England and took the immigrants back home at will.

For a long time, French Canadians in places like Sanford clung tenaciously to the language, the religion and the culture of their ancestors. "The existence of the world beyond was regarded as culturally disorienting and a danger to the soul."[9] The home culture was a haven where families spoke French, friends were limited to French speakers, and the schools were French Catholic. It was safe inside and even gave the illusion that French was the language of the dominant class.By the 1950's, the French sphere had started to break apart since it was hardly possible in the United States to live only in French. In the past, English had allowed them to deal with the monolingual English speakers in their world on their own terms. Even this process maintained the illusion that the Anglo-Saxons were outside the French circle, the true reality. This *modus vivendi* produced two operating modes that existed side by side forming thus a series of fragmentations, which rarely overlapped or meshed. One was governed by French, the family and friends, "le côté tendre et langoureux," the other by English, the environment, the practical, "le côté short and sweet."[10]

The greatest contributing factor to this separateness or difference was probably the influence of the Catholic church and its church-run schools.

"More than any other institution, the elementary schools, founded and maintained by separate parishes, influenced and shaped individuals and gave them a sense of belonging to the Franco-American group."[11] In the 1950's and even into the 1960's in Sanford there were 3 separate Catholic parishes which founded their own elementary schools. In addition, a joint high school was also in operation. These schools were bilingual in the sense that half of the day the classes were taught in French, the other half in English. Among themselves the children often spoke French and English or created their own language, a mixture of both. The discipline in the Catholic schools was very strict and severe and as a result the Franco-American children very rarely associated with public school students who were thought to be wild and sinful.

This type of siege mentality in the long run often provokes the very conflicts that people are trying to avoid, however, in the case of Sanford, with this particular *modus operandi* the two worlds seldom met and things went smoothly. Such a process, however, while perhaps comforting for the French speakers was in part responsible for the invisible veil that existed around the Francos. The existence of language barriers implied that French formed part of a secret world accessible to the initiated only. In a society dominated by English, this also signified that in the minds of the anglophones the Franco-Americans became shadows who were barely understood and hardly recognizable.

Over time the Francos were faced with the problem all immigrants have had to come to terms with, that is the anglicized pronunciation of their names, a sort of linguistic assimilation. The mispronunciation of their names which at first caused confusion and disorientation would in time be so accepted that many would not even know that this was not the correct pronunciation. Gaston Miron once explained how speakers are unaware of the transformation their language assumes when it is threatened by a more powerful one. Miron referred to this as "linguistic alienation".[12] The linguistic changes of Franco-American names symbolized a similar alienation and the difficulties of existing in such fragmented space. The Francos started gliding to a sphere outside their own, to the English side.

This phenomenon of unmanageability caused problems since the intertwining of the key elements of language and faith proved problematical in time. They defined the Franco-American in negative terms, as being different, as lacking ambition and motivation, as being the "White Niggers of the North." The label of "white niggers" which has often been attributed to Francos can be found in the works of several Haitian writers. In an un-published paper, Jean Morisset mentions a Haitian author who refers to Quebec as a kind of subculture which is not black but which presents never-theless certain characteristics of black culture. He also says the Quebecois is a white man who doesn't know he is white, a kind of non-white per-son.[13] The immigrants who crossed the Canadian border carried with them this feeling of being "not quite white." With succeeding generations however the Franco-Americans desperately tried to cast off this image. Difference was too heavy a price to pay. Alfred Poulin, another Franco-American poet, has stated: "We worked hard at negating and trying to erase all traces of our French-Canadian heritage, first the accent, then the language, then the faith, the customs and the manners. We were 'White Niggers' hell bent on becoming categorically assimilated."[14]

Linguistic fragmentation also became more and more contradictory and confusing as Franco-Americans were told by their host country that they did not speak real French, i.e. the standardized version of France. The French, the "Canayen" or "joual" spoken by them lacked this status. Quebec was not a true nation, they were told, and even if it could be argued that it had a cultural distinctiveness then certainly the language they spoke was not a recognizable form of a standard language. The anglo-phones, who were in a position to set the standards, insisted the accent and expressions had to be Parisian French. Since "Canayen" did not possess these characteristics, then the Francos were speaking a kind of bastard-ized dialect. Switching easily from "Canayen" to English began to pro-duce a sense of conflict. It became increasingly difficult in Sanford to be in the linguistic cracks. Speaking two languages did not make Franco-Americans more intelligent or more valuable assets, it just made them more mixed up, more apart. The fragments which up to this point had provided a *modus operandi* were themselves breaking up, causing more separations, emphasizing differences.

Along with the linguistic struggles, racial epithets arose: "stupid frogs" and "dumb Canucks." Over time the Francos started to believe these terms and referred to other Franco-Americans as "dumb Canucks." The desire to be released from contradictory space and difference increased. Three possible solutions presented themselves. The most obvious was to stop speaking French entirely. It was a seemingly useless skill and it wasn't even French, in any case, since the association was to someone ignorant and uncultured. In Maine in the 1950's and 60's the best jobs were not given to those with a French last name.

Other Franco-Americans for whom "Canayen" French was less of a conflictual sphere remained firmly within the circle of security their language and faith provided. However, feelings of fear and bitterness were fostered as these French speakers started to resent the very act of exclusion itself. Many of the graduates of St. Ignatius High School in Sanford who stayed in their hometown evolved little over the years. In the 1970's the expressions they chose to describe the English speakers remained as they had been when they were children. The anglophones were still "eux" (them).

The Franco-Americans who felt that the sound of their mother's song was too sweet to abandon but who were uncomfortable in the cracks and between two worlds opted for the third choice: to master Parisian French, symbol of the elite classes. Since the language of France was a reference of quality, ideally these Francos would be admired and respected. In the process they drew closer to the English world as the French they spoke removed them from the language of their ancestry. Speaking recognized French also engendered more fragmented space for the Franco-Americans who, although they were now proficient in a national language, were losing the sounds and expressions of Franco-American culture. Other Francos were reluctant to speak to them in French as they now spoke "une langue instruite" (an educated language). In acquiring their new skill had they lost parts of the world they had grown up in? Were these two French worlds they were part of the same?

Jean Morisset, a Quebec professor of geography, has made an endeavor to understand this recent linguistic itinerary of Franco-Americans and to answer some of the questions of the separation of language in one of his poems called *A propos de "Immigrant Dream"*.[15] Morisset was responding to a poem written by Susann Pelletier, a Franco-American poet from Lewiston, Maine, a town founded by Franco-Americans, who does not speak or write in French. Her poem is a dark picture of the lives of weary and exhausted mill workers. (Pelletier's poem can also be found in the appendix.) In his poem Morisset has made use of fragments of English in the French text which appears to reflect the contradictory spaces of the cultural environment of the Franco-Americans. This repeated breaking apart and coming together of the French established a kind of rhythm typical of Franco-Americans. For francophones in Maine the choice of mixing both languages also implies a kind of geopolitical statement. Holding on to the two languages is without a doubt a conscious or unconscious refusal to assimilate entirely into the dominant Anglo-Saxon culture. It is also a statement about difference.

Without analyzing Morisset's poem from a literary point of view but from a more socio-cultural approach, we can pick out characteristics which are part of Franco-American identity. French and English have always played a separate role in the sphere of the francophone experience in New England. Morisset has dedicated his poem "à Susann with pride" and "to Suzie avec émoi" which contrast and communicate the presence of different planes of emotions. The broken sequences of language are like the fragmentation of the lives of many Francos who were forced to navigate between these two linguistic spaces. Are Susann and Suzie the same persons? Does Susann refer to that part of Pelletier's French nature or to her private invisible life, and Suzie to the English part or to her public visible life? Even the sounds of these words do not communicate the same register of emotions. The author's spelling of her first name "Susann" could also be interpreted as fragments of English and French with the double "n" added to the English "Susan". Yet, Pelletier has failed to make it entirely French as the "z" is an "s" and the final "e" of "Suzanne" is missing. She may be attempting to negotiate the space or the difference between these two linguistic worlds. The "with pride" associated to the French reminds us of the "home of the pilgrims pride" found in the patriotic American hymn "My Country 'tis of Thee," It also recalls the region the Francos migrated to – New England – thus, giving to the Franco-Americans a kind of dual nature to their identity, the world of difference between two languages, between two countries. The "avec émoi" after "to Suzie" adds emotion or sentiment to the expression, less puritanical than "with pride." Are thus Franco-Americans two people in one who need both languages? If so, they are in the state of alienation that the Quebecois poet, Gaston Miron, has described as "dispossession"[16]

The sociologist, Pierre Bourdieu, in talking about dispossession points out the fact that symbolic dispossession can only take place if "the dispossessed collaborate or take part in their dispossession and adopt criteria which are highly unfavorable in evaluating their language production and that of others."[17] (my translation) This is certainly true of the Franco-Americans in the 1950–1970 period when the anglophones in New England were highly critical of the quality of French-Canadian French. According to Louise Péloquin-Faré, a Franco-American writer, the acceptance of Anglophone criticism led to a weakening of the desire to speak French, in spite of the proximity to the mother country.

There are further examples of difference and fragmented space in the poem. In the English verse at the beginning, Morisset seems to have inverted the immigrant process, that is, it is not the immigrants who migrated but the country which encompassed them. Indeed when the first waves of French-Canadians[18] arrived in New England in the 1800's they did not feel that they had left their home. The people they encountered spoke French and the border between the United States and Canada was porous. Since there were no border guards to stop them, they could return to their villages as often as they pleased. Thus, could we say they were migrating to another country or merely moving to another part of the French-Canadian collective space?. When the borders closed in the 1920's, however, the francophones soon realized that they were not in Lower Quebec or *"le Québec d'en bas,"*[19] as they thought, but that their new country had now migrated upon them, a most bewildering experience.

Morisset's reference to MacDonald's, a symbol of the United States, and to "tourtière," a typical French-Canadian dish, well-known to all Francos in New England, gives us another example where two spaces come together and break apart. "La tourtière", a special meat pie usually made during holidays, reminds Franco-Americans of family gatherings when old Quebecois songs were sung and everyone took part in "les rigodons," a very lively and happy type of dancing. Eating meals, while giving the people access to the American way of life puts the Franco-Americans in the uncomfortable position of being in-between, in the cracks. Might the source then of their identity lie in the separations as they glide by means of language and culture form one side to the other, from the whiff of "tourtière" to the smell of hamburgers, sometimes touching upon a middle ground belonging to neither, a third way, a third language that is uneasy to live with first. If you are nowhere but in the cracks, then are you anywhere?

Morisset gives further examples of fragmentation in the opposition he makes between the poetic and the down-to-earth. The suffix "-aches" which he has added to the word "Bostonaches" in the third stanza recalls for him the foundation myths of the intermarriage of the first French to North America with the native Americans. Consequently, according to the legend these "métis" developed a strong love of freedom and of nature, like the wild daffodils in the poem. Contrasted with this uncontrolled and unfettered temperament are the ordered tulips and townships so symbolic to the French-Canadians of their English masters. The poet is once again emphasizing the two voices and the dual nature of Franco-American identity.

He also mentions some of the great American poets such as Whitman, Thoreau, Longfellow, and William Carlos Williams who used the Acadians, the lumberjacks, the *coureurs de bois* and the *voyageurs* as a source of inspiration and as romantic figures who extolled a life without constraints. According to Christian Morissonneau, another Quebecois geographer: "History was to render these men of the wilderness legendary. The *coureurs de bois* is part of the heroic and mythic heritage of French-Canadian culture. After the *coureur de bois* in the pantheon of anonymous heroes there appeared two other types of adventurer whom only a new country could bring forth: the *voyageur* and the lumberjack."[20] No one born in Maine can forget the courage of the lovely Evangeline Bellefontaine in Longfellow's poem of the same name. The poem has become part of Maine's popular culture. The ancestors of the Franco-Americans were praised and admired for their adventurous, out-door life of freedom. Whereas their grandfathers and grandmothers were personifications of liberty and enterprise, risk takers constantly on the move, their descendants however, according to some reports of the times, seemingly lacked ambition and were so subjugated to their language and faith that they had little distinctive personality.[21] Endlessly bridging contradictory spaces and differences seems to have been the fate of the Francos.

In *Book of Dreams*, Jack Kerouac, a famous Franco-American, talks about the difficulty of being a bi-cultural Franco in the America of the Anglo-Saxon dream. Kerouac feels the dream calls out to the Francos, the Chicano, and to other ethnic groups to allow themselves to become "prisoners" of the dream to feed the foundation myths of the country. Kerouac cries out the frustration and rage of many Franco-Americans caught in the American immigrant myth when he says: "Had I gone back to Canada I wouldn't have taken shit from any non-Frenchman."[22]

Morisset also feels this weight when he uses the word *"devoir"* (obligation) to be thankful for the debilitating and rigorous conditions that the mills offered the Francos. For a people who came mainly from rural villages where trees and wide open spaces were the norm, the confinement of the factories and of their living conditions removed their sense of liberty. The fragmentation of the French-Canadians is such that many no longer view these literary legends as having emerged from their very own French culture. Also, what source of identity these adventurers could provide had been taken over by Anglo-Saxon writers.

Attempting to recognize and understand the itineraries and separated parts of the Franco-American experience in New England can serve as David Plante, a Franco-American writer, has said "to reconstruct the silence of one's father."[23] By gathering up their broken history Francos can reclaim the pieces that will help them understand the present, to redefine their position in a changing environment, to reclaim a legitimacy denied them by those who determine the course of events, and finally come out of the wings. As the Franco-American singer, Josée Vachon, sings: "On est toujours là et aussi forts qu'autrefois"[24] (We are still here and as strong as we were before).

Priscilla Morin-Ollier
Université François-Rabelais, Tours

Notes

1. Pierre Jakez-Hélias, *Le Cheval d'Orgueil* (Paris: Plon, 1975), 101.

2. Denis Ledoux, *Lives in Translation, An Anthology of Contemporary Franco-American Writings* (Lisbon Falls: Soleil Press, 1991), 12.

3. Robert Beaudoin, "Le nom 'Franco-Américain,'" *BSHFA* (1967), 151–54.

4. Gerald Brault, *The French-Canadian Heritage in New England* (Hanover: UP of New England, 1986), 185.

5. Pierre Anctil, "The Franco-Americans of New England," *French America: Mobility, Identity, and Minority Experience across the Continent*, eds. Dean R. Louder and Eric Waddell (Baton Rouge: Louisiana State UP 1983), 45.

6. Christian Morissonneau, "The 'Ungovernable' People: French-Canadian Mobility and Identity," *French America*, 28.

7. Brault, 7.

8. Steven Riel, "Field Trip Home," *Lives in Translation*, 63.

9. Brault, 10.

10. Jean Morisset, a Quebecois geographer who has written much on the question of Quebecois space, used these expressions to describe these two languages in an unpublished article in this author's possession. "Une vie en translation ou la vertige et la gloire d'être French," written July 1996: 32.

11. In Brault, 92.

12. Gaston Miron, *L'homme rapaillé* (Montréal: Typo, 1996), 237.

13. In Jean Morisset, "Piste autochtone et filière transe-culturelle," *Proceedings from Séminaires de la chaire Concordia-UQAM en études ethniques*, juin 1994: 26. Taken from *Haïti délibérée/Québec inassouvi ou l'Amérique franco-créole en quête de son destin* (Montréal/Port-au Prince, 1988), 250.

14. A. Poulin, *Lives in Translation*, 141.

15. Jean Morisset, *A Propos de* Immigrant Dream, unpublished poem, written 2 July 1996. Morisset who has written many articles on the problems of language and space was inspired to write this poem after reading *Lives in Translation, An Anthology of Contemporary Franco-American Writings*. He was greatly moved by the sentiments expressed in the works of his "cousins from the USA."

16. Miron, 237.

17. Pierre Bourdieu, "Le fétichisme de la langue," *Actes de la recherche en sciences sociales*, 4 (juillet 1975), 2–32.

18. "French Canadian" is used here to refer to the more traditional definition of the francophone minority in Canada. Although it is not normally used in Quebec today it is still the best term to define this group historically before the Quiet Revolution of the 1960's when the expression was rejected by a large majority.

19. Expression found in *French America*, 5. In the introduction Louder, Waddell, and Christian Morissonneau state that "approximately 700,000 people left for New England between 1850 and 1930, a demographic hemorrhage that nevertheless gave birth to a *"Quebec d'en bas."*

20. Morissonneau, "The 'Ungovernable'", 17.

21. James W. Vander, *American Minority Relations* (New York: Knopf, 1983), 19–20.

22. Jack Kerouac, *Book of Dreams* (San Francisco: City Lights Books, 1991), 118.

23. David Plante, *The Francoeur Novels: The Family; The Woods; The Country*. (New York, 1983) Plante examines "the silence of one's father" in his works.

24. Josée Vachon, *Collection Vol. 1* (Cevon Musique, 1993). Vachon wrote the words and music for this song herself.

Works Cited

Beaudoin, Robert. "Le nom 'Franco-Américain'." *BSHFA*. 1967.

Brault, Gerald. *The French-Canadian Heritage in New England*. Hanover: UP of New England, 1986.

Bourdieu, Pierre. "Le fétichisme de la langue." *Actes de la recherche en sciences sociale*, 4 juillet 1975.

Jakez-Hélias, Pierre. *Le Cheval d'Orgueil*. Paris: Plon, 1975.

Kerouac, Jack. *Book of Dreams*. San Francisco: City Lights Books, 1991.

Ledoux, Denis. *Lives in Translation, An Anthology of Contemporary Franco-American Writings*. Lisbon Falls: Soleil Press, 1991.

Louder, Dean R. and Eric Waddell, eds. *French America: Mobility, Identity, and Minority Experience across the Continent*. Baton Rouge: Louisiana State UP, 1983.

Miron, Gaston. *L'homme rapaillé*. Montréal: Typo, 1996.

Morisset, Jean. *A Propos de Immigrant Dream*. Unpublished poem written, 2 July 1996.

————. "Piste autochtone et filière transe-culturelle." *Proceedings from Séminaires de la chaire Concordia-UQAM en études ethniques*, juin 1994: 26

Plante, David. *The Francoeur Novels: The Family; The Woods; The Country*. New York, 1983.

Vachon, Josée. *Collection Vol. 1*, Cevon Musique, 1993.

Vander, James W. *American Minority Relations*. New York: Knopf, 1983.

Part V
AFRICA

21

The English Language in South Africa: Empowerment and Domination

English in South Africa seems to be above all the mother tongue of the South Africans whose ancestors were born in the British Isles. It was one of South Africa's two official languages between 1910 and 1993 which helps explain why though it has always been a minority language (it is the mother tongue of less than 3.5 million people), English became the most popular vehicle for public life – in the public service, at school, in the national media. Today, English is protected by the Constitution as just one of eleven official languages, but practice has made it a vehicular idiom for people with different mother tongues in the multilingual context of the country and it is more and more needed to lead South Africa back onto the global stage. The questions that arise are: must English become the country's *lingua franca* or would such a move endanger the nation-building and democracy-building processes now at work?

The identity of English in South Africa has changed tremendously since it started as a colonial language spoken by a limited number of British settlers. Today it is the dominant language of politics, administration and trade spoken by many other people than the mere descendants of those exiles. Yet throughout its two centuries of presence at the southern tip of Africa, English has retained one feature: it has always been at least one of the languages of the country's élites and bourgeoisie and, as such, the dominant medium of communication in and between the centres of power. More recently English has become a *lingua franca* across racial barriers for the middle class, including the limited Black middle class. The English language has gradually lost its narrow focus as a cultural marker of a mere British identity and has become a crucial tool language for many citizens whose mother tongue or home language is not English in the democracy-building process through which South Africa is passing.

English Speakers in South Africa: A Diverse Group

In South Africa, English speakers make up such a heterogeneous category that one can hardly speak of a 'community'. English was first brought by Englishmen and Scotsmen who emigrated to South Africa in the early 19th century when the British Empire took over the Cape Colony from Holland. After the first consequent and lasting settlement of 4,000 people on the eastern coast of the Cape Colony in 1820, most emigrants stayed in existing towns or villages, or founded new ones, both on the coast and in the hinterland. Other large inputs of British immigrants occurred in the 1840s in Natal, and after diamonds in 1867 and gold in 1885 were discovered in the Republics of the Transvaal and Orange. 19th century British immigration to South Africa was never massive, sometimes less than 1,000 a year, because the wages offered to labourers were so low that few Whites were ready to accept 'kaffir (black) work'. Unlike their Australian or Canadian counterparts, White English-speaking South Africans (ESSAs) have never been the leading demographic force in their new land. The expression 'English-speaking South Africans' itself is deceptive. For most people, it means 'White mother tongue English speakers of British background' who nowadays represent barely more than half of the mother tongue English speakers. Several waves of non-British white immigrants adopted English as their vehicular, and often home, language on arriving in the country: Russian, German and Lithuanian Jews in the 19th century, Italians and Greeks after World War II, and a large number of Portuguese citizens after the end of Portugal's rule in Angola and Mozambique in 1975, are among the most notable.

Secondly, a growing proportion of the Coloured community (almost 16%, i.e. more than 500 000 people), whose language has traditionally been Afrikaans, are now also using English as a home language. Yet the largest homogeneous English-speaking group are the Indians (approximately 1 million people) descended from indentured labourers who came to work in the cotton and sugar cane growing areas of Natal in the 1860s. Working mainly under the guidance of English masters, they had to learn some English but kept speaking their original languages (Gujerati, Hindi, Urdu and Tamil essentially). After they became free, those workers adopted English in the anglicized context of Durban where they had settled massively. As immigration from India was brought to an end, the younger generations gradually forgot the languages of their forefathers which were kept for cultural purposes. This process took some time since by the mid-70s, 50% of the South African Indians said they could speak at least some of one of these languages. Today, English is the vehicular language of virtually all Asians. A radio station called Radio Lotus, operating from Durban for the Indian community, has been broadcasting almost exclusively in English since it was launched in 1983.

Since English has been adopted by so many 'non-British' as their main language, ESSAs are being deprived of what was almost the only element that tied them together and could be wielded as a distinctive cultural feature, especially after South Africa left the Commonwealth in 1961. ESSAs are notorious for being the least multilingual of all South Africans, a flaw in a country with at least 20 acknowledged languages. Even though Afrikaans was compulsory for them at school, they were not really forced to use it in the workplace, as most of them entered the English-dominated private sector. On the contrary, Afrikaners knew that learning English could secure a position in the public service where bilingualism was an obligation. Backed by the power and confidence of the British Empire and Commonwealth, ESSAs never felt threatened and have always felt confident about their language. At the same time, they have not really developed a sense of exclusiveness: ESSA élites have almost never used English for ethnic claims or to mobilize their community, unlike the Afrikaners who used Afrikaans *consciously* as a political weapon.

A Language of Empowerment

Yet, in spite of being the only imported official language of South Africa (the other ten are indigenous languages, including Afrikaans which is only a far cry from the Dutch spoken by the early settlers), English has imposed itself as the language of power and empowerment. Historically, British subjects dominated the early phases of the country's economic development. In the towns, 'business tended to fall in the hands of British settlers' (Davenport 489) who became shopkeepers whereas most Afrikaners were farmers. The English language had no competitor as the natural tool for commercial communication when the trade networks developed between the towns. South African English has always been the language of the cities where decision-making and trade are performed, in modern industrial societies. Most Europeans settled in the towns, often remaining in or around the harbour where they had landed, and adopted English because it was the vehicular language. The gold diggers of the 1880s settled in what became mushroom urban areas. To a large extent, the rise of English and capitalism in South Africa have had similar courses. In a developing economy, the towns became the places of the accumulation of capital in the hands of English speakers. In the early 20th, Blacks and Afrikaners who came to the cities found themselves in subservient positions, forced to acquire English to get a job from British employers who held a large proportion of the country's economy in their hands.

Business and urbanisation are not enough to explain the growth of English. English was the *de facto* language of colonial administrators, until the 1910 Constitution made English one of the Union of South Africa's two official languages, the other being Dutch. Even though both languages were 'to be treated on a footing of equality and possessed equal freedom, rights and privileges' (Liebenberg and Spies 49), English became the most popular vehicle for public life – in state administrations, government affairs and at school. In the 20th century, large-scale industrial and urban growth gave the language its pivotal position.The language used by the state is of paramount importance because citizens who cannot speak it are virtually excluded from the nation. Such anglicization was steadfastly enforced and made English the language of cultural empowerment. This should come as no surprise since a community that controls both the political life and the economy tends to impose its own cultural references on the rest of the population. In 1822, Governor Lord Charles Somerset issued a proclamation that English was to be the only language of courts, schools and administration, though the Dutch settlers, the rulers' primary targets, outnumbered the British by 8 to 1. Imperial Britain then made sure that English remained the natural language for public life. After the Boer Republics were defeated in 1902, another fit of anglicization fell on the unruly Afrikaners, when Lord Milner, the High Commissioner for South Africa, imposed English as the sole medium of instruction in state schools. Afrikaans was repressed and any child caught speaking Afrikaans was punished, a frequent situation in exoglossic contexts.

School has always been a prime vehicle for the dissemination of culture, but the mass media have become extremely potent. And the well-established South African media are overwhelmingly English. Newspapers were started by the British, who brought the first printing press in 1795. Drawing on the English experience, and as an urban phenomenon, one or two newspapers were systematically established in each town or village. Today, the deepest influence lies with cinema, radio and TV which channel a deep Anglo-American influence into the urban mass culture, even among Blacks with little or no spoken or written practice of the language. A major element is that all the media are commercial, including the public service radio stations and television channels. The British press has been closely associated with the country's commercial elite and defends a broad liberal outlook. Most English titles belong to, or relate closely to, Anglo American, the country's largest industrial and financial holding. Since the pioneer days of commercial radio in the 1950s, most announcers have wanted their products to be advertised in English because it is the most widely understood language among the essentially urban markets they have been targeting. The relationship with the English-dominated economic sector is vital for the country's commercial activity.

Radio, which is extremely popular with Blacks, uses mainly the vernacular tongues, but not television. TV, which was started in 1976 as a single English/Afrikaans bilingual public service channel, could not stay away from cheap American products as the financial burden became heavier over time. Consequently it increased its offer in English which urban Blacks adopted quickly, especially after 1985 when an all-English national evening channel was launched. Today, English is the most widely used language on the public service channels, as well as on M-Net, an encrypted pay service, which broadcasts massively in English, marginally in Afrikaans and uses no Black languages, on the market-driven grounds that its customers are primarily upper-class Whites. In 1997, TV attracted more than 15 million daily viewers, a majority of whom are Blacks whose first language is not English.

It is the context of use which gives a language its status. For a language to become powerful, it must be used by élites as a communication device, and marketed to the people as a step to empowerment and a needed transcultural device, even more so in a multilingual society. In a modern, rapidly industrializing urban setting, English became the language of the various dominant élites of the country: in politics, in administration, in business, trade and industry, in culture, in the media, at school. More recently, English was adopted by the emerging Black bourgeoisie as something to look up to, in spite of ethnic revival tendencies which advocate the exclusive use of vernaculars. Therefore, when the building of democracy during the 'transaction period'[1] demanded the empowerment of the Black languages, the question was asked: should English be allowed to retain its dominant though efficient position in influential sectors of society when 60% of the population could not speak it at all?

The Language Debate in the Transition Period: Should English Be an Official *lingua franca*?

The euphoria of democratization and vast promises of equality somewhat blurred the realities of the language context until after the first 'one man one vote' elections of 1994. The domination of English started to worry Black scholars and thinkers as they noticed a growing tendency to unilingualism in public spheres and in the workplace. They felt that, added to the consequences of apartheid's cultural fractionism, this was leading to further disempowerment of Blacks and contradicted the equal opportunity principle which the young democracy claims to live by, by preventing many people from getting a job in their own country.

Compared with its numerical importance, the symbolical and functional power of English is enormous. Mother tongue English speakers represent less than 10% of the population and it is considered that 40% to 45% – an optimistic figure – can understand English. Zulu is the leading language but it is spoken by only 22% of the population and understood by hardly more than 50%. Unless it becomes essential in the economy, in the educational system, in government matters or the media, Zulu, as well as Afrikaans, will lag behind English, as South Africa's dominant language. Thus, since in truly multilingual contexts, i.e. when at least three languages are largely used in a given country, one of them tends to dominate and impose itself as a *lingua franca*, the government was left with three options when devising the new official language policy – by and large, one free market *v* two forms of state intervention: 1 *laissez faire*; 2 imposing English; 3 implementing an interventionist policy with constitutional and legal obligations regarding the use of all the languages spoken in South Africa.

The Case for English as South Africa's Linking Language

Cost and practicality factors point to the necessity of limiting the use of other languages and entrench English as the dominant medium of power, decision-making and public life. In fact, under market pressure, English is already imposing itself because it is cheap and effortless to implement. Of course, ESSAs defend such an option. Many of them assume that English is universally spoken or that this should be the rule. The private sector is a strong lobbyist, considering that for the country to develop properly and create jobs, English should not be repressed but imposed because it is the most efficient tool of communication, because it is the only South African language with a world audience, and because it is the only one spoken by most members of the country's élites. This option is often presented as common sense, whereas multilingualism is associated with underdevelopment and poverty, and seen as a recipe for a fractious Tower of Babel.

Government agencies themselves seem to prefer English for practical reasons. For instance, in 1996, English accounted for 87% of all the speeches made in Parliament. Legislation will remain in English and Afrikaans, while Hansard, the parliamentary record of debates, will be published in English with insets in the home languages used by MPs. The Ministry of Justice also plans to drop the use of Afrikaans in courts and retain only English due to lack of translators (*Rapport*). Even the document detailing the RDP (Reconstruction and Development Project), the transition government's platform, is only available in English.

An interesting point is that Blacks perceive English in a favourable light. Schools for Blacks were founded by British missionaries who sought to mould black Christian communities along European lines. In spite of this imperialistic content, and even though ESSAs belonged to the racial oligarchy, English carries notions of learning and development, not oppression. Black élites have always used English: as early as 1912, the South African Congress of Natives, soon to become the ANC, used it as its language of communication. Most of its founders were educated in mission schools, and many ANC leaders went to the College of Fort Hare, for a long time the only Black higher education institution, which provided education in English. During the apartheid period, English became an instrument of protest, whereas Afrikaans was identified with the racist regime. Emotionally, English also held a positive value, enhanced from the late 1960s onwards, as a window onto the outside world. In the 1970s and 1980s, many Black Consciousness thinkers saw English as the best medium to carry an efficient struggle, by attracting foreign attention and support. AZAPO (Azanian's People Organisation), an ultra-left ANC splinter group with Africanist leanings, even advocated the use of English as a unifying language for Blacks.

Beyond all the emotive aspects of the language issue, most Blacks see English as a tool for a better life, albeit perhaps as a necessary evil, to the point that its instrumental function seems to supersede all other considerations. Back in 1971, a poll revealed that 88.5% of 200 Soweto Standard 10 pupils preferred to receive education in English rather than in Afrikaans or in the Bantu languages (Goguel 22). In 1979, the apartheid regime extended the teaching of English from the fifth year of schooling to the whole country in Black schools. Unfortunately, the Black youth of the late 1970s started boycotting schools so that proficiency in English dropped dramatically: a survey showed that by 1986 65% of the Black adult population could not speak it. Today, it is very likely that, given the right to choose the language of education of their children, most parents will pick English as a second or third language after the mother tongue. They want their children to achieve higher social status and see English as a means to an end. Many of them 'send their children to schools where English... is the language of instruction (because of) how empowering fluency in English is' (Kaschula and Anthonissen 59).

The Domination of English and Unilingualism: Redressing Imbalances

However, some have come to consider that the laissez faire option was just renewed Eurocentric colonialism and the hegemony of English potentially dangerous. As has been stressed above, a language can spread only if it is felt as necessary by its users. But if political, educational and economic structures remain as they are and 'without an effective policy for implementation, the multilingual policy enshrined in the constitution will remain a token gesture. The ultimate effect will be that the hegemony of English will proceed unchecked' (Kashula and Anthonissen 107). In fact, a growing number of Black scholars, many with Africanist background, see English as a problem for the democracy-building process, not as a solution. According to Dr Neville Alexander, a former Robben Islander and ANC activist, probably South Africa's most famous language planner, whose writings in the 80s helped frame the modern language issue, especially in the field of education, 'left to itself, the present situation would simply doom us to repeating the same mistakes so many other African and post-colonial states have made. We would end up with a small English-fluent élite for whom their proficiency in this world language would amount to cultural capital, enabling them to get the best jobs and enjoy the perks of high status while the rest of the population is insulated from all the power positions and social processes, thus making a mockery of development and democracy' (Alexander).

Alexander insists on the need for language planning – 'a government-authorized, long term sustained and conscious effort to alter a language itself or to change a language's functions in a society for the purpose of solving communications problems – (DACST 7) to redress the imbalances created by apartheid. Language planning also entails the symbolical recognition of the cultural assets of each community. The ANC's official position is that the market alone cannot address past cultural inequalities and that government must intervene. Hence the recognition of 11 official languages (the mother tongues of 98% of the population) as one of the six founding provisions of the 1996 Constitution, and the inclusion of language rights into the Bill of Rights. Other sections of the Constitution refer to the necessity of respecting language diversity and of not discriminating against any language in any situation, particularly in the fields of justice, education and culture.

As can be seen, the case for linguistic diversity did not arise from the mere wish to respect all cultures. In December 1995, Minister of Arts, Culture, Science and Technology BS Ngubane announced the creation of Langtag (Language Plan Task Group) to prepare a language plan for South Africa. Initially, Langtag, composed of eight renowned language scholars and chaired by Neville Alexander, intended to work on establishing equal opportunities for Black languages. But it turned out that its proceedings were dictated by a wish to counteract the domination of English, as can be inferred from its report which was tabled in Parliament in August 1996: the task, it says, 'is truly mountainous. It is no less than challenging the hegemony of English' (11). The lack of financial backing, material obstacles and an entangled linguistic situation meant a letdown in that area of government and a soft acception of English domination as 'during the past months, it has become clear that there is a definite tendency to unilingualism in our country' (DACST, 1).

Among Langtag's main concerns were 'the drift towards unilingualism in the Public Service despite the constitutional commitment to multilingualism' (31), which meant that many public services were not available to African language speakers, the 'blatant hegemony' of English on public service television, a tendency to use only English at meetings, including Cabinet meetings, at national and local government levels, and 'a questionable commitment to multilingualism in the ranks of the political leadership of the country' (27). 'At national level, the official attitude is clearly pro-English and... interpreting services in Parliament are for practical purposes limited to English and Afrikaans' (15).

Acknowledging the fact that the status and functions of a language are symptoms of its power, the report recommends that the Bantu languages 'be used in high-status functions such as parliamentary debates, languages of learning and teaching in all phases of education, from pre-school up to the universities and the technikons, in the print and electronic media and for domestic (national, regional and local) business transactions' (12). Political, economic and cultural leaders should be made to use African languages on important occasions to set the right example. It is an established fact that community and national leaders play a prescriptive role for the population. In January 1998, Nelson Mandela used Xhosa to answer questions in English during a live interview on SABC3, an allegedly all-English public channel. Beyond the symbolical aspect, there is the belief that a Bantu language can be used for a major event, which is the case whenever the head of state speaks to the nation.

As regards public and government services, Langtag called for the drafting of 'guidelines for all public servants to use languages other than English on a regular basis in national, provincial and local Government forums'. The report wanted to compel private employers to consider 'proficiency in an African language as a criterion for employment'. This goes further than mere affirmative action: being Black would not be the only reason for getting a job anymore. Such measures would, at long last, empower the Black population psychologically, the important point being that people are useful because they *are* proficient in Tsonga, Zulu or Ndebele, not that they are useless because they don't master English.

Yet the need for the government to prove that things are changing does not preclude the implementation of essential long term measures regarding education and literacy. By 1994 80% of Black South Africans and about 40% of whites could not read or compute at a Standard 5 level (WMG). In the South African educational system, literacy in the mother tongue is 'highly correlated with proficiency in English and basic numeracy'. For that same reason, a high proportion of those who are proficient in English are literate. On the reverse, literacy is absolutely necessary for a language to be empowered. In modern highly computerized societies, a language that has no well-established written form cannot become a necessary instrument and is therefore doomed to go under or become extinct. Many Blacks suffer from double illiteracy: they can neither speak the vehicular language, English, nor write in their own mother tongue.

As South Africans are gradually discovering and accepting, they belong to a country with many cultural identities where each individual has probably several identities. One of the paths to follow is multilingual education. Dr Alexander champions 'additive bilingualism' which involves building on a child's home language. 'Under conditions where there is no English-speaking environment you have to use the home language, bring in English as soon as possible and build on the child's actual understanding of concepts in the home language' (CT). English would not be considered as an enemy but as a stepping stone and a needed trans-cultural device. 'Sustainable development will only be possible if education occurs via African languages together with English at all levels' (DACST 18). For Blacks, to go beyond four years of education means learning a foreign language. But when children drop out and stop acquisition, an all too frequent situation, they lose all chances to climb up the social ladder.

Another set of reasons for the domination of English pertains to the characteristics of the Bantu languages. The Bantu languages are territorialized in fairly strict borders, with the exception of the Johannesburg area, whereas English and Afrikaans are spoken throughout the country and more importantly in all the cities. In addition, Bantu languages have almost no written tradition. As Canadian linguist W. Mackey wrote: 'The lack of standardization jeopardizes the potential status of a language' (Mackey 52). The Bantu languages are in need of written material (dictionaries, schoolbooks) as well as well-trained technical experts (DACST 13).

Finally, such a policy requires enormous sums of money and many point out that it would be less costly, and more efficient, to let English dominate. Librarians in the Western Cape complain about a lack of Xhosa books, but 'publishers are reluctant to publish Xhosa books because they are not commercially viable and they won't publish 300 books, say, just for library services' (CT). Since culture has become a product that is sold and bought, its content depends on profitability' (Mackey 52). Langtag rejected the cost argument because of its defeatist outlook. It is is very critical of the Constitution which claims that 'questions of usage, practicality and expense' must be taken into account (8–3). Eventually, this is what 'leads to unilingualism and the unacceptable subordination of marginalised groups under a dominant group which we can no longer tolerate in a democratic South Africa' (DACST 23).

The success of the state language policy will depend on the money available, on the unyielding will of the government, on the commitment of the teachers, workers and of the population as a whole to accept and promote all the languages of South Africa. Most of all, such a policy needs time. As for the English culture in South Africa it stands in a fairly ambiguous position because it is often used, as by the national media, to convey a trans-cultural image of South African society.

There is also a danger of playing English against the other languages. Fortunately, having twenty or so different idioms might not necessarily lead to anarchy or impede upon the rise of a single unified nation. 'Language is not an instrument of exclusion: in principle, anyone can learn a language... Print is what invents nationalism, not *a* particular language per se... In a world in which the nation state is the overwhelming norm, all this means that nations can now be imagined without linguistic communality...' (Anderson 1985 134–135). If South Africa intends to follow such a path to unity, it will have to handle the contradictions between the need for a powerful English language and the vital social and cultural position of all the other languages – Afrikaans, Bantu and Indian.

Bernard Cros
Université d'Avignon et des Pays de Vaucluse

Works Cited

Alexander, Neville. *The Star*, 25 October 1996. http://www2.inc.co.za/Archives/1996/9610/25/language.html

Anderson, Benedict. *Imagined Communities*, London: Verso, 1983.

CT. *Cape Times*, 20 November 1997.

http://www2.inc.co.za/Archives/SepttoDec1997/9711/20/neville1211.html

Davenport, TRH, *South Africa – A Modern History.* 4th ed. London: Macmillan, 1991.

Development Bank of South Africa, In: *SABC, Delivering Value, Part Two. Supplementary Submission of the South African Broadcasting Corporation to the Independent Broadcasting Authority*, Dec. 1994, p. 46.

DACST (Department of Arts, Culture, Science and Technology). *Towards an national language plan for South Africa, Final Report of the Language Plan Task Group (Langtag)*, August 1996.

Goguel, Anne-Marie. "La crise du système éducatif sud-africain." *Politique Africaine*, 25 mars 1987, pp. 14–37.

Kashula, Russell, and Anthonissen, Christine. *Communicating across cultures in South Africa: Towards a critical language awareness*. Johannesburg: Hodder and Stoughton, 1995.

Liebenberg B.J., Spies S.B. (dir.). *South Africa in the 20th Century*. Pretoria: J.L. Van Schaik Academic, 1993.

Mackey, William F., 1992. "Langues maternelles, autres langues et langues véhiculaires." *Perspectives*, vol. XXII, 1 (81), pp. 45–57.

Rapport, February 17, 1998.

WMG. *Weekly Mail and Guardian*, 2 February 1995. 'A rainbow nation of illiterates'. http://wn.apc.org/wmail/issues/950602/wm950602–3.html.

Note

1. Dominique Darbon of the Centre d'Etudes d'Afrique Noire in Bordeaux has pointed out that the 'transition period' has something 'magical' about it but that if it is to be fruitful it has to bring opponents around a negotiating table in order to exchange their points of views – make 'transactions' and get things going.

22

Homeless: The Motif of Eviction in
Two Early South African Narrative Texts[1]

Two early South African texts treat the problem of domestic exile which
occurs when people are evicted from their homes. A short-story by a
white English-speaking writer, Pauline Smith focuses on the eviction of
a poor white Afrikaner from a farm in the Karoo during a drought. The
account of a black Setswana writer, Sol Plaatje documents widespread
evictions resulting from the implementation of the Native Lands Act of
1913. Despite the different forms used and the political intent of Plaajte's
text, there are substantial similarities in their responses to the plight of
their subjects – in the ethical positions they require of their readers, and
in the cultural translation that necessarily takes place because of their
choice of English as medium. Plaatje and Smith offer complex but com-
plementary perspectives on eviction, perspectives which remain relevant
today because they help define the role of the writer in a society which
has had more than its fair share of trouble.

Perhaps readers might be familiar with the music of Ladysmith Black Mam-
bazo, the *mbaqanga* group from South Africa who shot to international
fame when they collaborated with Paul Simon in the recording of *Grace-
land*. While in Europe in 1998, I heard them singing a Zulu background
to the Heinz adverts on TV. One of the more haunting of the English lyrics
of their songs contains these lines:

> We are homeless, homeless
> moonlight shining on a midnight lake
> somebody sing, somebody cry
> somebody sing, why why why?

The sentiment of being without a home which must surely be shared by all
those who are in exile, and all those, in particular, who have suffered the

form of exile with which this chapter is concerned: eviction. In similar vein, Sol Plaatje both prefaces and concludes his documentary account of the evictions following the 1913 Native Lands Act in South Africa with a quotation from St Paul: "Pray that your flight be not in winter".

At the outset, exile cannot be seen simply as retreat or banishment across national boundaries. Perhaps its harshest and most public emanation in South Africa has been the widespread evictions and forced removals by which *apartheid* policy was implemented from 1948 onwards, and particularly in the 60s, 70s and early 80s. Although its present impact is most evident these days in the reversals of land claims, reinstatements and restitutions, eviction – the exile of people from their homes – has not entirely disappeared from the enlightened order of the new South Africa. Nor was the practice of eviction begun, in the past, by the Afrikaner Nationalist government. On the contrary this practice had its roots in a long tradition of relocating and dislocating people from their homes which the Nationalist government inherited from British colonial rule. Nor is it only black people who have suffered the effects of eviction. The intense will-to-power which characterised the rise of Afrikaner nationalism had its roots, I would suggest, in the severe economic hardship endured by a poor-white class like that which developed in the United States: rural people who fell prey to the ravages of drought and disease, and lost homes and farms because of them.

One of the reasons for the choice of early twentieth century writers, therefore, is to remember that the phenomenon of exile is not new. Sol Plaatje's 1916 *Native Life in South Africa*, in particular, was a powerful protest against the implementation of the Native Lands Act and the widespread evictions which followed it. Travelling through the countryside during the bitter winter of that year Plaatje documented the plight of people forced off the lands on which they had been living, often for generations. *Native Life* is an act of testimony, a bearing witness, an invocation of imperial intervention to aid those most at the mercy of colonial greed and political opportunism. Pauline Smith's collection, *The Little Karoo*, published some nine years later, is not motivated by so overt a political purpose. In introducing the first edition, Arnold Bennett says of her characters: "They are simple, astute, stern, tenacious, obstinate, unsubduable, strongly prejudiced, with the most rigid standards of conduct – from which standards the human nature in them is continually falling away, with fantastic, terrific, tragic, or quaintly comic consequences" (1925: 10). Her project is literary and moral, in other words, and her mode realistic. Unlike Plaatje, Smith found writing hard, and the retired life she led was dominated by a constant battle with the private craft of fiction. Although the form their writing takes is different, these two writers have in common an intelligent and incisive compassion for the suffering they have seen, and an immanent urge to set it down so others too can see. Comparing the treatment they give to eviction in a South African society which was still largely rural, should demonstrate the continuities and connections which make their commentary relevant today.

There are significant differences between Plaatje and Smith. Plaatje was a black man who built a professional career as writer on the education he had received from missionaries, editor and translator, and travelled to Europe and the United States in pursuit of his political commitments. He was a founding member of the South African Native Congress, forerunner to the ANC, and achieved substantial communal recognition for the work he undertook amongst his people. The setting of his text is the then Transvaal and Free State, drought-stricken regions which Plaatje sets in stark contrast to the lush paradisiac conditions he enjoyed as a child on a farm on the banks of the Orange River. Documenting the fate of tenant farmers at the hands of a government which bans land ownership and effectively outlaws cattle ownership, Plaatje's political intentions – and his political credentials – are clear.

Smith, by contrast, was a shy white woman whose idyllic rural childhood in Oudtshoorn in the Eastern Cape came to a sudden end when she was sent to boarding school in Scotland at the age of thirteen, and her father, to whom she was very close, died soon after. She suffered from debilitating neuralgia most of her adult life, which she lived in retirement in an English village with her mother and her sister, returning twice to the Cape to assemble material for her writing. Her output as a writer was not large: she published just one novel, *The Beadle*, a memoir of Arnold Bennett, her patron and mentor; and two collections of short stories, set in the Little Karoo region of the Eastern Cape, a region which includes both fertile areas of well-watered farming land and areas whose droughts and rockiness render them desolate and hostile to those who eke out a living on their arid soil.

In 1981 J.M. Coetzee levelled a sharp criticism against the work of Smith: to the effect that her representation of rural white people at the turn of the century is susceptible to nostalgic conservatism, and, more seriously, that it propagates the myth of the Afrikaner as Israelite, as the chosen people seeking and finding their chosen land. It is true that Smith is broadly sympathetic towards the Afrikaners about whom she writes, but I would think that Coetzee's criticism is undercut, at least in the story 'Desolation', by her choice of subject. Where Plaatje describes the experiences of black farm workers evicted in terms of an act of the colonial parliament, Smith focuses her story upon an old woman whom she describes as "the child of poor-whites and ... the mother of poor-whites [who] had drifted for seventy years from farm to farm in the shiftless, thriftless labour of her class" (1925: 162). The poor-white, says Smith, "is poor also in physique, and ... consumptive" (1925: 167). She continues:

> The poor-white here, though he belongs to the soil, has no roots in the soil. He is by nature a wanderer, with none of that conservative love of place which makes to many men one spot on earth beloved above all others. Yet the Verlatenheid man remains as a rule in the Verlatenheid, dwelling in no part of it long, and coming, it may be, again and again for short spells at a time to the farms which lie, for no clear reason, within the narrow course he sets himself (1925: 173–174).

It is possible that the real target of Coetzee's criticism is the Afrikaner farmers who had already settled the land they chose for themselves. By contrast, the poor-whites Smith describes are no Israelites: they are the flotsam and jetsam of a community, who have no claim to the land nor roots in it. This point is amplified by the title of her story. Smith claims a spontaneous immanence for the term when she says the region "*takes its name* from the desolation which nature displays here in the grey and volcanic harshness of its kopjes and the scanty vegetation of its veld" (161–162, my emphasis). As Geoffrey Haresnape points out, her translation of the term '*verlatenheid*' as 'desolation' serves the fictional purpose of linking psychic with spatial landscape. Variant translations of the word, which Smith did not choose but which a South African reader may well bring to the text, include "abandonment", "desertion", "dereliction", "forsakenness", "waste", or literally "having been left behind". The first two of these meanings might alert us to biographic connections between the boy Koos's separation from Alie, his grandmother, and Smith's separation from her father. More poignantly, we might recognise that Alie herself is psychically as well as socially homeless: she has 'lost' connection with her people who named the desert, and hence exists in a state of dereliction, foresakenness, abandonment. Either way, these terms are in direct contrast to the notion of a chosen land, and, for a South African reader at least, they activate a conceptual archive of destitution rather than one of political power.

Smith's title and her treatment of poor whites raise another question: Can you 'evict' people who do not properly 'belong'? In this regard it is worth contrasting Smith's subjects with Plaatje's. The rural black people he describes have for the most part longstanding arrangements with the farmers on whose land they are living, and hence have a clear moral right to residence. One example: "that of the oldest man in the 'Free' State. He had been evicted (so we were told during that evening on the farm) along with his aged wife, his grey-headed children, the children's children and grandchildren" (1916: 62). Generations of one family have led a settled existence on the farm, only to have their stability destroyed and their security shattered by the implementation of the new law.

Plaatje shows this law to be morally and pragmatically indefensible. The law replaces tenancy (and the share-cropping associated with it) with servitude; so that farmers can for a minimal wage commandeer the labour of whole families and their cattle. For people who measure their wealth in terms of the cattle they own this is tantamount to making the landlord "a present of all their life's savings", and they are unwilling to accept the radical change. Yet the law introduces penalties as well as entitlements: it becomes "criminal for anyone to have black tenants" (1916: 49), and farmers face substantial fines if they flout it: "£100 for accommodating a native on his farm; and ... an additional fine of £5 for every day that the native's cattle remain on that farm" (1916: 63–64).

Besides expressing his own views, Plaatje follows the rhetorical strategy of including in his text a range of responses to the law and the evictions which ensue. Of course the majority of farmers are ready and willing to implement a law whose effects are likely to accrue to their advantage. Some white people, though, have reservations about it. A policeman whom Plaatje meets on the road "was a Transvaaler, he said, and ... knew that Kaffirs were inferior beings, but they had rights, and were always left in undisturbed possession of their property when Paul Kruger was alive" (55). While recognising the "rights" of those have been evicted, the young policeman is by no means sympathetic to their plight, because

> ... they had no business to hanker after British rule, to cheat and plot with the enemies of their Republic for the overthrow of their Government. Why did they not assist the forces of their Republic during the war instead of supplying the English with scouts and intelligence? Oom Paul would not have died of a broken heart and he would still be there to protect them. Serve them right, I say (1916: 56).

There is possibly a strand of truth in his claim, which invokes the mutual support one agrarian community might be expected to have for another. Yet Plaatje knew full well what kind of deals Boers struck, as is evident in his ironic description of their opportunistic attempts to claim all the land for themselves in the division of the spoils of war in his novel *Mhudi* (141). At this point in *Native Life*, he is prevented only by the policeman's departure from challenging his logic: Why, he wonders, did the same fate affect those in Natal and the Cape who were British subjects and hence cannot be said to have cheated and plotted "with the enemies of our colonies"? (1916: 56).

Plaatje's dead-pan transcription of the policeman's words contains both irony and humour, since the man has no sense that he is neither as intelligent nor as sophisticated as the person he is addressing. Plaatje is an educated and literate man, and hence is frequently applied to for advice. Witnessing the terrible effects of the evictions, he counsels those who can to stay on the land and undertakes to appeal to a "higher authority than the South African parliament and finally to His Majesty the King who, we believed, would certainly disapprove of all that we saw on that day had it been brought to his notice" (1916: 57–58). In Plaatje's conviction that the King will hear him we see both his faith in the imperial system and his sense of himself as a person of stature who can command an audience with the highest authorities. Perhaps it is this self-assurance as well as basic narrative generosity which leads him to render the policeman as naïve rather than vicious – perhaps it is his *ubuntu* which respects the 'personhood' even of a person who is patronising and insulting him.

What is striking is that the opinions expressed by Afrikaners generally recognise that blacks have rights of residence, and that the law breaks with an established set of relations sanctioned by long tradition. Amongst the responses Plaatje cites are those of a Boer who speaks out against the law at a public meeting, reminding his fellows "that they were only debarred from taking any **new** native tenants; that it was wicked to expel a Kaffir from the farm for no reason whatever, and so make him homeless" (1916: 61, my emphasis). He receives threats of physical violence for his pains. And then there is the Boer 'vrouw' Hannelie whose intervention with her husband on behalf of their farm workers forms the subject of a chapter entitled 'Our Indebtedness to White Women'. Plaatje learns of her words to the farm workers that "the Devil appears to have possessed himself of the hearts of most farmers" (1916: 6), and her injunction to her husband not to obey the law, and her promise that, "if it comes to physical ejectment, or if they take me to prison, [I am] prepared to go to Pretoria in person and interview General Botha" (1916: 72). The chapter ends with the adulation expressed by Plaatje's informant, the old farm-worker Aunt Mietjie, who calls Hannelie "an angel" and hopes to accompany her "when Elijah's chariot comes for her soul, so as to render her what little aid I can on board" (1916: 74). Her sentimentality must be read against Plaatje's clear-sighted account of the cynical calculations of Hannelie's husband, who offsets against the prospect of fines he might face an assured annual income of £3000 from the labour of his tenants ... and elects to "resist the law and take the consequences" (1916: 71). The system of sharecropping that had been in place was by no means equitable; nevertheless it offered the natives relative freedom and autonomy, and their landlords substantial rewards. Small wonder, then, that one landlord asks Plaatje: "What has suddenly happened? We were living so nicely with your people, and why should the law unsettle them in this manner?" (1916: 60).

In contrast to Plaatje's documentary accounts of conversations with a number of people, Smith deals with only one family who suffers eviction, and only two members of it: the mother and the son of one Stephan van Staden, a *bijwoner* or tenant of a farmer called Godlieb Bezedenhout. Unlike the natives in Plaatje's account, old Alie suffers eviction not because of a change in the law, but because of the death of her son from tuberculosis, and because of Bezedenhout's need (or desire) to replace his assistant as rapidly as possible. Like Plaatje, Smith offers a complex perspective on this eviction. Although there is some evidence that she based her story on real-life events, unlike Plaatje she offers a fictionalised version of them. The position of the character Bezedenhout is thus reflected in free indirect discourse:

> He was, he said, but naturally sorry for herself and the child, but doubtless they had relatives to whom they might go, and she must see for herself that it was impossible for him, a man wellnigh ruined by the drought, to do anything whatever to help her. She must know, also, that her son's illness had made him a poor bijwoner and added much to his losses among his sheep. In fact the more he thought of it the more convinced he was that no other farmer in the Verlatenheid would have borne with Stephan so long as he, Godlieb Bezedenhout, had done (1925: 166).

Unlike Plaatje, Smith does not offer explicit narrative comment on the farmer's position. Several aspects of his representation warrant a reader's suspicion, however, and imply a moral perspective. Bezedenhout's claim that it is impossible for him to do "anything whatever to help her" is extreme, and sits oddly in the mouth of a man whose name invokes the love of God. Earlier Smith has alluded to the "disease of the chest which had killed first [van Staden's] father and then his three brothers" (1925: 162), and to his own rapidly increasing illness. He is by no means responsible for his inability to work. His master, though, is a "harsh man made harsher by a drought which had brought him close to ruin" (1925: 163), a drought which is "the worst that any middle-aged man of the Verlatenheid remembered. When Stephan went as bijwoner to Koelkuil the farm had had no rain for over two years and through all his eighteen months of service with Mijnheer only three light showers fell" (1925: 163). Like Stephan Mijnheer has severe troubles to contend with.

Typically, Smith's treatment of the conflict between the two men explains without justifying actions on both sides which are clearly inhumane.

> In the strain of these months there was constant friction between Stephan van Staden and his master. Nothing done by the one was right in the eyes of the other. Stephan, ill and irritable, was loud in his criticism of Mijnheer. Mijnheer, a ruined man, was unjust in the demands he made of his bijwoner (1925: 164–165).

Like most of the Afrikaners who populate Smith's stories, Stephan is intensely religious, but he is also a man in torment: "at each fresh blow dealt him by his God he lifted up his voice and cried aloud his injury" (1925: 163). Oddly, it is not this vociferous expression of suffering which Mijnheer finds intolerable, but the silence and aloofness of old Alie, Stephan's mother, whom he resents and fears: "He read in it a judgement of himself, and who was this Alie, this poor-white, that she should judge him? Why did she never speak that he might answer?" (1925: 165). His resentment turns to hatred, and the death of Stephan in a spell of bitter cold brings him the relief of knowing that "now old Alie must go" (1925: 165). There is a ruthless irony in the fact that while the conflict between the two men is grounded in severe tribulations, it is nevertheless the woman and her grandchild who suffer most from its consequences.

The eviction of Alie and her grandson Koos is thus a complexly motivated affair, which takes place in a highly charged situation exacerbated by the drought and the cold. At an individual level, Godlieb Bezedenhout's actions toward the old woman and the young child are as inhumane as those of Plaatje's landlords who evict tenants of long standing in pursuit of better financial deals or in order to avoid fines. Unlike Plaatje, and probably because hers is a fictional account, Smith indicates with some -

insistence the personal relations which contextualise and motivate the eviction. Her focalisation of Bezedenhout's resentment and fear of Alie shows us something of his point of view. It also the cruelty at the heart of human relationship – a frequent motif in her work. Alie's silence makes her seem strong and powerful to Bezedenhout, but it masks the dire poverty and powerlessness of her position. "What, indeed, was there for her to answer? Mijnheer spoke of relatives to whom she might turn for help for herself and Stephan's child, but in fact she had none" (1925: 167). Alie has no right of residence on Bezedenhout's farms. She is completely at the mercy of his decision, and says nothing to contest it.

As a fiction, Smith's narrative is free to follow the old woman and the young boy after they leave the farm. Two aspects of Alie's distress are common to those in Plaatje's account: the impact of eviction on children, and its impact on animals.

Alie's prime motive in travelling to Hermansdorp is to provide for her grandson, who, as the last surviving member of Stephan's family, "had none but herself to stand between him and destitution. All that was to be done for him," she recognises, "she herself must do. All that was to be planned for him she herself must plan" (1925: 167). The relationship between the two is intensely registered in the story: she has saved him when his mother died in childbirth, and protected him from his father who "in his illness, turned against his own son". He is a "slim small child with eyes as dark as her own, and long thin fingers like the claws of a bird", and his trust in his grandmother is absolute: "She was his tower of strength, his shadow of a great rock in a dry and thirsty land. By her side he was safe" (1925: 168).

There has been critical contention about the ending of the story which sees Alie arrive in the town of her girlhood and leave her grandson in the "orphan-house" before dying. Some have argued that Alie has achieved for him the security of food and shelter which they lost on being evicted. Structurally speaking, this is true, yet this reading necessarily downplays the morally wrenching separation which occurs when the young custodian of the orphan-house ushers Koos in to a meal with the other children. Alie is left with the image of "Koos's face turned towards her in bewilderment and appeal – adding sorrow to her sorrow" (1925: 197). Although she is powerless to prevent it, her betrayal of his trust is complete.

Plaatje too shows a keen awareness of the effects of eviction upon children, and being himself a family man draws comparisons with his own

family, in a reach of sympathy which engages and involves the reader. The
night he spends with the fugitives is a bitterly cold one:

> A cutting blizzard raged during the night, and native mothers evicted from
> their homes shivered with their babies by their sides. When we saw on that
> night the teeth of the little children clattering through the cold, we thought of
> our own little ones in their Kimberley home of an evening after gambolling in
> their winter frocks with their schoolmates, and we wondered what these little
> mites had done that a house should suddenly become to them a thing of the
> past (1925: 58).

In the circumstances it is not surprising that newly born animals should die,
as do the kids of the goats which are on the road. More sombrely, a key
moment in this chapter occurs when the sick baby of the Mr and Mrs Kgo-
badi "began to sink as the result of privation and exposure on the road, and
the night before we met them its little soul was released from its earthly
bonds". The "torturing anguish" which they feel is exacerbated by a "fresh
perplexity ... The deceased child had to be buried, but where, when and
how? (1916: 58). The young couple are forced to dig a grave under cover
of darkness and inter the child without blessing or ceremony. No such incident occurs in 'Desolation', though in the journal Smith kept of her trip
to the Cape she documents a similar story of a poor-white man who likewise has to bury his child along the way. In Plaatje's case, the incident is
accorded political force, becoming metaphoric of the plight of all natives
"whose only crime is that God did not make them white" and who are
therefore denied the "undisputed claim" even of criminals to "six feet of
ground on which to rest their ... remains" (1916: 59), and this in the land
that is their ancestral home.

Like Smith, Plaatje is very conscious that eviction has not only human
but also animal victims. In the morning of the night he spends with the fugitives he lands on the south bank of the Vaal River, and recalls the past
when his family sold milk to wagonneers unable to cross the river in times
of flood. That was a time of milk and honey: "while the flocks were feed-
ing on the luscious buds of the haardoorns and the orange-coloured blos-
soms of the rich mimosa and other wild vegetation that abounded on the
banks of the Vaal River, the cows, similarly engaged, were gathering more
and more milk" (1925: 53). This context is harshly contrasted by the fate
of animals evicted with their owners. "We frequently met those roving pa-
riahs," he says,

> with their hungry cattle, and wondered if the animals were not more deserv-
> ing of pity than their owners. It may be the cattle's misfortune that they have

a black owner, but it is certainly not their fault, for sheep have no choice in the selection of a colour for their owners, and no cows or goats are ever asked to decide if the black boy who milks them shall be their owner, or but a herd in the employ of a white man; so why should they be starved on account of the colour of their owners? (1916: 64).

Plaatje's tone here is matter of fact, and his argument pragmatic, but the ownership of stock is at the crux of the evictions, and the people he meets are invariably driving herds of oxen, sheep, goats, horses, donkeys, all suffering more bitterly even than their human owners.

Smith's treatment of the issue is characteristically more personalised: Alie's stock are poor and starved at the outset, and the hardship of the journey, with no water and little food, sees them dying one by one. The patient suffering of the donkeys receives specific narrative attention: "From time to time they turned towards her seeking with their tongues such moisture as her clothes might hold. And always when they did so she would speak to them quietly, as if speaking to children, of the Hermansdorp dam" – yet when she reaches it the dam has dried up (1925: 178).

The alignment of human and animal suffering is thus evident in both texts, although its treatment differs: Plaatje uses the perspective of the beasts to castigate the human laws which have caused their suffering – he argues the case from their point of view. Smith echoes in the patient and pitiful efforts of the donkeys Alie's resigned endurance of unjust fate. Plaatje's critique is a political one. Smith's delineation of Alie's plight rather calls for moral and ethical responses from a reader who must bear witness to suffering caused by the joint tyranny of natural disaster and human unconcern.

Although much of Smith's story is focalised through Alie's consciousness, Smith maintains significant narrative distance from her central character. She uses the term "poor white" repeatedly, and includes in her story alternate perspectives and judgements on Alie by several minor characters. To these people Alie appears naïve, dogged and misguided, and her age and her dignified silence serve as a barrier which prevents them from approaching her in any effective way. Smith uses these different perspectives to demonstrate the confines of a mentality schooled by poverty and ignorance and forced by a lack of imagination to seek solutions to present problems in her memory of the past. What sustains Alie on her long and agonising trek through the Karoo, the "grey and barren veld, the wild and broken kopjes of the Verlatenheid" (1925: 169), is the remembered vision of Kerk Straat in Hermansdorp, where she lived and worked for six months as a girl, with its "running furrows of clear water and its double row of pear-trees in blossom" (1925: 170). Yet this image is explicitly linked to the mirages which she and her grandson encounter on the second day of their long and agonising trek through the Karoo, a "strange fantastic world that slipped into being, vanished, and slipped into being again" (1925: 175), and is expressly contradicted by the "empty sun-baked hollow gaping to the indifferent heavens" which is now the dam (1925: 179), and the dustbowl which is now the town. Added to this is the pain which racks "old Alie's" body until it gives way to numbness, the handful of shillings she will get from the sale of her "exhausted donkeys and famishing sheep" (1925: 186), and her separation from her grandson, and it is hard to conceive an ending more relentless in its tragic vision.

Alie has many positive qualities: she is devoted to her grandchild; she is strong and direct in her pursuit of her goal; and she has a spiritual resilience which lends grandeur to her poverty and suffering. Yet she epitomises the powerlessness of the old and the female, and quite clearly plays out the moral tragedy which Smith elects for her as a victim of eviction. Once she leaves the farm, nothing but death awaits her, and if she secures the future of her grandchild, it is at the price of a terrible separation. The experience of Plaatje's 'natives' is as fundamental, yet they are distinguished from her in significant ways. Whereas the remembered past in which Alie places her faith proves illusory, the Africans of whom Plaatje writes have a sense of the past which sustains identity. Being black they are forced to endure the privations and oppressions of their white masters, yet at a primal level they remain 'native'. They may be denied rights in their "ancestral home" yet this ancestral home is not lost to them: it remains there and it remains theirs. Perhaps it is this sense of cultural location and existential security which inclines Plaatje towards satire and social commentary rather than the symbolism and tragedy in which Smith tells her story.

Finally, however, it is these writers' choice of medium for their narratives which links them in interesting ways, because it positions them ethnographically in relation to their subjects and in relation to the readerships their texts construct. Although they are both South African writers, they are writing in English about non-English subjects, and they are writing for English readers. Given the period in which they are writing – 1916, 1925 respectively – this is not surprising. Yet the use of English conditions their narrative relations with their characters, and the constructions they offer of eviction. Plaatje is a native-speaking Barolong, but he is also an educated, middle-class man who has thoroughly mastered the English language. If he aligns himself with the "natives" who have been evicted from their homes, this is for the political purpose of representing them to the English public and the English King whom he hopes will intervene to restore to them their rights of residence. The experience Plaatje shares with the refugees is incontestable, yet it is transient. Unlike those whose lives are permanently altered by their evictions, his documentary purposes mean he is, ultimately, only passing through. Smith, by contrast, is a first-language English speaker whose audience, too, is far removed from the "poor whites" of whom she writes. Unlike Plaatje, it is not her intention to invoke political intervention. Rather her documentation of the Afrikaner Alie's experience calls upon readers to witness and to be emotionally and morally involved. Her text places before us the suffering of others, and bids us acknowledge we are connected with it. Thus both Plaatje and Smith engage in acts of cultural translation which are seminal to their narrative projects, and recognising this will, I trust, shed a little further light on their respective constructions of eviction, which it has been the purpose of this article to explore.

Myrtle Hooper
University of Zululand

Works cited

Coetzee, J.M. 1981. Pauline Smith and the Afrikaans Language. *English in Africa*, 8(1), 25–32.

Haresnape, G.L. 1977. Pauline Smith's "Desolation" and the Worthwhile African English Text. *UCT Studies in English*, 7, 99–103.

Plaatje, Sol T. 1987 (1916). *Native Life in South Africa*. Harlow: Longman.

Smith, P. 1981 (1925). *The Little Karoo*. Cape Town: Balkema.

Note

1. A disclaimer: I have followed terminology used by the authors concerned, even where this has taken subsequently taken on derogatory connotations.

About The Authors

Marianne Ackerman is a journalist and playwright who divides her time between Montreal and Provence. Her first novel, *Jump*, is set in Montreal during the 1995 referendum, published by McArthur & Co (2000).

Alba Ambert is a Puerto Rican novelist, poet, essayist, lyricist and short story writer. She is co-editor of *Mango Season*, the literary review of the Caribbean Centre, Goldsmiths College, University of London. She has recently been commissioned to write the lyrics for the musical *Nilda* based on a novel by Nicholasa Mohr. She is Writer in Residence at Richmond, The American International University in London and is currently completing her fourth novel.

Nilufer E. Bharucha is a Professor of English at the University of Bombay where she teaches Postcolonial Literatures and Theories, the Literature of the Raj and Applied Linguistics. Dr. Bharucha has co-edited *Indian English Fiction 1980–1990: An Assessment, Postcolonial Perspectives on the Raj and its Literature* and *Mapping Cultural Spaces: Postcolonial Indian Literature in English* has also written several short-stories which have been published in The Illustrated Weekly of India, Eve's Weekly and the Indian PEN. She has also done translations from the Urdu for the Sunday Observer.

Gillian Bouras is the author of six books. The latest title from Penguin Books Australia is *Starting Again* (1999) and the University of Queensland Press has recently published *Saving Christmas*. She has had her writing published in five countries and her third book, *Aphrodite and the Others* is available in a Modern Greek translation from Dorikos Press, Athens. *Aphrodite and the Others* won a NSW State Literary Award in 1994.

Ruth Brown teaches part-time in the Centre for Continuing Education. at the University of Sussex Her publications include articles on Australian and New Zealand literature, history, and cultural politics.

Sooyoung Chon is an associate professor of English at Ewha Womans University in Seoul, Korea. She has published essays on Joseph Conrad in *Conradiana, The Conradian,* and *L'Epoque Conradienne* as well as in the book *Under Postcolonial Eyes*. A book on Conrad comprising such issues as language, ideology, and the experience of imperialism is forthcoming.

Mary Condé is the co-editor with Thorunn Lonsdale of *Caribbean Women Writers: Fiction in English* (Macmillan,1999).She teaches at Queen Mary and Westfield Colege, University of London.

Bernard Cros teaches British and South African history and English language at the University of Avignon, France. He has published on South African culture and media.

Florence D'Souza is a Lecturer in English at the University of Lille III and is the author of *Quand la France découvrit l'Inde – les écrivains-voyageurs français en Inde (1757–1818)*, Editions L'Harmattan, Paris, 1995.

Miriam Frank has recently retired from her position of Senior Lecturer and Consultant in Anaesthesia at the Royal London Hospital, London. She is completing *Her Innocent Absence, Anatomy of Human Dislocation.* She has translated into English the novels *Fire in Casabindo* and *The Man Who Came to a Village* by the Argentinean author, Héctor Tizón, and numerous short stories for collections by Latin American writers. She has written articles published in the *Guardian Review, Buenos Aires Herald, Index on Censorship* and *In Other Words*, the *Journal of the Translators' Association* of the *Society of Authors of Great Britain*.

Geetha Ganapathy-Doré is a senior lecturer at the University of Paris XIII. She has published a large number of articles on Indian Writing in English, British perceptions of India, cross cultural communities, voices of women in the arts and a few translations of Tamil short stories into French in journals such as the *Journal of Commonwealth Literature, Commonwealth, Wasafiri, The Canadian Theatre Review, Hommes et Migrations, Les Cahiers du Sahib* and *Rencontre avec l'Inde*.

Madelena Gonzalez lectures in English Literature and Translation Studies at Avignon University. Her publications include articles on contemporary fiction in English and she is currently working on a project to translate the work of little-known Indian writers into French.

Myrtle Hooper is professor and head of the Department of English at the University of Zululand. She has published on Joseph Conrad, the interplay of privacy, politeness and power as these manifest themselves in narrative and the ways in which conversational realities shape identity.

Sara Le Menestrel is a researcher at the National Center for Scientific Research in France (CNRS). She has published *La voie des Cadiens. Tourisme et identité en Louisiane*, Paris, Belin, 1999. She is currently working on

French-Louisiana and Acadian identity and the social and political stakes of musical practices among Cajuns and Creoles.

Corinne Liotard, professeur agrégé, teaches English at Lycée d'Estienne d'Orves, Nice, France. She is completing a doctoral thesis on Anita Desai's works.

Priscilla Morin–Ollier is a professor of American civilisation at the Université François Rabelais in Tours, France. She has written several articles on the question of religion and politics, religion and identity in the United States, and the role of the Catholic Church in fostering its own sense of identity.

Vincent O'Sullivan is Professor of English and Director of the Stout Research Centre, at Victoria University, Wellington, New Zealand. He has co-edited the five volume edition of Mansfield's *Collected Letters* for the Clarendon Press, and published much on her work. He is also known as a poet, playwright, short story writer, novelist and critic.

Béatrice Pardini-Laurent teaches the history of British art at the University of Avignon. A book on the religious iconography of the British Pre-Raphaelites is forthcoming.

Xavier Pons is Professor of English at the University of Toulouse-Le Mirail and a past President of the European Association for Studies on Australia. He has published widely on Australian literature and civilization – his books include *Out of Eden* (1984), *A Sheltered Land* (1994), *Le Multiculturalisme en Australie* (1996), *L'Australie – Entre Occident et Orient,* (2000) – and he is currently editing the proceedings of the Fifth EASA Conference, to be published by Melbourne University Press under the title *Departures*.

Jennifer Rutherford is a research fellow in the School of Cultural and Critical Studies at Macquarie University. She is the author of *The Gauche Intruder: Freud, Lacan and the White Australia fantasy*; and Director/Writer of "Ordinary People", a forthcoming television documentary on the One Nation party. She has published widely on social psychoanalysis, nationalism, racism and Australian cultural studies and is currently writing a monograph: *Extimacy: an intimate dialogue with the new Right* (forthcoming M.U.P.)

Francine Tolron is a senior lecturer at Avignon University, where she teaches Commonweath cultural studies. She has published articles on New Zealand history, society and culture and is the author of *Les écrivains néo-zélandais* (1996) and of *La Nouvelle-Zélande; du duel au duo?*, Presses Universitaires du Mirail (2000).

Russell West teaches English at the University of Lüneburg, Germany. He has published *Conrad and Gide: Translation, Transference and Intertextuality* (1996), *Figures de la maladie chez André Gide* (1997), and co-edited *Marginal Voices, Marginal Forms: Diaries in European Literature and History* (1999) and *Subverting Masculinity: Hegemonic and Alternative Versions of Masculinity in Contemporary Culture* (2000). He is co-editor of the Rodopi series *GENUS: Gender in Modern Culture*. A study entitled *"Here is My Space": Representations of Social Space and Historical Change on the Jacobean Stage* is forthcoming.